SELECTED WRITINGS

OF

Judith Sargent Murray

WOMEN WRITERS IN ENGLISH
1350–1850

GENERAL EDITORS
Susanne Woods and Elizabeth H. Hageman

MANAGING EDITOR
Elizabeth Terzakis

SECTION EDITORS
Carol Barash
Patricia Caldwell
Stuart Curran
Margaret J. M. Ezell
Elizabeth H. Hageman

WOMEN WRITERS PROJECT
Brown University

SELECTED WRITINGS

OF

Judith Sargent Murray

EDITED BY

Sharon M. Harris

New York   Oxford

OXFORD UNIVERSITY PRESS

1995

OXFORD UNIVERSITY PRESS

Oxford   New York
Athens   Auckland   Bangkok   Bombay
Calcutta   Cape Town   Dar es Salaam   Delhi
Florence   Hong Kong   Istanbul   Karachi
Kuala Lumpur   Madras   Madrid   Melbourne
Mexico City   Nairobi   Paris   Singapore
Taipei   Tokyo   Toronto

and associated companies in
Berlin   Ibadan

New material © copyright 1995 by Oxford University Press, Inc.

Published by Oxford University Press, Inc.,
198 Madison Avenue, New York, New York 10016

Oxford is a registered trademark of Oxford University Press

Library of Congress Cataloging-in-Publication Data

Murray, Judith Sargent, 1751-1820.
[Selections. 1995]
Selected writings of Judith Sargent Murray/
edited by Sharon M. Harris.
p.   cm. -- (Women writers in English 1350–1850)
1. Feminism—United States—History—18th century—Literary
collections. 2. Women—United States—History—18th century—
Literary collections. I. Harris, Sharon M. II. Title. III. Series.
PS808.M8A6   1995   818'.209--dc20   95-3580
ISBN 0-19-507883-7 (cloth)
ISBN 0-19-510038-7 (paper)

This volume was supported in part by the National Endowment
for the Humanities, an independent federal agency.

Printing (last digit):
9   8   7   6   5   4   3   2   1

Printed in the United States of America
on acid-free paper

For my aunt,
Shirley Sperber—
with love

CONTENTS

FOREWORD

Women Writers in English 1350–1850 presents texts of cultural and literary interest in the English-speaking tradition, often for the first time since their original publication. Most of the writers represented in the series were well known and highly regarded until the professionalization of English studies in the later nineteenth century coincided with their excision from canonical status and from the majority of literary histories.

The purpose of this series is to make available a wide range of unfamiliar texts by women, thus challenging the common assumption that women wrote little of real value before the Victorian period. While no one can doubt the relative difficulty women experienced in writing for an audience before that time, or indeed have encountered since, this series shows that women nonetheless had been writing from early on and in a variety of genres, that they maintained a clear eye to readers, and that they experimented with an interesting array of literary strategies for claiming their authorial voices. Despite the tendency to treat the powerful fictions of Virginia Woolf's *A Room of One's Own* (1928) as if they were fact, we now know, against her suggestion to the contrary, that there were many "Judith Shakespeares," and that not all of them died lamentable deaths before fulfilling their literary ambitions.

This series is unique in at least two ways. It offers, for the first time, concrete evidence of a rich and lively heritage of women writing in English before the mid-nineteenth century, and it is based on one of the most sophisticated and forward-looking electronic resources in the world: the Brown University Women Writers Project textbase (full text database) of works by early women writers. The Brown University Women Writers Project (WWP) was established in 1988 with a grant from the National Endowment for the Humanities, which continues to assist in its development.

Women Writers in English 1350–1850 is a print publication project derived from the WWP. It offers lightly annotated versions based on single good copies or, in some cases, collated versions of texts with more complex editorial histories, normally in their original spelling. The editions are aimed at a wide audience, from the informed undergraduate through professional students of literature, and they attempt to include the general reader who is interested in exploring a fuller tradition of early texts in English than has been available through the almost exclusively male canonical tradition.

SUSANNE WOODS
ELIZABETH H. HAGEMAN
General Editors

ACKNOWLEDGMENTS

The collaborative effort that is the Women Writers Project thrives on the contributions of all its members. Ongoing thanks are due to Brown University and its administrators, especially President Vartan Gregorian, Provost Frank Rothman, Dean of the Faculty Bryan Shepp, and Vice President Brian Hawkins. Members of the Brown English Department, particularly Elizabeth Kirk, Stephen Foley, and William Keach, have provided indispensable advice; many thanks to Marilyn Netter for her help in finding the WWP a new director. Gratitude is also owed to Don Wolfe, of Brown's Computing and Information Services. At Brown's Scholarly Technology Group, Geoffrey Bilder and Elli Mylonas are unfailingly resourceful and obliging in all matters, and Allen Renear is a rare source of energy and inspiration.

Working with Oxford University Press is always a pleasure; many thanks to Elizabeth Maguire for making the Series possible and to Claude Conyers for his unlimited patience, his unfailing sense of humor, and the laugh that goes with both.

A more committed set of colleagues than the WWP staff is hard to imagine. Project Coordinator Maria Fish facilitates all contacts with the outside world with her unerring knowledge of protocol and her considerable diplomatic skills. The computer textbase from which this volume was drawn approaches perfection largely through the efforts of Carole Mah and Syd Bauman. I thank Julia Flanders for defining the position of managing editor and easing me into the very big shoes she left behind. New Director Carol DeBoer-Langworthy deserves thanks for bringing a hearty serving of Midwestern pragmatism into the office. Others who have made this series possible include Elizabeth Adams, Anthony Arnove, Rebecca Bailey, Kim Bordner, Susie Castellanos, Paul Caton, Nick Daly, Cathleen Drake, Faye Halpern, Loren Noveck, Anastasia Porter, Kasturi Ray, Caleb Rounds, and Kristen Whissel.

ELIZABETH TERZAKIS
Managing Editor

ACKNOWLEDGMENTS

I wish to acknowledge the generosity of two institutions in granting me access to and permission to use some of Judith Sargent Murray's works: The Sargent-Murray-Gilman-Hough House Association (especially Patricia D. Runkle and Bonnie Smith); and the Manuscript Collection, Mississippi Department of Archives and History (Judith Sargent Murray Papers [Z/1827], Letterbooks [microfilm]).

Special thanks are due to Patricia Caldwell for her insightful editorial guidance, and to Lydia Kualapai for her invaluable research assistance; their "female abilities" were integral to the completion of this project.

SHARON M. HARRIS

INTRODUCTION

"I feel the pride of womanhood all up in arms," Judith Sargent Murray declared in a 1777 letter to a female cousin (letter 54).[1] Responding to what she termed the "abominable" and "intolerable" arguments against women's education by the French philosopher Jean Jacques Rousseau, she asserted, "For those sentiments, so humiliating to our sex, avowed by Rousseau, I will never forgive him" (letter 54). The pride of womanhood—and the many capabilities of women—were themes to which Murray dedicated her writings and her life. Her sixty-nine-year life spanned crucial decades of revolution and national independence that redefined concepts of citizenship, literary genius, and women's rights. Perhaps no American woman writer until Margaret Fuller equalled Murray in intellectual powers, in the breadth of genres in which she wrote, or in public recognition.

In addition to poetry, essays, dramas, and a novel, Murray was a prolific letter-writer. Her correspondence, like her other literary endeavors, reveals her commitment to human rights. Numerous letters discuss topics such as her concerns about women in the local almshouse (letter 22), female education (letter 235), and prejudices against African-Americans (letter 408). As the Reverend Gordon D. Gibson, who located the supposedly lost letter books, has noted, the letters confirm that Judith Sargent Murray was "a gifted writer, a strong feminist, an ardent Universalist."[2]

Judith Sargent, the oldest of eight Sargent children, was born on 1 May 1751, into an elite merchant-class family. Her mother, Judith Saunders Sargent (1731-1793), had also grown up in a prominent family connected with the thriving New England maritime industry, and her father, Captain Winthrop Sargent (1727-1793), was a shipowner and merchant. At an early age, Judith demonstrated exceptional intellectual

---

1. I am following Murray's numbering of her letters in The Letter books, Judith Sargent Murray Papers (Z/1827), Manuscript Collection, Mississippi Department of Archives and History.

2. "The Rediscovery of Judith Sargent Murray," The John Murray Distinguished Lecture for 1991, presented at the Unitarian Universalist General Assembly, June 1991, p. 2; published in "Not Hell, But Hope" (Murray Grove Association).

skills, but because she was a girl, her early education was minimal. Her first tutor, Judith recalled, was "an ancient Woman, from whom I had received the rudiments of reading".[1] Although Judith retained a fondness for her first teacher, she knew that her early education had been inadequate. In a letter to her brother many years later, she reflected:

> But during my first years, although our parents were, as you know, the best of human beings, they yet did homage to the shrine of fashion, custom tyranises over the strongest minds—It was the mode to confine the female intellect within the narrowest bounds, and by consequence, I was robbed of the aid of education—I shall feel the effects of this irrational deprivation, as long as I shall continue an inhabitant of this world. (letter 58)

Eventually her parents became increasingly aware of her exceptional intelligence and determined that Judith should receive an education comparable to the lessons her younger brother, Winthrop, Jr., was to receive in preparation for Harvard. The Reverend John Rogers, a local minister and a graduate of Harvard, was their tutor. They were probably tutored in Latin and Greek, the usual instruction for Harvard-bound boys; Judith's classical training is evident in all of her writings. Although no record of the Sargent siblings' lessons is extant, one fact about Judith's reading is known: in 1767, the sixteen-year-old scholar owned her own copy of a text which she inscribed on the inside cover as "The best book that was ever written." The book was entitled *The Oeconomy of Human Life In Two Parts; Translated from an Indian manuscript, written by an ancient* BRAMIN, *To which is prefixed An account of the manner in which the said manuscript was discovered,* IN A LETTER *from an English gentleman, residing in China, to the Earl of* *****; *Printed in the year* MDCCLXII.[2] After their education under the Reverend Rogers was completed, Winthrop, Jr., shared his advanced education with Judith to the

---

1. See page 88 in the present volume. Page numbers for subsequent quotations from the present volume will be given in parentheses.

2. I am indebted to Priscilla D. Runkle, Vice President of The Sargent-Murray-Gilman-Hough House Association (SMGHHA), for this information. The book is owned by The Sargent House Museum, Gloucester, Massachusetts. Several chapters are missing: "Desire and Love," "Woman," "Husband," and a section on "Father" in a chapter about "natural relations." I have been unable to locate a complete copy of this edition, although several earlier and later editions are available; *The Oeconomy of Human Life* was originally published in 1751.

extent he could during vacations from college. Although Judith's education was certainly exceptional for a woman of her era, she always lamented the lack of a formal education. Out of this lament were sown the seeds that she would harvest through a lifetime of self-education and an advocacy of better educational opportunities for females of all ages.

Whatever intellectual goals Judith Sargent may have dreamed of as a young woman in mid-eighteenth century America, the only career opportunities for women of her class at the time were marriage and motherhood.[1] While she embraced these goals, throughout her life she would also expand and reconceptualize the possibilities of women's contributions to American culture and to their own constructions of liberty and happiness. On 3 October 1769, Judith Sargent married John Stevens, a Gloucester sea captain and trader; their first home was a beautiful, newly built mansion, "the largest and most elegant house in town," as one observer noted.[2] The marriage lasted for seventeen years, but like many marriages of that era, it was not founded on love. In a letter dated 1 July 1776, Stevens revealed an affectionate attachment to her family that suggests "home" remained associated with the Sargent household (particularly the female members) and not with her own residence since marriage. Writing to her sister, she remarked, "Often, and often, since I left home, hath my bosom sighed for the kind soothings of an amiable sister, for the dear presence of an affectionate Mother— Indeed Home hath ever been to me a word possessing most potent charms" (90). In a letter written shortly before her second marriage, Judith presented a rare personal description of her marriage to John Stevens. She is careful to note that he was a man of many virtues whom she respected, but she was equally explicit in her assertions that she did

---

1. The details of the years before her marriage are scarce, in large part because Murray chose to destroy almost all of her letters written before 1774; she did so, she asserted in the preface to her letterbooks, because they contained only "a kind of history of my juvenile life." In this preface she also noted that she had purposely constructed her letters to create ambiguity about some of the people whom she described: "everything relative to myself as an individual, I have endeavored to render clear and unembarrassed, but when remarking upon the communications of others, I possess no right to be thus explicit."

2. Quoted in Vena Bernadette Field, *Constantia: A Study of the Life and Works of Judith Sargent Murray, 1751–1820* (Orono, Maine: Univ. Press, 1931), 17. This house was Murray's home until 1793; it has been preserved by the SMGHHA as The Sargent House Museum, 49 Middle Street, Gloucester, Massachusetts.

not love her husband nor, in spite of "far from indifferent" desires for "fires" other than those of friendship, did she feel any passion for him (98). Yet she "determined, in the strictest sense, to discharge every obligation, and my perseverance in the path of duty more than tranquilized my soul" (letter 615). At whatever personal costs, this philosophy was linked to the image of home she created for herself in these years: "Self approbation ensures peace, while discord at home is pregnant with most corroding sorrows" (letter 237). Perhaps not surprisingly under these conditions, it was during the early years of her first marriage that Judith Sargent Stevens began to act upon her ardent desire to become a writer. Although "On the Equality of the Sexes" would not be published for more than a decade, it was also during this time that Stevens composed the first part of her most famous essay. Her first writings were occasional poems, which she began composing as early as 1775. Although poetry was the first genre in which Stevens wrote and would remain one of her favorite forms, it was not where her greatest talents lay.[1] Some of her early verses were published in 1784 in the Boston periodical, *Gentleman and Lady's Town and Country Magazine;* but the events of the American Revolution turned her interests to themes of liberty and human rights and turned her favored form to that of the essay. Her first published essay in *Town and Country* was "Desultory Thoughts upon the Utility of Encouraging a Degree of Self-Complacency, Especially in Female Bosoms."[2] Published under the signature of "Constantia," which would remain Stevens's most prevalent pen name, the essay argued for more advanced educations for girls, both in terms of the intellectual content and the values—especially self-respect ("self-complacency")—that informed contemporary teachings for females. In all of Stevens's essays, the introductory poems encapsulate the themes expounded upon more fully in the essay itself. Thus in "Desultory Thoughts," she explicitly links self-worth and achievement—"Ne'er taught to 'rev'rence self,' or to aspire, / Our bosoms never caught ambi-

---

1. This is a contemporary evaluation; both John Murray, Judith's second husband, and Susan Lear, a friend of Judith's from Philadelphia, left accounts praising Judith's "sublime poetry" (Lear, quoted in Field, 23).

2. *Gentleman and Lady's Town and Country Magazine* (October 1794): 251–53 (see page 44 in this edition).

tion's fire"—and exposes the means by which lack of education and its incumbent self-estimation have been falsely constructed as natural for women: "We judg'd that nature, not to us inclin'd, / In narrow bounds our progress had confin'd." The subsequent essay sets forth the philosophy that she would continue to present to the public throughout her life: "I think, to teach young minds to aspire, ought to be the ground work of education" (45).

While Judith Stevens's literary career was blossoming in the late 1770s and early 1780s, she and her husband were facing increased financial strain.[1] Between the business failure of John Stevens's father, the decimation of the maritime industry during the Revolution, and apparently in part through John's own mismanagement, the Stevenses emerged from the war years in considerable debt. In 1786, John Stevens left Gloucester for the West Indies, attempting to escape debtors' prison and hoping to recoup his financial standing. Shortly thereafter, however, Judith was informed of her husband's death at St. Eustatius in the West Indies. As a childless[2] young widow, Stevens at first decided that, rather than remarry, she would live a retiring, single life and support herself through sewing and whatever other means presented themselves. While Stevens believed that turning her attention to supporting the faith that she had embraced a decade earlier would be the best way to enact this retiring life, her commitment to Universalism in fact changed both the course of her life and of her writings.

Unlike the New England Congregationalist belief in distinctions between the regenerate or "Elect" and the unregenerate (those members who had been "saved," and those who had not, respectively), Universalism denied the concept of the Elect and avowed universal salvation as well as individual religious liberty. This form of Christianity originated

---

1. During these years, Judith Stevens published one book that has rarely been discussed. It is a catechism outlining her Universalist beliefs, published at Norwich, Connecticut, and entitled *Some Deductions from the System Promulgated in the Page of Divine Revelation: Ranged in the Order and Form of a Catechism: Intended as an Assistant to the Christian Parent or Teacher* (Norwich: Trumbull, 1782; rpt., Portsmouth, New Hampshire, 1782); see Gibson, 10–11.

2. While the Stevenses did not have any biological children during their marriage, they did take in two young girls who were distant relatives of John Stevens and who had been orphaned. To date, I have been unable to determine how long these children remained with the Stevenses or if Judith continued to raise them after John's death.

during the sixteenth-century European religious revolution known as the Reformation. John Biddle (1516–1562) established Universalism in England and, two centuries later, John Murray (1741–1815) extended its teachings to America, where it was embraced by the liberal faction of Congregationalism. Like Judith and John Stevens, all members of the Sargent family aligned themselves with Universalism from its earliest introduction in the colonies in 1770; indeed, Gloucester was the only town in John Murray's earliest travels throughout the Mid-Atlantic and New England colonies in which he found individuals who had previous knowledge of "Rellyism"—Universalism as taught by the English preacher James Relly who had influenced Murray's conversion from Anglican Methodism to Universalism. Eventually the Sargent family's support of John Murray's Universalist preachings led to their suspension from the First Parish Church of Gloucester. Rather than repenting and returning to the First Parish (an option they were given when suspended), they helped build the first Universalist meeting house on land donated by Judith Stevens's father. The meeting house was dedicated by John Murray on 25 December 1780, instituting a new chapter in religious liberalism in America.

Judith Sargent Stevens's Universalist beliefs are reflected in numerous essays and poems that she composed throughout her life. Religion was, for Judith, both a practical and a philosophical aspect of life. In "Necessity of Religion, Especially in Adversity," an attack on Robespierre's advocacy of atheism, she presents a pragmatic view of the benefits of religion in everyday life but also adheres to arguments for the separation of church and state and for religious freedom in general.[1] "Spirit Independent of Matter," on the other hand, constitutes one of her most sophisticated philosophical examinations of her religious beliefs. Beginning with the poetic invocation, "I love to trace the independent mind (78)," this essay espouses her belief in the immortality of the mind and of the soul and, moving beyond the questions answerable through scientific explorations, it celebrates the powers of imagination, "darting

---

1. *The Gleaner*, 3 vol. (Boston: I. Thomas and E. T. Andrews, 1798), 1:31 (see page 69 in this edition). Maximilien-François-Marie-Isidore de Robespierre (1758–1794) was a French lawyer and Revolutionary leader.

into futurity (80)," to confirm immortality.[1] In one of the last writings she produced, an 1803 poem entitled "On Blending Spirit with Matter," she returned to this theme and deemed the imaginative mind as "Offspring of Deity!"[2]

Judith Stevens's and John Murray's commitment to Universalism and their mutually engaging intellectual strengths soon developed into a strong and affectionate friendship. The letters they exchanged in their early years of acquaintance and growing admiration were an opportunity, as Judith defined it, to "mingle souls upon paper" (87). Although she had begun corresponding with John Murray as early as 1774, Stevens knew that it was highly suspect for a widow to continue to correspond with a man who was not a relative. Yet she defied the custom that denied "to a single Woman, an intellectual connexion with an individual of the other sex" (98) and continued to exchange letters with John Murray after her husband's death. It was not until after John Stevens's death, too, that the correspondents would admit, first to themselves and then to each other, that the friendship had developed into love.

On 6 October 1788, Judith Sargent Stevens married John Murray. Unlike her first marriage, Judith's second union was based on love, admiration, and "ardour" (99).[3] It was an egalitarian marriage, one in which John encouraged Judith's literary ambitions and in which she became an active supporter of his efforts to establish Universalism in the new nation. By her own accounts, Judith's concept of a marriage union—where "friendship's sweetest joys abound"[4]—was achieved in her marriage to John Murray. Over the next few years, Murray accompanied her husband on many of his preaching tours to New York, New Jersey, and Pennsylvania—a practice that afforded her the opportunity to meet several renowned citizens, including Abigail and John Adams

---

1. "Spirit Independent of Matter," *The Gleaner,* 2:62, pp. 266, 269.

2. *Boston Weekly Magazine* 5 (Mar. 1803): 80.

3. This was also John Murray's second marriage. His first wife, Eliza Neal, had died in England in 1769; their only child, a son, had also died, at age one.

4. From "Wedding Hymn," SMGHHA typescript of Murray's unpublished poem.

(*The Gleaner* would be dedicated to the latter); Martha Custis Washington (describing the First Lady as "benignly good" and "adorned with social virtues");[1] and Benjamin Franklin's family ("among the foremost of our favorers").[2] These travels produced some of Murray's most memorable letters, describing New York's social and political scenes. Accounts of her travels and the Universalist activities in which the Murrays were engaged offered her the opportunity to become a contributor to the *Universalist Quarterly.* It would be erroneous, however, to view Murray's contributions to Universalism as merely support of her husband's endeavors. Long before she married John Murray, she had begun a correspondence with many interested women and men in Gloucester and throughout New England; in these letters, she shared her ideas about and commitment to this new religious movement in America. In the era of calls for American independence, she had embraced Universalism as a faith complementary to human liberty and empowerment. Numerous writings, private and published, reveal her role in helping to shape the central tenets of Universalism in America. It is little wonder, too, that a woman of Judith Sargent Murray's intelligence and independence of spirit embraced Universalism and helped to cast its commitment to women's equality. Universalism was the first American denomination to ordain women, and in the nineteenth century, three Universalist ministers—Olympia Brown (1835–1926), Phebe Hanaford (1829–1921), and Augusta Jane Chapin (1836–1905)— would become leaders in the feminist movement.[3]

While Murray proudly contributed her time and writings to the Universalist movement, she also intended to pursue her long-held desire for a literary career, and it was important to her to establish that career in her own right. Her goal, she asserted, was to be "*independent as a writer.*"[4] In 1789, at the age of thirty-eight, she not only experienced

---

1. *Universalist Quarterly* 19 (1882): 142.

2. Quoted in Russell E. Miller, *The Larger Hope: The First Century of the Universalist Church in America 1770–1870* (Boston: Unitarian Universalist Association, 1979), 30.

3. See Drusilla Cummins, "Celebrate the Bicentennial of Universalism," *The Communicator* (March/April 1992): 5; and Miller, *Larger Hope*, chapter 20.

4. "Conclusion—The Gleaner Unmasked," *The Gleaner*, 3:100, p. 314.

her first pregnancy, but she also began contributing poetry to the *Massachusetts Magazine*. The Boston monthly thrived from 1789 to 1796 and thus gained the honor of being "the longest lived of all eighteenth-century American magazines";[1] the magazine published poetry, fiction, book reviews, essays on topical issues, and music. In addition to Murray, contributors included the poet Sarah Wentworth Morton (1759–1846); the essayist, poet, and editor Joseph Dennie (1768–1812); the dramatist and poet Mercy Otis Warren (1728–1814); and the dramatist William Dunlap (1766–1839). The periodical would become one of the most important sources for the publication of Judith Sargent Murray's work.

In part, Murray's intense return to writing in 1789, which eventually led to the "Gleaner" series, may have been precipitated by a desire to immerse herself in work after the death of her son George, who was stillborn. Indeed, her first publication in the *Massachusetts Magazine* was a poem entitled "Lines Occasioned by the Death of an Infant." The 105-line poem begins with the joys of motherhood—watching a baby sleep and anticipating its growth under the mother's care and tutelage. But the poem shifts suddenly from hope to reality:

> 'Twas thus I plann'd my future hours to spend,
> With my soft hopes maternal joys to blend;
> But agonized nature trembling sighs!
> And my young sufferer in the struggle dies:
> As the green bud though hid from outward view,   5
> On its own stem invigorated grew,
> Yet ere its opening leaves could look abroad,
> The howling blast its latent life destroy'd:
> So shrieking terrour all destructive rose,
> Each moment fruitful of increasing woes,   10
> And ere my tongue could mark his natal day,
> (With eager haste great nature's dues to pay)

---

1. Bruce Granger, "The Massachusetts Magazine," in Edward E. Chielens, ed., *American Literary Magazines: The Eighteenth and Nineteenth Centuries* (New York: Greenwood Press, 1986), 249–50.

> Its native skies the gentle spirit sought,
> And clos'd a life with early evil fraught.[1]

A letter by John Murray detailing the difficult birth, the death of their son, and Judith's postpartum illness not only reveals the emotional trauma the Murrays endured at this time but is also one of the most graphic accounts we have of the dangers of childbirth for women in early America:

> The first saturday in August our suffering Friend was taken ill. She continued to suffer more than any language can describe till the wednesday night following. She was then, with the assistance of Doctor Plummer, *and his Instruments* delivered of a Male child weighing very near fifteen pounds, whose spirit returned to the God who gave it, a few hours before it was born. We now flattered ourselves the worst was over, but, alas, never did woman suffer more than she has suffered ever since. Near three weeks we were obliged to have three nurses, and four weeks we were obliged to have two. I am not able to make you acquainted with her complaints. Sufficient to say, that for many weeks her life was dispaired of, and day and night she suffered the most excrutiating tortures. She is not yet able to sit on any seat but one which she is often obliged to use. With great difficulty she can walk from there to her bed which she can neither enter nor leave without assistance, and pain, and God only knows whither she will ever be well. However, I am incouraged to hope. I am willing to hope. She would do better now was it not for the willing [swelling?] in her legs. Her leg is larger than her father's thigh, but Doctor Plummer assures us she will, in time have all her complaints behind her.[2]

In spite of her near-fatal illness, Murray published a dozen poems and her seminal essay, "On the Equality of the Sexes," in the year following their son's death. On 22 August 1791, the Murrays' second child, Julia Maria, was born. In 1779, Murray had written the first section of "On the Equality of the Sexes," and in the year preceding her daughter's birth, she appended an extensive letter to the essay and published it in the *Massachusetts Magazine*.[3] In this essay, Murray challenges

---

1. *Massachusetts Magazine* 2 (January 1790): 57.

2. John Murray to Colonel Paul Dudley Sargent; the letter is dated "Gloucester October 1st 1789." The SMGHHA owns this letter.

3. *Massachusetts Magazine* 2 (March 1790): 133.

the prevailing idea that intellectual differences in men and women are natural. It is women's lack of education and prevailing social constructions, she argues, that create such misconceptions: "Grant that [women's] minds are by nature equal, yet who shall wonder at the *apparent* superiority, if indeed custom becomes *second nature;* nay if it taketh place of nature, and that it doth the experience of each day will evince(6)." Murray also realized that Scriptural interpretations were often used as "evidence" of women's inferiority; thus, in the 1790 publication of "On the Equality of the Sexes," she appended a letter in which she offers her own interpretation of the Adam and Eve story, elevating Eve to equal (if not superior) status. Murray recognized that it was the story of Eve that was so often employed against women's equality through the insistence that Eve was the cause of Adam's/humankind's fall from grace. As early as 1777, in a letter to her cousin Miss Goldthwaite, Murray had begun drafting her revisionist ideas about the Biblical story used to condemn women to inferior cultural and religious positions: "That Eve was indeed the weaker Vessel," she wrote her cousin, "I boldly take upon me to deny" (91). While her writings for the *Massachusetts Magazine* focused on a wide variety of political, cultural, and religious topical issues, the theme Murray returned to most often was that of the natural equality of the sexes and the need for changes in education and in attitudes towards girls' and women's intellectual and emotional strengths. Murray's ideas were reinforced by international calls for women's rights. Two years after she had published "On the Equality of the Sexes," she read Mary Wollstonecraft's *A Vindication of the Rights of Woman* when it first appeared in 1792; the *Vindication* confirmed and expanded her own beliefs in the need for women's education and increased opportunities for employment.

Then, in February 1792, Murray began a series of essays in the *Massachusetts Magazine* under the title and persona of "The Gleaner." She was one of the first women in America to have, in effect, what constituted her own magazine column; in fact, she authored two ongoing columns. From September 1792 through July 1794, Murray published in *Massachusetts Magazine* another series entitled "The Repository," in which she addressed social and religious issues, but it was as "The

Gleaner" that she was most outspoken in addressing contemporary cultural topics. Since Murray had given birth to a daughter six months before she began writing *The Gleaner* series, it is not surprising that one of the most important issues she analyzes in the early *Gleaner* essays is that of raising and educating a female child. The *Story of Margaretta* constitutes one of the most fascinating and important early novels in American literature for several reasons: because it refuses to depict a "fallen woman" as the protagonist, preferring instead an intelligent heroine who is capable of forging a significant life for herself; because of its complicated nature of being embedded in an on-going series of essays by "The Gleaner," a technique that allowed Murray to critique her own novel as she was writing it; and because of the issue of gender constructions complicated by a female author's use of a male persona to relate the life of a female protagonist.

The *Story of Margaretta* begins with the second essay in the *Massachusetts Magazine* series and constitutes one-third of volume one in the book version of *The Gleaner.*[1] The novel traces the life of Margaretta Melworth, a young orphan who is taken in by Mr. Vigillius ("The Gleaner") and his spouse, Mary Vigillius; it follows Margaretta's early education, her mistaken love for the aptly named Sinisterus Courtland, and her rejection of the scoundrel in favor of the honorable Edward Hamilton, whom she marries at the end of the novel in volume one. Many scholars have deemed Judith Sargent Murray one of the leading proponents of "Republican Motherhood," an ideology that emerged at the end of the eighteenth century and which Linda Kerber has defined as follows:

> Searching for a political context in which private female virtues might comfortably co-exist with the civic virtue that was widely regarded as the cement of the Republic, [women] found what they were seeking in the notion of what might be called "Republican Motherhood." The Republican Mother integrated political values into her domestic life. Dedicated as she was to the nurture of public-spirited male citizens, she guaranteed the steady infusion of virtue into the Republic. Political

---

1. In volume one of *The Gleaner,* the *Story of Margaretta* constitutes chapters 2, 7-8, 20-21, 28-29 (see page 153 in this edition).

"virtue"…could be safely domesticated in eighteenth-century America; the mother, and not the masses, came to be seen as the custodian of civic morality.[1]

While Republican Motherhood, on the one hand, offered women a degree of empowerment and aided their increased educational opportunities, it was also a means of denying women direct political participation in the new republic. Many well-known gender biases emerged from this ideology: women are politically inept; women have political power through the domestic arena in that they can influence their husbands and sons.[2] Yet, the other side of Republican Motherhood was that it "seemed to accomplish what the Enlightenment had not by identifying the intersection of the woman's private domain and the polis";[3] in that light, Republican Motherhood is one of the earliest precursors to the twentieth-century feminist theory that "the personal is political." The limitations of Republican Motherhood were many, but the strengths of this eighteenth-century ideology were its emphases "upon better education, clearer recognition of women's economic contributions, and a strong political identification with the Republic. The idea could be pulled in both conservative and reform directions."[4] Judith Sargent Murray's contributions to American literature and culture, then, must be understood in light of her advocacy of Republican Motherhood's major tenets while recognizing the complexities of Murray's vision of reform for women's roles in society. Her vision included not only increased educational opportunities for women but also increased employment opportunities outside the home that included the theater.[5]

---

1. Linda Kerber, *Women of the Republic: Intellect & Ideology in Revolutionary America* (New York: W. W. Norton, 1980), 11.

2. Barbara Welter's classic essay on the rise of this "cult of domesticity" ("The Cult of True Womanhood: 1820–1860," *American Quarterly* 18 [Summer 1966]: 151–74) indicates that it was an early nineteenth-century phenomenon; more recent studies, such as Kerber's, into early (pre-1800) American culture suggest it began during the crucial revolutionary years.

3. Kerber, 283.

4. Kerber, 284.

5. At this time, women stage performers were considered to have, at the least, loose morals; they were often deemed akin to prostitutes. Judith Sargent Murray not only wrote for the theater, she also associated with many actresses and she sometimes brought her daughter with her when she was working in the Boston theaters.

As she noted in one *Gleaner* essay, the needle was giving way to other opportunities:

> I take leave to congratulate my fair country-women, on the happy revolution which the few past years has made in their favour; that in these infant republics, where, within my remembrance, the use of the needle was the principal attainment which was thought *necessary* for a woman, the lovely proficient is now permitted to appropriate a moiety of her time to studies of a more elevated and elevating nature. Female academies are every where establishing.[1]

If "a moiety of her time" reflects Murray's frustration with the slowness of the process, the rise of female academies confirmed her belief in education as the vehicle of change.

The *Story of Margaretta* is the text by Murray that most openly adheres to Republican Motherhood ideals; yet it would be a mistake simply to align the ideas the novel conveys with one ideology. The *Story of Margaretta* is a complex novel in which the characterization of Margaretta embodies Murray's philosophy of education. When a poem addressed to Margaretta and praising her many angelic charms is published in a local newspaper, Margaretta, we are told, "was too much accustomed to praise to be highly elated by, or interested in the matter" (192), that is, her self-confidence acts as a barrier against inordinate flattery, the downfall of most young women in early American novels. Margaretta is young and human—she at first is drawn to Sinisterus— but her self-confidence and educated intellect allow her quickly to estimate Sinisterus's true nature and to enact "her emancipation" from his influence (199). In the earlier essay, "Desultory Thoughts," Murray had presented just such an argument—when a young woman is taught "to reverence [her]self," she will not fall victim to male flattery (46).

If Margaretta's marriage embraces the role of Republican Motherhood, the subtexts to the *Story of Margaretta* challenge that tradition in unusual ways. First, there is a "fallen woman" in the novel—Frances Wellwood, who was earlier duped by Sinisterus Courtland and had several children with him out of wedlock. Frances is not, however, con-

---

1. *The Gleaner*, 3:88, p. 188.

demned to die at the novel's end. Rather, Margaretta and her family refuse to abandon or condemn this young woman. They offer to help her, believing that both she and Courtland are redeemable human beings, given the proper assistance. It is Courtland's erroneous early "mistaken mode of education" that "hath been his ruin" (208), and in this context, Murray extends her philosophy of education to men as well as women. Importantly, if attitudes about equality and equitability between the sexes and in all social contexts are going to change, Americans must recognize the need to reeducate men as well as to educate women. Second, an integral aspect of Republican Motherhood was that mothers were to educate their *sons* to become valued citizens of the new republic and their daughters were to be educated only insofar as they could continue the process of educating sons in the rudiments of reading and writing when the daughters became mothers themselves. In Murray's vision, women's education should emphasize self-fulfillment as well as its potential for contributing to the polis. In earlier writings, she had satirized the social attitudes toward the "Old Maid," who is seen as one of the "burthens upon society" and argues that "love, friendship and esteem, ought to take place of marriage" when no suitable husband is discovered by the young woman (48).

Not only should girls be educated in their own right but, to Murray's mind, that process should include the history of women's contributions to world culture. It is through an exchange of letters in the *Story of Margaretta* that Murray first presents this idea. Approximately one-third of early American novels employed the epistolary format.[1] Murray synthesizes the traditional narrative novel form and the epistolary. Most often, the epistolary form allowed either the narrative voice or a primary character to inculcate the values of the dominant society. Certainly Mary Vigillius's letters to the young Margaretta serve this purpose, in part, although even then the Vigilliuses' emphasis upon female education went beyond the societal norm. In most early novels, such as Susanna Rowson's *Charlotte Temple* (1791) and Hannah Webster Foster's *The*

---

1. See Cathy N. Davidson, *Revolution and the Word: The Rise of the Novel in America* (New York: Oxford Univ. Press, 1986), especially chapters five and six.

Coquette (1797), the young female protagonist is without parental influence during a large portion of the novel's action. In *Margaretta*, the adoptive parents and especially the mother, are prominent guides through the daughter's years of development.[1] In volume two of *The Gleaner*, however, Murray returned to the exchange of letters between the mother and the married daughter.[2] Some attention to women's history and contributions to various national cultures had been noted in the early letters, but these became a central focus of the adult letters, most notably through a lengthy exchange discussing Mary, Queen of Scots.[3] The mother-daughter letters examine English history in general; but the process begun in the *Story of Margaretta* was continued by Murray in volume three of *The Gleaner*, when she turned her attention fully to women's history on an international basis in a series of essays entitled "Observations on Female Abilities."[4]

In addition to the characterization of Margaretta herself, the *Story of Margaretta* is an important early American novel because of its unique narrative style. Embedded as it is in a series of non-fiction essays, the *Story of Margaretta* allows Murray not only to write fiction but also to take on the role of literary critic. "The Gleaner" is both outside the novel, critiquing it, and a character within the novel who is instrumental in shaping its action. The critique begins with the art of letter-writing itself. Mary Vigillius carefully educates her daughter to the strengths of the genre—honesty, openness, rooted in reason but conveying genuine feelings. Indeed, when Frances Wellwood too dramatically recounts

---

1. Certainly, in *The Coquette* Eliza Wharton is influenced by surrogate parent figures, the Richmans; but as I argue in "Hannah Webster Foster's *The Coquette:* Critiquing Franklin's America," *Redefining the Political Novel: American Women Writers to 1900,* ed. Sharon M. Harris (Knoxville: Univ. of Tennessee Press, 1995), the Richmans are not viable parental substitutes. Indeed, Lucy Freeman Sumner, the voice of the dominant culture's values, is far more influential. The plots of *The Coquette* and the *Story of Margaretta* begin in quite similar fashions, but the conclusions each author draws are notably divergent—Eliza Wharton is seduced by the rake, Major Sanford, in large part because she can see no viable alternative for her future, and she dies shortly after giving birth out of wedlock, while Margaretta Melworth is able to reject her licentious suitor and establish herself in a viable marriage.

2. Murray set off the lengthy mother-daughter letter exchange in volume two as distinct from the *Story of Margaretta;* therefore, these letters have not been included as part of the novel in the present volume.

3. *The Gleaner,* 2:47-50.

4. *The Gleaner,* 3:88-91 (see page 15 in this edition).

her sorrows, Margaretta responds with due sympathy but remarks on the "pathetically plaintive" nature of Frances's style (210). As is true for most early novels, the literary critique also includes an analysis of novels in general. The novel was still a suspect genre because of its potential for inflaming the reader's emotions and imagination. Thus early novelists felt compelled to emphasize the realistic basis of their stories. But in the *Story of Margaretta*, rather than ban novels from the young woman's reading repertoire, the Vigilliuses seek to *educate* their daughter about the issue of the quality of novels:

> We once entertained a design of debarring her the indulgence of novels; but those books, being in the hands of every one, we conceived the accomplishment of our wishes in this respect, except we had bred her an absolute recluse, almost impracticable; and Mrs. Vigillius, therefore, thought it best to permit the use of every decent work, causing them to be read in her presence, hoping that she might, by her suggestions and observations, present an antidote to the poison, with which the pen of the novelist is too often fraught. (165)

In conjunction with Murray's preference for educating young women to critique novels so they may judge for themselves the value of a work, she uses the narrator's outsider/insider nature as a means of incorporating readers' criticism of the novel into the text itself. Thus, *The Gleaner* 12 begins with analyses of the novel by "the genuine critic," the reader (215). Of course, like any good critic, Murray (via her "critics") dictates how one should view the *Story of Margaretta:* the "sober young woman" recognizes the value of the story, while the "*facetious divine*" delivers an unwittingly self-condemning tirade against it (215). But in a more serious vein, Murray uses reader-response criticism for two significant purposes—first, to suggest the eclectic nature of her readership (women and men of all ages and classes); and second, to emphasize her theme of equality. Thus one woman reader demands more independence for women and a greater recognition of "their true dignity" (217). More explicitly, the double standard concerning virtue is challenged:

> "For my own part," continued the fair rationalist, "I am free to own, however singular it may be deemed, that unblemished virtue is, in my estimation, as essential in a man, as in a woman; and that as *man is*

commonly the primary aggressor, I regard a *male prostitute* with even greater detestation than I do an abandoned female. I profess myself an admirer of the Gleaner. I conceive him to be a moral writer." (217-218)

Murray thus avoids the usual didactic narrative voice by allowing "the fair rationalist" to determine for herself the quality of the novel.

The third means by which the *Story of Margaretta* constitutes an important early American novel is through its maze of gender constructions that force the reader to foreground the issue of gender. It is not evident that Murray was widely known as the author of the *Massachusetts Magazine* series when it began; by the time of the book publication of *The Gleaner*, however, her identity was well-known. Thus, the period in which her contemporaries read the *Story of Margaretta* undoubtedly affected their evaluation of its gender issues. Certainly the issue of a male narrator, however, makes explicit the dominant influence of "Fathers," Founding or otherwise, in early America; more subtle, however, are the implications of a female author employing a male persona and the critique of male perspectives in the novel.

In the opening pages of the *Story of Margaretta*, "The Gleaner" observes that he had been "an idle young fellow, fond of indulging myself in every luxury which the small patrimony that descended to me from a very worthy father, would permit" (155).As an indulgent young man, The Gleaner held very traditional views about a woman's "proper" sphere. When he suggested to his wife, for instance, that they make a trip to South Carolina, he observed that "she submitted with that kind of acquiescence, which our sex is so fond of considering as the proper characteristic of womanhood" (156). The *Story of Margaretta*, then, is not only a novel about a young woman's coming of age but equally so about how the narrator learns what it is to be a "worthy" father through taking on the role of parent and learning from his wife as well that the best parent rears an independent child. To use a female persona in this instance would have forced Murray into a didactic mode of reminding her male readers of their need to change, to re-educate themselves about "true womanhood." Such a voice of authority from a woman to a man was virtually unknown in early America, even to a writer of Murray's abilities who had referred to males as "ye haughty sex" in "On the Equality of the Sexes" (8). Murray undoubtedly believed she could convey her ideas in the tried-and-true (that is, safe) method of employing a male narrator, but she explicitly notes later in the novel when she is addressing the issue of readers' responses that *"Facts, real events*, have often been communicated to the world *under feigned names;* and instruction not seldom arrays itself in the decent and alluring veil of allegory" (216).

In the characterization of Edward Hamilton, we have another call for a recognition of the equality of the sexes: if Margaretta is capable of succinct reasoning, Edward is capable of demonstrating his emotional responses to situations. When Margaretta falls in love with Sinisterus, Edward is plunged into "the abyss of despair," but his demonstration of love for Margaretta is deemed a "fine manly" act. It is when "the big emotions of his bosom" are expressed that Edward becomes worthy of marriage to Margaretta (225). In the *Story of Margaretta*, then, Murray uses the comfort of a male narrative persona to deconstruct several layers of gender constructions in late eighteenth-century American culture. The education of Margaretta is extended to all readers, male as well as female. While many traits of Republican Motherhood are, then, perpetuated by Murray in this novel, her choices of narrator, style, and themes also reveal the complex negotiations necessary for an eighteenth-century woman author, even one as well-educated and self-reliant as Judith Sargent Murray.

Murray apparently practiced what she preached in the rearing of her own daughter. The liberality of Julia's education is suggested in a brief portrait of her when she was a young woman: "Julia was brought up to speak with theatrical action; frequented the theatre; was occasionally in the green room, her mother having written plays, which were in rehearsal. I once heard Mrs. Murray say with great delight, that Mrs. Powell, an actress of that day, had spoken highly of Julia's exhibition."[1] Murray believed that one of the surest ways to advance young women's

---

1. Lucius Manlius Sargent, "Reminiscences of Lucius Manlius Sargent"; the manuscript is owned by the SMGHHA (pages are unnumbered). As noted below, the accuracy of Lucius Sargent's accounts of Judith and Julia Murray is always open to question. While Lucius apparently intended this as a depiction of Julia's loose morals and Judith's dangerous educational practices, it is clear from the account that Judith was quite pleased with her daughter's talents and outspokenness.

sense of self-worth and to push for women's equality in general was to educate Americans about the history of women's literary, social, and political contributions on an international basis. Therefore, as a sequel to "On the Equality of the Sexes," Murray included near the end of *The Gleaner* essays a four-part series, "Observations on Female Abilities."[1] Part one aligns "Abilities" with "On the Equality of the Sexes" and notes that, "however well I may think of that composition…I do not conceive that the subject is exhausted."[2] Parts two through four outline the history of "female genius" from ancient Rome and Greece to eighteenth-century America, England, France, and Italy. Murray's argument is presented in a logical construction reminiscent of the sermon format with a detailed proposition followed by proofs and an application. Her purpose is "the establishment of the female intellect, or the maintaining [of] the justice and propriety of considering women, as far as relates to their understanding, in *every respect*, equal to men" and is replete with a catalog of notable women and their accomplishments. Murray's greater purpose—her "application" —places her in the forefront of modernity, for it is not history in and of itself that she values but rather the fact that such knowledge will arm young women to form "a new era in female history."[3] It is a theme that runs throughout Murray's body of work: knowledge of women's abilities and accomplishments is the greatest tool for empowering young women in the new republic.

The Murrays had moved from Gloucester to Boston in 1793, residing at 5 Franklin Place. It was an opportune moment for Murray, who was always seeking new avenues for her literary talents. The move to Boston widely extended Murray's awareness of political and cultural issues at the end of the eighteenth century. A knowledgeable and astute cultural analyst, she was able to enter contemporary debates through her writings in the pages of the *Massachusetts Magazine*. Her essays and plays from this period are increasingly political in nature. One of the

---

1. Part one of the four-part "Observations" is not included in the present volume since it merely sets up the comparison with "On the Equality of the Sexes" and the central tenets of Murray's arguments are presented in parts two through four, which are included herein.

2. *The Gleaner*, 3:88, p. 188.

3. Ibid., p. 189.

most notable examples is "Sketch of the Present Situation of America, 1794."[1] What role America should play in the French Revolution was a hotly contested issue in 1794, when all of Europe was involved in the struggle and when Robespierre and the "Reign of Terror" had emerged. Although Murray recognized the need to support all people's claims to liberty, she also recognized the complexities of the situation that would embroil America:

> But deliberation here maketh a pause—Against whom shall we commence hostilities? So many are the wrongs which we are said to have suffered from the maritime belligerent powers, that an unprejudiced American will hesitate against which to prefer the loudest complaints.(52)

Many citizens who supported the French Revolution, viewing it as an extension of America's own War for Independence, were appalled when the revolutionaries attacked organized Christianity and when reports began to emerge about the extraordinary atrocities committed by both sides. Federalists feared that the social anarchy of the French Revolution would spread to America if they became involved in the war, and Murray was an ardent Federalist. In the early years of the new republic, she argued,

> every one seemed sensible of the blessings of a good government, and *federalism* was the basis, on which we were successfully building the superstructure of every thing useful, every thing virtuous, every thing ornamental. What a fearful and destructive hydra is faction! War is its eldest born, and with the eye of the basilisk it seeketh to annihilate the cherub peace. (50)

More specifically, however, "Sketch of the Present Situation of America, 1794" is a direct attack on the influence on American politics by Edmond Genet (1765–1834), the French republic's minister to the United States. Genet arrived in America in April 1793 and immediately sparked wide public support for the French revolutionary cause. However, he also risked America's stance of neutrality when he hired Americans to attack British shipping interests in the Caribbean and elsewhere.

---

1. *The Gleaner,* 1:26-27 (see page 49 in this edition).

When President George Washington insisted Genet desist from such actions, Genet defied Washington and threatened to take his demands to the people. Genet was eventually recalled to France; yet, even though Genet had attacked Washington's authority, the President blocked his extradition because Genet's party, the Girondists, had lost their power in France and his return would have endangered his life. His influence was felt long afterward in various stateside factions that supported United States involvement in France.

Murray, like most Federalists, feared Genet's influence and based her opposition on its abridgement of constitutional processes. Addressing "ye associated declaimers," she asked:

> But, suffer a fellow-citizen to make the inquiry—What is your object? Why are you thus studious to create divisions? Why are you ambitious of forming an *aristocracy* in the midst of your brethren? Ought not the nation at large to constitute one vast society of people, bound by common ties, common wishes, and common hopes? Hath any part of the Union *constitutionally* delegated their powers to you? To whom will you appeal? The late envoy of France, *in effect, at least*, threatened an appeal to the people! But surely, neither the quondam ambassador or his adherents have sufficiently attended to the origin, nature, and completion of our happy constitution. (54)

However one views the Federalist position during the French Revolution, the sketch constitutes a remarkable document. It is little wonder that Murray felt the necessity of a male persona in her *Gleaner* essays: no other American woman of her time, even under cover of anonymity, spoke so openly about contemporary political controversies.

Murray's entry into the field of playwriting was equally political, and in both of her produced plays (as in the *Story of Margaretta* and elsewhere), Murray linked the social and the political. Although performances of plays had been banned in Boston as early as 1750, opposition to the argument that the theater was the instigator of moral and religious decay had been equally long-standing. When the Murrays moved to Boston, the city had just lifted its ban, and Murray quickly turned her skills to writing dramas and to defending the artistic and cultural benefits of the theater. She had apprenticed her dramatic talents while in Gloucester, writing poetic prologues and epilogues for local productions of several well-known plays, including Royall Tyler's *The Contrast* (1787). In Boston, however, she began writing original comedies. While attitudes about women and the corrupting effects of the theater prevailed in eighteenth-century America, they were changing, due in large part to the published (if unperformed) patriotic dramas of Murray's friend, Mercy Otis Warren, during the American Revolution. Murray supported the theater in general, but she also sought to transform it: "The stage is undoubtedly a very powerful engine," she wrote, "in forming the opinions and manners of a people. Is it not then of importance to supply the American stage with American scenes?"[1] Both of her produced plays adhered to that goal (Murray apparently wrote a third play with the provocative title of *The African;* she refers to the play in her letters, but unfortunately no copy is extant).

Murray's first play, *The Medium, or Virtue Triumphant,* was performed at Boston's Federal Street Theatre on 2 March 1795.[2] As Murray's first biographer, Vena Bernadette Field, observed, Judith Sargent Murray "was one of the earliest [Bostonians] to patronize the theatre, thereby championing an art branded by many of her contemporaries as an influence for evil."[3] *The Medium, or Virtue Triumphant* was the first play by an American author performed at the Boston theater, but it earned only one performance. Her second play, *The Traveller Returned,* was performed at the same theater on 9-10 March 1796. Scholars have typically assumed that the quality of the plays warranted their short runs. However, such assumptions ignore the bias against female playwrights—and it should be noted that her first play reinforced her call for women's rights. The reviews that followed the first performance of *The Medium,* for instance, revealed just such gender biases: one critic, who obviously knew Murray was the author, denied her abilities by

---

1. "Observation on the Tragedies of Mrs. Warren," *The Gleaner,* 3:96.

2. Lucius Manlius Sargent indicates that the original title of Murray's first play was *The Medium, or happy tea party.* While a title that wittily plays off of Boston's most famous Revolutionary act is certainly within the realm of the content and satirical style of Murray's work, I have found no other reference to the play with this title; its published title is *The Medium, or Virtue Triumphant.*

3. Field, 32.

insisting that her husband must have co-authored the comedy, and the second critic assumed it must have been written by a man.[1] These critical evaluations, which appeared the day after *The Medium*'s first performance, had the expected effect, but the perpetuation of these evaluations has been rampant, far too often without any knowledge of the plays themselves.

In spite of the attacks on her dramatic writings, Murray chose to include the two plays in *The Gleaner*, one of which, *The Traveller Returned*, is included in the present volume. Set during the American Revolution, *The Traveller Returned* supports the Revolutionary cause and also raises issues about the emerging class structure of the new nation. Characters represent virtually every class—the upper-class Montagues, the middle-class Emily Lovegrove, the working-class Vansittarts, servants such as Patrick O'Neal, Obadiah, and Bridget (the latter two characters' household positions and their lack of last names suggests they may have represented the slave class). While the class struggles in this comedy reveal the rising yearnings for social mobility in the working class, these struggles are the major source of the comic action in the play, whereas the characters from Murray's own upper-class background are the central and serious voices in the comedy. In a more satisfying manner, the play incorporates two other issues well-known by this time to Murray's readers: the education of women and the necessity of allowing errors made early in life to be corrected. The widowed Mrs. Montague could live an idle life, but she rigorously educates herself in philosophy and science, and Murray incorporates some of Mrs. Montague's reading directly into the play. The theme of young women's development is more complex. While Emily Lovegrove constitutes the proper young woman, it is obvious that Murray prefers the lively, outgoing nature of Harriot Montague, who is invested with a sense of humor.

It is the middle-aged Mrs. Montague, however, who is revealed to have erred in her youth. Benjamin Franklin had outlined in his *Autobiography* the numerous "errata" that he had committed as a young man

---

1. For a fuller discussion of critical responses to Murray's plays, see Field, 33–40, and Sharon M. Harris, "Early American Women's Self-Creating Acts," *Resources in American Literary Studies* 19.2 (1993): 223–45.

and the means by which he corrected them as he rose to national status as an elder statesman; however, in early American literature virtually every characterization of women who do not live a reclusive and strict life condemns the woman to death or deems her inadequate for marriage at the text's conclusion.[1] Murray's comedy, however, depicts a woman who, in spite of her "errors," never lost her place in society and, as she matures, changes and is restored to her marriage. When she asks her husband if he can forgive her, he responds that he, too, had erred and that he had been "too severe!" (150). As in the *Story of Margaretta*, women who step outside the bounds of established "propriety" are not condemned; it is the strictures of society itself that come under question.

In 1798 Murray collected her extremely popular writings from the *Massachusetts Magazine* into the three-volume collection entitled *The Gleaner* and published under the signature of "Constantia." By this time, her identity was well-known; she was recognized as a significant author of poetry, essays, fiction, and drama. Running almost one thousand pages in length, *The Gleaner* was published by subscription at Boston by Isaiah Thomas and E. T. Andrews. The three volumes include one hundred essays on such topics as women's equality, current health issues, the American work ethic, religion, justice, beauty, philanthropy, history, genius, travel, propriety, politics, hospitality—in other words, a compendium of cultural issues relevant to late eighteenth-century America. Nowhere are Murray's extraordinary talents for satire so evident as in these essays. Throughout the volumes, too, she continues the self-critique begun in the *Story of Margaretta* by creating letters from "readers" that present a plethora of perspectives on the contemporary issues she addresses.

---

1. Hannah Foster also exposes this double standard in *The Coquette*, but she does not alter the fate of her heroine, Eliza Wharton, who dies in childbirth. (For a fuller discussion of how Foster deals with this theme, see Sharon M. Harris, "Hannah Webster Foster's *The Coquette:* Critiquing Franklin's America," in Sharon M. Harris, ed., *Redefining the Political Novel: American Women Writers to 1900* [Knoxville: Univ. of Tennessee Press, 1995].) Similarly, the erring Dorcasina Sheldon in Tabitha Tenney's *Female Quixotism, Exhibited in the Romantic Opinions and Extravagant Adventures of Dorcasina Sheldon* (1801; rpt., New York: Oxford Univ. Press, 1992) changes her attitudes but is denied her desire to marry at the novel's conclusion.

The subscription publication of *The Gleaner* was highly successful, representing the public's recognition of a major new author on the American literary scene. There were subscriptions for 824 sets at one dollar a volume; the 759 subscribers (several subscribed to more than one set) included Martha and George Washington, President John Adams, Sarah Wentworth Morton, John Hancock, Susanna Rowson, David Ramsay, and the Governors of New Hampshire and Massachusetts, among many other notable political and literary persons as well as friends and family. Subscriptions came from throughout the colonies and continental territories as well as from England.[1]

After the appearance of the three-volume edition of *The Gleaner* in 1798, Murray published only eight more original pieces, all poetry; seven poems appeared in the *Boston Weekly Magazine* from 30 October 1802, to 19 March 1803,[2] and one poem was published in *Boston Magazine* on 14 December 1805. Murray's remaining publications were edited editions of her husband's writings. Two reasons for this sudden shift in literary productivity assert themselves: first, the *Massachusetts Magazine* temporarily suspended publication in the beginning of 1795 due to financial exigency. Murray apparently hoped that it would be reinstated, but her own needs changed and the magazine ended its publication at the end of 1796. She published her last eight poems pseudonymously as "Honora-Martesia" and "Honora," as if retiring "Constantia" in honor of her association with the *Massachusetts Magazine* and *The Gleaner* series.[3]

---

1. A complete list of subscribers and number of copies purchased is appended to the 1798 edition of *The Gleaner*.

2. It is notable that the novelist, playwright, and educator Susanna Haswell Rowson was a contributing editor to the *Boston Weekly Magazine* when Murray published her poetry in that periodical.

3. The predominant theme of these last poems is that of childbirth. Although Murray had not written a poem on the occasion of the birth of her daughter, she published "Lines Written while Rocking a Cradle" in the *Boston Weekly Magazine*, 6 Nov. 1802, p. 2, when Julia Maria was eleven years old. The poem runs 102 lines and is a tribute to her daughter: "My Maria—careful joy, / All my moments you employ; / Time advanceth not for me, / 'Tis devoted all to thee...." (ll. 1–4). Unlike the tragic move from hope to loss in the poetic tribute to her son, in this poem Murray envisions Julia's long life and maintains the spirit of hope throughout, ending with a sense of their eternal connection: "*Together live*—beyond the death of time, / Sublime our pleasures—and our hopes sublime."

The second reason for Murray's shift from original to edited writings was undoubtedly the Murrays' increasingly desperate financial problems in the late 1790s. John Murray had never been a concerned money manager, at times offering his services free of charge, and Judith's earnings from her writings were insufficient to provide for a family of three that traveled frequently and expended considerable sums on behalf of their commitment to Universalism. By the end of the decade, their financial situation was critical. It was John who had suggested Judith publish her popular "Gleaner" essays in book form as a means of increasing the family's income. In addition, John's eyesight had been failing for several years, complicating his own production of sermons and other writings; then, in 1809, he suffered a severe stroke that left him paralyzed until his death in 1815.

These were extremely difficult years for Judith Sargent Murray. The only means by which the Murrays' financial concerns were eventually eased was through their daughter's economic generosity. On 26 August 1812, Julia married Adam Louis Bingaman, son of a wealthy planter and a Harvard graduate; the marriage was kept a secret because of opposition from both the bride's and the groom's families. Judith's cousin, Lucius Manlius Sargent (1786–1867), attempted in his reminiscences to suggest that Julia and Adam married only after she became pregnant; not only are his assertions unsupported, but Lucius was notoriously vituperative when it came to his cousin Judith and her family. Sargent was himself an author and translator. In his last years, he revealed his conservative politics in an extensive series of temperance tracts and in an anti-abolition text, *The Ballad of the Abolition Blunderbuss* (1861). Undoubtedly, his attacks against Murray were linked to their opposing political views and perhaps to the success his elder cousin had achieved as a writer. It is impossible to know how much of an impact his denigrations of Murray may have had on the subsequent suppression of her writings and reputation, but he certainly caused her much personal pain.[1]

Lucius admits that he did not deserve his cousin's kindness and that

---

1. Lucius's disparaging remark about his cousin—"she wrote poetry by the acre" —has become well-known among Murray scholars and is still quoted in most accounts of her life; it was cited as well in a recent history of Universalism in America (see Miller, 29).

he enjoyed playing "foolish tricks" on her. His idea of tom-foolery, however, reeks of cruelty. In 1807, when the Murrays were impoverished,
the twenty-one-year-old Lucius wrote to Judith in the guise of the
printers, Blecher & Armstrong, asking permission to publish the collected writings of "Honora Martesia." After several letters negotiating
terms, "the bait was greedily swallowed," as Lucius put it. Judith
devoted precious time to selecting appropriate works for the collection;
needless to say, she was stunned and disbelieving when Armstrong
asserted that he knew nothing of the offer. After Judith's death, Lucius
(who never revealed himself to her as the instigator of the prank) sought
to diminish her reputation by mocking her writing; apparently, he
deeply resented her feminist attitudes. One passage in his writings
about Julia further suggests the extent to which he went to ruin the
character of mother and daughter. The early friendship and evolving
love between Julia and Adam paralleled that of her parents in many
ways. Because of the Stevenses' financial difficulties, they had taken in
boarders, most notably John Murray; likewise when the Murrays faced
equally difficult financial straits, they took in boarders, including Adam
Bingaman. But in Lucius's account, "Julia when the thermometer was
above 40 of Farenheit wore her gown very low in the neck, a thing,
which has proved fatal to bishops & laymen—Adams fall was, doubtless, a very natural consequence."[1] Lucius's ludicrous creation of the
seduction of Adam and his biblically aligned fall suggests either that he
had never read his cousin's treatise on patriarchy's false constructions of
the Adam and Eve creation story—or perhaps his attack was rooted in
the fact that he had read it!

Whatever the doubts of the parents may have been, the young couple
seem to have established a lasting relationship. They moved to Natchez,
then part of the Mississippi Territory; settled on Adam's inherited property, known as the Fatherland Plantation; and raised two children,
Charlotte and Adam, Jr. In spite of the unpromising beginning between
the Murrays and the Bingamans, Julia and Adam financially assisted the
elder Murrays through their last stringent years.

---

1. Unpublished manuscript, at SMGHHA.

Dedicated to her husband and to Universalism in general, Judith Sargent Murray turned her literary attentions in her final years to the publication of John's writings. In 1812–13, she published his *Letters, and Sketches of Sermons* in three volumes; after John's death, she added three chapters to the end of his autobiography (which he had been working on since 1773) and published it in 1816 under the title, *Records of the Life of the Rev. John Murray, Written by Himself, with a Continuation by Mrs. Judith Sargent Murray.* That same year, Murray moved to Natchez, Mississippi, to live with her daughter and son-in-law. She lived there until her death on 6 July 1820, at the age of sixty-nine. Murray was buried in the Bingaman family cemetery on St. Catherine's Creek, which bordered the Mississippi River.

If Murray's diverse and numerable writings and her distinguished literary reputation were lost to American literature for almost two centuries, the recent resurgence of interest in her writings acknowledges Murray's contributions to American literary history and to the prolonged argument for women's equality. In the prefatory comments to *The Gleaner,* Murray had written, "My desires are, I am free to own, aspiring—perhaps presumptuously so. I would be distinguished and respected by my contemporaries; I would be continued on grateful remembrance when I make my exit; and I would descend with celebrity to posterity."[1] If the descent to posterity has been prolonged, it is the late twentieth-century contingent of readers who are responding with "grateful remembrance."

Selected Bibliography

Baym, Nina. "Introduction." *The Gleaner.* Schenectady, N.Y.: Union College, 1992, iii–xx.

Field, Vena Bernadette. *Constantia: A Study of the Life and Works of Judith Sargent Murray, 1751–1820.* Orono, Maine: Univ. Press, 1931.

Gibson, Rev. Gordon D. "The Rediscovery of Judith Sargent Murray." The John Murray Distinguished Lecture for 1991, presented at the Unitarian

---

1. *The Gleaner,* vol. 1, pp. vii-viii.

Universalist General Assembly, June 1991; published in *"Not Hell, But Hope"* (Murray Grove Association).

Jacoba, Madelon. "The Novella as Political Message: *The Margaretta Story.*" *Studies in the Humanities* 18 (Dec. 1991): 146–64.

————. "'An Inestimable Prize,' Educating Women in the New Republic: The Writings of Judith Sargent Murray." *Journal of Thought* 20 (Fall 1985): 250–62.

Murray, Judith Sargent. The Letterbooks. Manuscript books housed at the Mississippi Department of Archives, Jackson, Mississippi.

Schofield, Mary Anne. "'Quitting the Loom and Distaff': Eighteenth-Century American Women Dramatists," in Mary Anne Schofield and Cecilia Macheski, eds., *Curtain Calls: British and American Women and the Theater, 1660–1820.* Athens: Ohio Univ. Press, 1991, 260–73.

Note on the Text

The texts of "On the Equality of the Sexes" and "Desultory Thoughts…" have been transcribed from their original magazine printings in *The Massachusetts Magazine* and *Gentleman and Lady's Town and Country Magazine*, respectively. Excerpts from the letters of Judith Sargent Murray have been transcribed from microfilm copies of her letter books. All other texts included herein are transcribed from the 1798 first edition of *The Gleaner*, printed by Isaiah Thomas and E. T. Andrews at Boston, Massachusetts. In all cases of printed texts and letters, eighteenth-century practices of paragraphing, punctuation, spelling, and capitalization have been retained. The only silent emendations are as follows: obvious printer errors have been corrected; quotation marks have been standardized when necessary for purposes of clarity; capitalization in chapter titles from *The Gleaner* has been regularized in conjunction with modern practices; and original Errata noted in *The Gleaner* have been corrected. All notes are the editor's unless indicated by brackets as the author's.

SELECTED ESSAYS

On the Equality of the Sexes

That minds are not alike, full well I know,
This truth each day's experience will show;
To heights surprising some great spirits soar,
With inborn strength mysterious depths explore;
Their eager gaze surveys the path of light,   5
Confest it stood to Newton's[1] piercing sight.
    Deep science, like a bashful maid retires,
And but the *ardent* breast her worth inspires;
By perseverance the coy fair is won.
And Genius, led by Study, wears the crown.   10
    But some there are who wish not to improve,
Who never can the path of knowledge love,
Whose souls almost with the dull body one,
With anxious care each mental pleasure shun;
Weak is the level'd, enervated mind,   15
And but while here to vegetate design'd.
The torpid spirit mingling with its clod,
Can scarcely boast its origin from God;
Stupidly dull—they move progressing on—
They eat, and drink, and all their work is done.   20
While others, emulous of sweet applause,
Industrious seek for each event a cause,
Tracing the hidden springs whence knowledge flows,
Which nature all in beauteous order shows.
    Yet cannot I their sentiments imbibe,   25

Title. This essay was originally published in *The Massachusetts Magazine, or, Monthly Museum of Knowledge and Rational Entertainment* 2.3–4 (March–April 1790): 132–35, 223–26.

1. **Newton's:** Sir Isaac Newton (1642–1727), English philosopher and mathematician.

Who this distinction to the sex ascribe,
As if a woman's form must needs enrol,
A weak, a servile, an inferiour soul;
And that the guise of man must still proclaim,
Greatness of mind, and him, to be the same: 30
Yet as the hours revolve fair proofs arise,
Which the bright wreath of growing fame supplies;
And in past times some men have *sunk* so *low,*
That female records nothing *less* can show.
But imbecility is still confin'd,   35
And by the lordly sex to us consign'd;
They rob us of the power t'improve,
And then declare we only trifles love;
Yet haste the era, when the world shall know,
That such distinctions only dwell below;   40
The soul unfetter'd, to no sex confin'd,
Was for the abodes of cloudless day design'd.
    Mean time we emulate their manly fires,
Though erudition all their thoughts inspires,
Yet nature with *equality* imparts,   45
And *noble passions,* swell e'en *female hearts.*

Is it upon mature consideration we adopt the idea, that nature is thus partial in her distributions? Is it indeed a fact, that she hath yielded to one half of the human species so unquestionable a mental superiority? I know that to both sexes elevated understandings, and the reverse, are common. But, suffer me to ask, in what the minds of females are so notoriously deficient, or unequal. May not the intellectual powers be ranged under these four heads—imagination, reason, memory and judgment. The province of imagination hath long since been surrendered up to us, and we have been crowned undoubted sovereigns of the regions of fancy. Invention is perhaps the most arduous effort of the mind; this branch of imagination hath been particularly ceded to us, and we have been time out of mind invested with that creative faculty. Observe the variety of fashions (here I bar the contemptuous smile) which distinguish and adorn the female world; how continually are they changing, insomuch that they almost render the wise man's assertion problematical, and we are ready to say, *there is something new under the sun.* Now what a playfulness, what an exuberance of fancy, what strength of inventive imagination, doth this continual variation discover? Again, it hath been observed, that if the turpitude of the conduct of our sex, hath been ever so enormous, so extremely ready are we, that the very first thought presents us with an apology, so plausible, as to produce our actions even in an amiable light. Another instance of our creative powers, is our talent for slander; how ingenious are we at inventive scandal? what a formidable story can we in a moment fabricate merely from the force of a prolifick imagination? how many reputations, in the fertile brain of a female, have been utterly despoiled? how industrious are we at improving a hint? suspicion how easily do we convert into conviction, and conviction, embellished by the power of eloquence, stalks abroad to the surprise and confusion of unsuspecting innocence. Perhaps it will be asked if I furnish these facts as instances of excellency in our sex. Certainly not; but as proofs of a creative faculty, of a lively imagination. Assuredly great activity of mind is thereby discovered, and was this activity properly directed, what beneficial effects would follow. Is the needle and kitchen sufficient to employ the operations of a soul thus organized? I should conceive not. Nay, it is a truth that those very departments leave the intelligent principle vacant, and at liberty for speculation. Are we deficient in reason? we can only reason from what we know, and if an opportunity of acquiring knowledge hath been denied us, the inferiority of our sex cannot fairly be deduced from thence. Memory, I believe, will be allowed us in common, since every one's experience must testify, that a loquacious old woman is as frequently met with, as a communicative old man; their subjects are alike drawn from the fund of other times, and the transactions of their youth, or of maturer life, entertain, or perhaps fatigue you, in the evening of their lives. "But our judgment is not so strong—we do not distinguish so well."—Yet it may be questioned, from what doth this superiority, in this determining faculty of the soul, proceed. May we not trace its source in the difference of education, and continued advantages? Will it be said that the judgment of a male of two years old, is more sage than that of a female's of the same age? I believe the reverse is generally observed to be true. But from that period what partiality! how is the one exalted, and the other depressed, by the contrary modes of education which are adopted! the one is taught to aspire, and the other is early confined and limitted. As their years increase, the sister must be wholly domesticated, while the brother is led by the hand through all the flowery paths of science. Grant that their minds are by nature equal, yet who shall wonder at the *apparent* superiority, if indeed custom becomes *second nature;* nay if it taketh place of nature, and that it doth the experience of each day will evince. At length arrived at womanhood, the uncultivated fair one feels a void, which the employments allotted her are by no means capable of filling. What can she do? to books she may not apply; or if she doth, *to those only of the novel kind,* lest she merit the appellation of a *learned lady;* and what ideas have been affixed to this term, the observation of many can testify. Fashion, scandal, and sometimes what is still more reprehensible, are then called in to her relief; and who can say to what lengths the liberties she takes may proceed. Meantime she herself is most unhappy; she feels the want of a cultivated mind. Is she single, she in vain seeks to fill up time from sexual employments or amusements. Is she united to a person whose soul nature made equal to her own, education hath set him so far above her, that in those entertainments which are productive of such rational felicity, she is not qualified to accompany him. She experiences a mortifying consciousness of inferiority, which embitters every enjoyment. Doth the person to whom her adverse fate hath consigned her, possess a mind incapable of improvement, she is equally wretched, in being so closely connected with an individual whom she cannot but despise. Now, was she permitted the same instructors as her brother, (with an eye however to their particular departments) for the employment of a rational mind an ample field would be opened. In astronomy she might catch a glimpse of the immensity of the Deity, and thence she would form amazing conceptions of the august and supreme Intelligence. In geography she would admire Jehovah in the midst of his benevolence; thus adapting this globe to the various wants and amusements of its inhabitants. In natural philosophy she would adore the infinite majesty of heaven, clothed in condescension; and as she traversed the reptile world, she would hail the goodness of a creating God. A mind, thus filled, would have little room for the trifles with which our sex are, with too much justice, accused of amusing themselves, and they would thus be rendered fit companions for those, who should one day wear them as their crown. Fashions, in their variety, would then give place to conjectures, which might perhaps conduce to the improvement of the literary world; and there would be no leisure for slander or detraction. Reputation would not then be blasted, but serious speculations would occupy the lively imaginations of the sex. Unnecessary visits would be precluded, and that custom would only be indulged by way of relaxation, or to answer the demands of consanguinity and friendship. Females would become discreet, their judgments would be invigorated, and their partners for life being circumspectly chosen, an unhappy Hymen[1] would then be as rare, as is now the reverse.

Will it be urged that those acquirements would supersede our domestick duties? I answer that every requisite in female economy is easily attained; and, with truth I can add, that when once attained, they require no further *mental attention*. Nay, while we are pursuing the needle, or the superintendency of the family, I repeat, that our minds are at full liberty for reflection; that imagination may exert itself in full vigor; and that if a just foundation is early laid, our ideas will then be worthy of rational beings. If we were industrious we might easily find time to arrange them upon paper, or should avocations press too hard for such an indulgence, the hours allotted for conversation would at least become more refined and rational. Should it still be vociferated, "Your domestick employments are sufficient"—I would calmly ask, is it reasonable, that a candidate for immortality, for the joys of heaven, an intelligent being, who is to spend an eternity in contemplating the works of Deity, should at present be so degraded, as to be allowed no other ideas, than those which are suggested by the mechanism of a pudding, or the sewing the seams of a garment? Pity that all such censurers

---

1. **Hymen:** in Greek mythology, the god of marriage.

of female improvement do not go one step further, and deny their future existence; to be consistent they surely ought.

Yes, ye lordly, ye haughty sex, our souls are by nature *equal* to yours; the same breath of God animates, enlivens, and invigorates us; and that we are not fallen lower than yourselves, let those witness who have greatly towered above the various discouragements by which they have been so heavily oppressed; and though I am unacquainted with the list of celebrated characters on either side, yet from the observations I have made in the contracted circle in which I have moved, I dare confidently believe, that from the commencement of time to the present day, there hath been as many females, as males, who, by the *mere force of natural powers,* have merited the crown of applause; who, *thus unassisted,* have seized the wreath of fame. I know there are who assert, that as the animal powers of the one sex are superior, of course their mental faculties also must be stronger; thus attributing strength of mind to the transient organization of this earth born tenement. But if this reasoning is just, man must be content to yield the palm [to] many of the brute creation, since by not a few of his brethren of the field, he is far surpassed in bodily strength. Moreover, was this argument admitted, it would prove too much, for occular demonstration evinceth, that there are many robust masculine ladies, and effeminate gentlemen. Yet I fancy that Mr. Pope,[1] though clogged with an enervated body, and distinguished by a diminutive stature, could nevertheless lay claim to greatness of soul; and perhaps there are many other instances which might be adduced to combat so unphilosophical an opinion. Do we not often see, that when the clay built tabernacle is well nigh dissolved, when it is just ready to mingle with the parent soil, the immortal inhabitant aspires to, and even attaineth heights the most sublime, and which were before wholly unexplored. Besides, were we to grant that animal strength proved any thing, taking into consideration the accustomed impartiality of nature, we should be induced to imagine, that she had invested the female mind with superiour strength as an equivalent for the bodily powers of man. But waving this however palpable advantage, for *equality only,* we wish to contend.

---

1. **Mr. Pope:** Alexander Pope (1688–1744), English poet.

I am aware that there are many passages in the sacred oracles which seem to give the advantage to the other sex; but I consider all these as wholly metaphorical. Thus David[1] was a man after God's own heart, yet see him enervated by his licentious passions! behold him following Uriah[2] to the death, and shew me wherein could consist the immaculate Being's complacency. Listen to the curses which Job[3] bestoweth upon the day of his nativity, and tell me where is his perfection, where his patience—*literally* it existed not. David and Job were types of him who was to come; and the superiority of man, as exhibited in scripture, being also emblematical, all arguments deduced from thence, of course fall to the ground. The exquisite delicacy of the female mind proclaimeth the exactness of its texture, while its nice sense of honour announceth its innate, its native grandeur. And indeed, in one respect, the preeminence seems to be tacitly allowed us, for after an education which limits and confines, and employments and recreations which naturally tend to enervate the body, and debilitate the mind; after we have from early youth been adorned with ribbons, and other gewgaws, dressed out like the ancient victims previous to a sacrifice, being taught by the care of our parents in collecting the most showy materials that the ornamenting our exteriour ought to be the principal object of our attention; after, I say, fifteen years thus spent, we are introduced into the world, amid the united adulation of every beholder. Praise is sweet to the soul; we are immediately intoxicated by large draughts of flattery, which being plentifully administered, is to the pride of our hearts the most acceptable incense. It is expected that with the other sex we should commence immediate war, and that we should triumph over the machinations of the most artful. We must be constantly upon our guard; prudence and discretion must be our characteristicks; and we must rise superiour to, and obtain a complete victory over those who have been

---

1. **David:** in the Bible, second king of Israel. See 1 Sam. 16:1 to 1 Kings 2:11.

2. **Uriah:** in the Bible, one of King David's generals who was executed in order to conceal David's acts of adultery. See 2 Sam. 11:1–25.

3. **Job:** in the Bible, the example of the suffering saint, whose experiences raise the question of why the religious suffer. See especially Job 42:1–6.

long adding to the native strength of their minds, by an unremitted study of men and books, and who have, moreover, conceived from the loose characters which they have seen portrayed in the extensive variety of their reading, a most contemptible opinion of the sex. Thus unequal, we are, notwithstanding, forced to the combat, and the infamy which is consequent upon the smallest deviation in our conduct, proclaims the high idea which was formed of our native strength; and thus, indirectly at least, is the preference acknowledged to be our due. And if we are allowed an equality of acquirement, let serious studies equally employ our minds, and we will bid our souls arise to equal strength. We will meet upon even ground, the despot man; we will rush with alacrity to the combat, and, crowned by success, we shall then answer the exalted expectations which are formed. Though sensibility, soft compassion, and gentle commiseration, are inmates in the female bosom, yet against every deep laid art, altogether fearless of the event, we will set them in array; for assuredly the wreath of victory will encircle the spotless brow. If we meet an equal, a sensible friend, we will reward him with the hand of amity, and through life we will be assiduous to promote his happiness; but from every deep laid scheme for our ruin, retiring into ourselves, amid the flowery paths of science, we will indulge in all the refined and sentimental pleasures of contemplation. And should it still be urged, that the studies thus insisted upon would interfere with our more peculiar department, I must further reply, that *early hours,* and close application, will do wonders; and to her who is from the first dawn of reason taught to fill up time rationally, both the requisites will be easy. I grant that niggard fortune is too generally unfriendly to the mind; and that much of that valuable treasure, time, is necessarily expended upon the wants of the body; but it should be remembered, that in embarrassed circumstances our companions have as little leisure for literary improvement, as is afforded to us; for most certainly their provident care is at least as requisite as our exertions. Nay, we have even more leisure for sedentary pleasures, as our avocations are more retired, much less laborious, and, as hath been observed, by no means require that avidity of attention which is proper to the employments of the other sex. In high life, or, in other words, where the parties are in possession of affluence, the objection respecting time is wholly obviated, and of course falls to the ground; and it may also be repeated, that many of those hours which are at present swallowed up in fashion and scandal, might be redeemed, were we habituated to useful reflections. But in one respect, O ye arbiters of our fate! we confess that the superiority is indubitably yours; you are by nature formed for our protectors; we pretend not to vie with you in bodily strength; upon this point we will never contend for victory. Shield us then, we beseech you, from external evils, and in return *we* will transact *your* domestick affairs. Yes, *your,* for are you not equally interested in those matters with ourselves? Is not the elegancy of neatness as agreeable to your sight as to ours; is not the well favoured viand equally delightful to your taste; and doth not your sense of hearing suffer as much, from the discordant sounds prevalent in an ill regulated family, produced by the voices of children and many *et ceteras?*

CONSTANTIA.

By way of supplement to the foregoing pages, I subjoin the following extract from a letter, wrote to a friend in the December of 1780.

And now assist me, O thou genius of my sex, while I undertake the arduous task of endeavouring to combat that vulgar, that almost universal errour, which hath, it seems, enlisted even Mr. P— under its banners. The superiority of your sex hath, I grant, been time out of mind esteemed a truth incontrovertible; in consequence of which persuasion, every plan of education hath been calculated to establish this favourite tenet. Not long since; weak and presuming as I was, I amused myself with selecting some arguments from nature, reason, and experience, against this so generally received idea. I confess that to sacred testimonies I had not recourse. I held them to be merely metaphorical, and thus regarding them, I could not persuade myself that there was any propriety in bringing them to decide in this *very important debate.* However, as you, sir, confine yourself entirely to the sacred oracles, I mean to bend the whole of my artillery against those supposed proofs, which you have from thence provided, and from which you have formed an intrenchment *apparently* so invulnerable. And first, to begin with our great progenitors; but here, suffer me to premise, that it is for mental strength I mean to contend, for with respect to animal powers, I yield them undisputed to that sex, which enjoys them in common with the lion, the tyger, and many other beasts of prey; therefore your observations respecting the *rib under the arm, at a distance from the head,* &c. &c. in no sort militate against my view. Well, but the woman was first in the transgression. Strange how blind *self love* renders you men; were you not wholly absorbed in a partial admiration of your own abilities, you would long since have acknowledged the force of what I am now going to urge. It is true some ignoramuses have absurdly enough informed us, that the beauteous fair of paradise, was seduced from her obedience, by a malignant demon, *in the guise of a baleful serpent;* but we, who are better informed, know that the fallen spirit presented himself to her view, *a shining angel still;* for thus, saith the criticks in the Hebrew tongue, ought the word to be rendered. Let us examine her motive—Hark! the seraph declares that she shall attain a perfection of knowledge; for is there aught which is not comprehended under one or other of the terms *good* and *evil*. It doth not appear that she was governed by any one sensual appetite; but merely by a desire of adorning her mind; a laudable ambition fired her soul, and a thirst for knowledge impelled the predilection so fatal in its consequences. Adam could not plead the same deception; assuredly he was not deceived; nor ought we to admire his superiour strength, or wonder at his sagacity, when we so often confess that example is much more influential than precept. His gentle partner stood before him, a melancholy instance of the direful effects of disobedience; he saw her not possessed of that wisdom which she had fondly hoped to obtain, but he beheld the once blooming female, disrobed of that innocence, which had heretofore rendered her so lovely. To him then deception became impossible, as he had proof positive of the fallacy of the argument, which the deceiver had suggested. What then could be his inducement to burst the barriers, and to fly directly in the face of that command, which *immediately* from the mouth of deity *he* had received, since, I say, he could not plead that fascinating stimulus, the accumulation of knowledge, as indisputable conviction was so visibly portrayed before him. What mighty cause impelled him to sacrifice myriads of beings yet unborn, and by one impious act, which *he saw* would be productive of such fatal effects, entail undistinguished ruin upon a race of beings, which he was yet to produce. Blush, ye vaunters of fortitude; ye boasters of resolution; ye haughty lords of the creation; blush when ye remember, that he was influenced by no other motive than a bare pusillanimous attachment to a woman! by sentiments so exquisitely soft, that all his sons have, from that period, when they have designed to degrade them, described as highly feminine. Thus it should seem, that all the arts of the grand deceiver (since means adequate to the purpose are, I conceive, invariably pursued) were requisite to mislead our general mother, while the father of mankind forfeited his own, and relinquished the happiness of posterity, merely in compliance with the blandishments of a female. The subsequent subjection the apostle Paul explains as a figure; after enlarging upon the subject, he adds, *"This is a great mystery; but I speak concerning Christ and the church."*[1] Now we know with what consummate wisdom the unerring father of eternity hath formed his plans; all the types which he hath displayed, he hath permitted *materially* to fail, in the very virtue for which *they* were famed. The reason for this is obvious, we might otherwise mistake his economy, and render that honour to the creature, which is due only to the creator. I know that Adam was a figure of him who was to come. The grace contained in this figure, is the reason of my rejoicing, and while I am very far from prostrating before the shadow, I yield joyfully in all things the preeminence to the second federal head. Confiding faith is prefigured by Abraham, yet he exhibits a contrast to affiance, when he says of his fair companion, she is my sister.[2] Gentleness was the characteristick of Moses, yet he hesitated not to reply to Jehovah himself, with unsaintlike tongue he murmured at the waters of strife, and with rash hands he break the tables, which were inscribed by the finger of divinity. David, dignified with the title of the man after God's own heart, and yet how stained was his life. Solomon was celebrated for wisdom, but folly is wrote in legible characters upon his almost every action. Lastly, let us turn our eyes to man in

---

1. **This...mystery:** Eph. 5:32.
2. **she...sister:** See Gen. 12:10–20.

the aggregate. He is manifested as the figure of strength, but that we may not regard him as any thing more than a figure, his soul is formed in no sort superiour, but every way equal to the mind of her, who is the emblem of weakness, and whom he hails the gentle companion of his better days.

Observations on Female Abilities

The historic page with many a proof abounds,
And fame's loud trump the Sex's worth resounds;
The patriot's zeal, the laurell'd warrior's claim,
The scepter'd virtues, wisdom's sacred name,
Creative poesy, the ethic page,   5
Design'd to form and meliorate the age,
With heroism, with perseverance fraught,
By honour, truth, and constancy enwrought,
And those blest deeds which elevate the mind,
With female genius these are all combin'd: 10
Recording story hands their virtues down,
And mellowing time awards their fair renown.

Plutarch,[1] in one of his invaluable compositions, speaking of men and women, thus expresses himself—"The talents and the virtues are modified by the circumstances and the persons, but the foundation is the same." This celebrated and truly respectable biographer has yielded every thing that we wish; and the testimony of so nice a distinguisher must be considered as a very powerful auxiliary.

It is not our purpose to analyze the properties of mind; we are inclined to think, that accurately to discriminate, or draw the intellectual line, is beyond the power of the best informed metaphysician within the purlieus of humanity. Besides, as we write for the *many,* and as it is notorious that a number of *well attested facts* have abundantly more weight with *the multitude,* than the finest spun systems which ever

Title. This essay runs for four numbers (3:88-91) in *The Gleaner;* the first essay acts as a lead-in and has not been included here.

1. **Plutarch:** Greek essayist and biographer (ca. 46–ca. 120 A.D.), author of *Parallel Lives* of Greek and Roman figures.

issued from the archives of theory, we shall proceed to summon our witnesses, arranging their testimonies with as much order, as the cursory turning over a number of volumes, to which a deficiency in memory necessitates us to apply, will permit; and here, (lest the patience of our readers should reluct at the idea of the motley circle, to which they may apprehend they are to be introduced) we take leave to inform them, that we shall be careful to abridge, as much as possible, the copious depositions which may present.

Many centuries have revolved, since the era, when writers of eminence, giving a catalogue of celebrated women, have made the number to amount to eight hundred and forty-five: From these, and succeeding attestators, we shall select a few, not perhaps the most striking, but such as occur the most readily. Our object is to prove, by examples, that the minds of women are *naturally* as susceptible of every improvement, as those of men. In the course of our examination, an obvious conclusion will, we conceive, force itself on every attentive and ingenuous reader. If the triumphs and attainments of the Sex, under the various oppressions with which they have struggled, have been thus splendid, how would they have been augmented, had not ignorant or interested men, after clipping their wings, contrived to erect around them almost insurmountable barriers. Descartes[1] expatiated on the philosophical abilities of *the sex;* and, if their supporting themselves with astonishing equanimity under the complicated oppressions to which they are not unfrequently subjected, may be called the practice of any branch of philosophy, the experience of every tyrant will evince their proficiency therein. But the highly respectable and truly honourable court, is, we presume, convened; the jury are empanneled, and we proceed to the examination of the witnesses, leaving the pleadings to those silent suggestions and inferences, which, we are assured, will voluntarily enlist themselves as advocates in every ingenuous bosom. The pending cause, as we have before observed, involves the establishment of the female intellect, or the maintaining the justice and propriety of considering

---

1. **Descartes:** René Descartes (1596–1650), French philosopher, scientist, mathematician, renowned for his famous philosophical phrase, "Cogito, ergo sum" (I think, therefore I am), signifying the certainty of existence.

women, as far as relates to their understanding, in *every respect*, equal to men. Our evidences tend to prove them—

First, Alike capable of enduring hardships.

Secondly, Equally ingenious, and fruitful in resources.

Thirdly, Their fortitude and heroism cannot be surpassed.

Fourthly, They are equally brave.

Fifthly, They are as patriotic.

Sixthly, As influential.

Seventhly, As energetic, and as eloquent.

Eighthly, As faithful, and as persevering in their attachments.

Ninthly, As capable of supporting, with honour, the toils of government. And

Tenthly, and *Lastly,* They are equally susceptible of every literary acquirement.

And, *First,* They are alike capable of enduring hardships. A proposition so self-evident, supercedes the necessity of either arguments or witnesses. On the women of Brittany, and the females among the savages of our own country, fatigues almost incredible are imposed. Imbecility seems to have changed sexes; and it is in these instances, *masculine weakness and feminine vigour*. The Sex, enervated and sinking amid the luxuries and indulgencies of an Asiatic climate, are elsewhere hardy and courageous, and fully adequate to all those exertions requisite to the support of themselves and their supine oppressors; and these well authenticated facts, are, I conceive, alone sufficient to prove the *powerful and transforming effects of education, and subsequent habits*. But we need not take a voyage to Brittany, nor penetrate the haunts of savages, to prove that women are capable of suffering. They are the *enduring sex;* and, by the irreversible constitution of nature, they are subjected to agonies unknown to manhood; while I do not recollect that they are exempted from any of the calamities incident to humanity.

Secondly, They are *equally* ingenious, and fruitful in resources. Female ingenuity will not, we apprehend, be controverted; every day furnishes fresh proof of their invention, and their resources are a consequence. We select, however, a corroborating instance, which, from its salutary effect, seems to claim a preference.

A certain sovereign, of avaricious memory, was so fond of amassing treasure, that he arbitrarily compelled a very large proportion of his subjects to labour in the mines; but while his majesty's ingots were rapidly augmenting, the grounds remained uncultivated; famine advanced with hasty strides; and the dreary prospect every moment gathered darkness. No one possessed sufficient intrepidity to remonstrate—the despot's nod was fate—from his decrees there was no appeal—and the love of life, although its eligibles may be in a great measure diminished, is generally a paramount passion. In this emergency, the ingenuity of the queen suggested a resource that snatched the nation from the horrors of that *dearth* which had seemed so inevitable. She secretly employed an artist to produce an exact imitation of those luxuries, in which the king most delighted, a variety of fish and fowl—bread and fruits of the most delicious kind, made of pure gold, were expeditiously completed, and displayed in order on the *costly* board—the table was highly decorated—and, when every thing was complete, the king, (after having been purposely diverted from taking his customary refreshment) was ushered into the banqueting-room. His Majesty took a seat—for a moment, astonishment suspended even the clamours of hunger, and his mind was occupied by admiration of the imagination of the queen, and the deceptive abilities of the artist. The event was proportioned to the most sanguine expectations of the lady. The mines were suddenly dispeopled, and the earth again produced the necessary support.

Thirdly, Their fortitude and heroism cannot be surpassed. Listen to a woman of Sparta,[1] reduced by melancholy casualties to a state of servitude—She was captured, and afterwards sold as a slave. The question was put by him on whom her very existence seemed to depend—*"What knowest thou?"* *"To be free,"* was her characteristic reply: But the unfeeling despot, uninfluenced by indubitable indications of a noble mind, proceeded to impose his ignominious commands; to which she dispassionately returned, *"you are unworthy of me;"* and instantly resigned her-

---

1. **Sparta:** city of ancient Greece and capital of Lacedaemon; renowned for its citizens' military strengths and austere discipline.

self to death. Fortitude and heroism was a conspicuous trait in, and gave uncommon dignity to, the character of the Roman ladies. Arria,[1] the wife of Paetus, a Roman of consular dignity, is an illustrious instance of that transcendent elevation, of which the female mind is susceptible. With persevering firmness, and a tenderness not to be exceeded, she continued unwearied in her endeavours to procure the life of her husband—long she cherished hope; but, when the pleasing vision fled, and the portending storm was bursting over their heads: In that tremendous moment, while the disappointed man, trembling on the verge of dissolution, had not the courage to point the deadly weapon—with that exquisite delicacy, true fortitude, and *faithfulness of affection, which is so highly sexual, she first imprinted on her own bosom the characters of death;* and, animated by that sublime consciousness becoming a being more than half celestial, she then presented him the pointed dagger, with this consolatory assurance— *"Paetus, this gives me no pain."*

But fortitude and heroism are not confined to the Greek and Roman ladies; we have pledged ourselves not to multiply examples unnecessarily, otherwise a crowd of witnesses presenting, we could with difficulty suppress their testimony. Yet we find it impossible so speedily to close this part of our examination; and from the multitude of examples in the Island of Great Britain, we produce the Lady Jane Gray,[2] who seemed an exemplification of every virtue and every grace which has been attributed to the male or female character. The excellent understanding she received from nature was opened and improved by uniform application. At sixteen, her judgment had attained a high degree of maturity. She was at that age an adept both in the Greek and Latin languages; and she was able to declare that her Greek Plato was a more pleasing entertainment to her than all those enchanting pleasures usually so captivating to the unexperienced mind. Nurtured in the bosom of parental affection, and of tender friendship—happy in the distinguishing regards of her sovereign, and permitted the sublime enjoyment of

---

1. **Arria:** a Roman matron who killed herself as an example of courage for her husband, who had been condemned to death in A.D. 42.

2. **Lady Jane Gray:** usually "Grey" (1537–1554), unwillingly proclaimed Queen of England in 1553; after nine days she was imprisoned and shortly thereafter executed.

intellectual pursuits, she had no ambition for the pageantry of royalty, and her advancement to the throne was an era, over which she dropped the melancholy tear. We are sensible that in adverting to these traits in a character, affectingly interesting, we do in fact anticipate other divisions of our subject; but, contemplating a mind thus richly furnished, it is difficult to consider separately, endowments so nicely blended, and reflecting on each other such unusual lustre.

The passage of the Lady Jane, from the throne to the scaffold, was very short—her imposed queenship continued only ten days; yet she seemed displeased at their duration, and she received, with *heroic fortitude*, the message of death. The lover and the husband, whose vows she had recently accepted, was also under sentence of death; and, on the morning assigned for their martyrdom, he solicited for a parting interview; with solemn firmness she refused his request—yet her resolution originated not in a deficiency of tenderness; but it was nerved by an apprehension that her sensibilities, thus stimulated, might surmount her fortitude. With modest resignation she pursued her way to the place of execution—the officers of death, bearing the body of her husband, while the headless trunk yet streamed with blood, met her on her passage—neither of them had completed their seventeenth year—she looked—she sighed—and then, reassuming her composed sedateness, desired her conductors to proceed—she mounted the scaffold with an accelerated step—she addressed the surrounding spectators—she committed the care of her person to her woman; and, with a countenance descriptive of serene dignity, bowed her head to the executioner. Thus perished a spotless victim of despotism and of bigotry in the bloom of youth and beauty, rich in innocence, and adorned with every literary accomplishment and sexual grace. Latest posterity will lament her fate, and many hearts will join to execrate the sanguinary measures which procured it. Under this head we produce but one more testimony.

Miss Anna Askew,[1] a young lady of great merit, and possessed also of a beautiful exterior, lived during the tyranny of Henry VIII. of England; a despot, who seemed to conceive the female world created on purpose

---

1. **Miss Anna Askew:** Anne Askew (Kyme) (1521–1546), English autobiographer and poet.

to administer to his pleasures, or to become the victims of his cruelty and implacability. Miss Askew was arraigned as a transgressor; her crime was a denial of the *real presence in the eucharist;* and for this atrocious offence, she was rigorously imprisoned, and subjected to a series of barbarities that would have disgraced even savage inhumanity. Yet, in a situation which involved trials, that in a succeeding reign proved too mighty for the *resolution even of the virtuous Cranmer,*[1] her heroism and fortitude continued unshaken. With unyielding firmness she vindicated the truth of her opinion, and her hourly orisons were offered up to her Father God. The chancellor, a bigoted Catholic, sternly questioned her relative to her abettors; but she nobly disdained to present an accusation, the consequences of which she so rigorously experienced: Her unbending integrity furnished the pretence, and she was, without further delay, put to the torture; but still her fortitude receded not; and her heroic silence evinced her abundantly superior to their unmanly cruelties. The enraged chancellor, in whose presence she suffered, transported with diabolic zeal, grasping with his own hands the cords, violently stretched the rack, and almost tore her body asunder; while yet unappalled, her fortitude forsook her not, and her triumph over her barbarous tormentors was complete.

Her death-warrant was next made out, and she received the sentence which condemned her to the flames, as an emancipation from every evil. All her joints dislocated by the rack, she was borne to the place of execution; and there, after being bound to the stake, was offered her life on condition of retracting her supposed error; but she consistently rejected an existence to be purchased only by the forfeiture of that consciousness of rectitude, which the virtuous so well know how to prize; and as the flames that were her passport to regions of blessedness, enkindled around her, a song of thanksgiving was on her lips, and her exultation evidently augmented.

Fourthly, They are equally brave. Bravery is not a quality which figures *gracefully* in the list of female virtues, nor are we anxious it should

---

1. **Cranmer:** Thomas Cranmer (1489–1556), Archbishop of Canterbury under King Henry VIII of England.

take rank in the catalogue—far from it; we should rather lament to see it become a characteristic trait. We would have women support themselves with consistent firmness under the various exigencies of life, but we would not arm them with the weapons of death: Yet, when contending for *equality of soil,* it may be necessary to prove the *capability* of the female mind, to rear to perfection whatever seeds may be adventitiously implanted therein. We therefore proceed to produce a witness or two on this part of the question; and, consulting our records, we assign the precedence, *all circumstances considered,* to a young woman of Lemnos, an island in the Archipelago.[1]

This magnanimous female beheld the streaming wounds of her expiring father, in the fatal moment in which he was slaughtered on the field of battle; and, instead of yielding to those tender sensibilities originating in nature, and generally associated with valour—instead of lamenting his fate by sighs and tears, or the wordy exclamations of clamorous sorrow, she undauntedly seized that sword and shield now rendered useless to the venerable warrior, and, arming herself therewith, reanimated the dispirited soldiers, led them once more to the charge; bravely opposed the Turks, who, having forced a gate, were rapidly advancing; and gloriously avenged the death of her father, by driving them back to the shore, and compelling them to take refuge in their vessels.

Jane of Flanders[2] next presents: This lady, during the imprisonment of her husband, nobly supported the declining honours of her house: With her infant son in her arms, she met the assembling citizens, and pathetically deploring her misfortunes, she secured their exertions in her favour. She sustained with unyielding firmness the attacks of a vigilant and active foe. In the frequent sallies made by the garrison, she herself led on her warriors. At the head of three hundred horse, with her own hand she set fire to the tents and baggage of the besiegers, thus necessitating them to desist from the general assault which they were in the moment of commencing; and, although intercepted in her return to

---

1. **Archipelago:** Aegean Sea.

2. **Jane of Flanders:** Possibly a reference to Countess Johanna of Flanders, who reigned from 1244-1278. In the thirteenth century, the people of Flanders revolted against the ruling Counts and for almost one hundred years ruled themselves.

the citadel, she nevertheless fought her way through one quarter of the French camp, and rejoined her faithful friends in triumph!

Margaret of Anjou[1] is a decisive proof that courage is not *exclusively* the property of man—Brave, indefatigable and persevering—fruitful in resources—supporting by her genius and her exertions a pusillanimous husband—repeatedly emancipating him from prison, and replacing him on a throne which he had lost by imbecility, and which he was unable to retain—and equal to every thing which depended on undaunted courage, she headed her armies in person; directed their arrangements; and proceeded from rank to rank, animating them by her undaunted intrepidity and judicious conduct; and, when borne down by misfortunes, and apparently destitute of every resource, suddenly she emerged, and, followed by numerous armies, again appeared in the field; nor did she submit to fate, until she had fought, as a general and a soldier, *twelve decisive battles!!!*

The French women—Charlotte Corde[2]—But our depositions unexpectedly multiplying, a recollection of our engagement can alone suppress their evidence.

* * *

> 'Tis joy to tread the splendid paths of fame,
> Where countless myriads mental homage claim;
> Time honour'd annals careful to explore,
> And mark the heights which intellect can soar.

Fifthly, They are equally patriotic. We have, in some measure, forestalled this article. The Grecian women have produced their testimonies, and that preference which they demonstrably manifested to the character Citizen; estimating it beyond the endearing appellations, Wife and Mother, incontrovertibly establishes their sex's *capability* of experiencing with an ardour *not to be exceeded,* the patriotic glow; and yet it is

---

1. **Margaret of Anjou:** Queen of Henry VI of England (1430–1482) and a political activist during the Wars of the Roses; letter-writer.

2. **Charlotte Corde:** Charlotte Corday (1768–1793), French Revolutionary activist who was executed for the assassination of the Jacobin leader, Jean Paul Marat.

true, that sexual occupations frequently humiliating, and generally far removed from whatever has a tendency to elevate the mind, may rationally be supposed to chill, in the female bosom, the fine fervours of the *amor patriæ.*[1]

Women are not usually exercised in those extensive contemplations which engage the legislator: They are not called on to arm in their country's cause; to appear in the well fought field, or to put their lives at hazard: But when they part with him in whom is centered their dearest hopes, who blends the characters lover, friend, husband and protector—when they resign to the hostile career the blooming youth whom from infancy they have watched with all a mother's tenderness, and whose rich maturity hath become the pride and consolation of their declining life—in those moments of anguish, their heroism and their fortitude are indisputably evinced. Nor is the patriotism of the chief arrayed for the battle; nor his, who devotes himself with all a statesman's integrity to the public weal, condemned to an ordeal more severe.

The *patriotism* of the Roman ladies, procured a senatorial decree that funeral orations should be pronounced from the rostrum in their praise: Repeatedly they saved their country. And the *patriotism* of the mother and wife of Coriolanus, while it snatched Rome from impending ruin, devoted to inevitable destruction the husband and the son: Hence towered the temple consecrated to feminine honour; and it must be confessed they had purchased this distinction at a very high price. The venerable Senate, too, again interposed; public thanks were decreed; and men were ordered, on all occasions, to yield precedence to women.

Sixthly, They are as influential. The ascendency obtained by females, is so notorious, as to have become proverbial. Instances are multiplied, wherein women have bent to their purposes the strongest masculine understanding. Samson, the victim of female blandishments, is not a singular instance. The example cited under the last article, is in point. Coriolanus rejected with unbending severity supplicating friendship, garbed in senatorial robes; succeeding deputies plead in vain—The ministers of religion, cloathed in sacerdotal habits, joined in solemn

---

1. **amor patriæ:** love of one's country, patriotism (Latin).

procession—they crowded around the warrior, commissioned to advocate a sinking people's cause; still, however, he continued obdurate, inflexibly firm and steady to his plans. But Veturia and Volumnia,[1] his wife and mother, attended by the most illustrious of the Roman ladies, appear—they shed torrents of tears—they embrace his knees—the hero is disarmed—his heart is melted—his resentment and his resolutions vanish together—and Rome is saved.

Seventhly, They are as energetic, and as eloquent. Women always decree with fervour: Did it depend on them, their movements would be decisive. Their expressions are often as strongly marked, as they are vehement; and both their plans and the execution thereof, are endowed with all the vigour that existing regulations will permit. Their eloquence is indisputable. Possessing a richness of fancy; their words are sufficiently copious; and education, when they are indulged with its aids, prescribes the proper rules. Aspasia, of Miletus,[2] it is well known, taught the immortal Socrates rhetoric and politics. And, when Rome groaned under the enormous cruelties of her second Triumvirate, the three barbarians by whom she was enslaved, and who had armed themselves for the destruction of her citizens, as if desirous of spreading every possible calamity, seized not only the lives, but the treasures of the people, and equally greedy of gold as of blood, after exhausting every other mode of plunder, turned their rapacious views on those respectable matrons, who had hitherto been exempted from pecuniary exactions; an exorbitant tax was levied on every individual female, and the consternation occasioned by this unheard of assumption, was proportioned to the distress of which it was productive.

In this extraordinary emergency, the oppressed females earnestly solicited the aid of those advocates who were appointed to plead the cause of the injured and defenceless; but the orators, fearful of incurring the displeasure of those who had usurped the power of life and death,

---

1. **Veturia and Volumnia:** In the fifth century B.C., as mother and wife of the Roman patrician, Coriolanus, they were the only ones capable of convincing him to spare Rome from destruction.

2. **Aspatia, of Miletus:** influential Athenian philosopher (fifth century B.C.), who Plato asserted was also an author, although no writings exist.

refused to interfere; and no means of redress appearing, submission to an imposition acknowledged grievous, seemed inevitable: It was, however, reserved to the talents and exertions of Hortensia[1] to furnish the desired aid.

This lady inherited all the abilities of her father; and she presented herself a voluntary advocate for her sex. With modest intrepidity she opened, conducted, and closed the pleadings. Persuasion dwelt on her tongue: Her arguments resulting from rectitude, were pointed by reason: And it will be conceived that her rhetorical powers must have been of the first rate, when it is remembered that *the countenances of the tyrants betrayed sudden and evident tokens of that remorse which was then first enkindled in their bosoms;* the hue of guilt pervaded their cheeks, and they hastily repealed the injurious decree. For the brow of Hortensia, fame prepared an immortal wreath: To the utmost gratitude of her cotemporaries she was entitled: Her triumph was the triumph of virtue and of talents: She enkindled even in the callous breasts of assassins, the almost extinguished sparks of humanity; and she stands on the page of history, a pattern of dauntless courage, and an example of genuine eloquence.

Eighthly, They are as faithful and as persevering in their attachments. Here countless witnesses crowd on retention, and the greatest difficulty is in choosing judiciously. Repeatedly have I seen the faithfully attached female, firmly persevering in that affection which was first implanted in the soil of innocence, and fondly watching with tender anxiety every symptom of the diseased man: With patient assiduity she hath hung over the couch, and sought to mitigate the pangs of him, whose licentious conduct had brought ruin on herself and her unoffending children! Had circumstances been reversed, *divorce* would have succeeded— a hospital must have sheltered the helpless woman; and, had she received from the man she had injured any trivial attention, the unmerited gratuity would have resounded through the circle of their connexions, been dwelt on with rapture, and echoed by every tongue. But

---

1. **Hortensia:** orator (first century B.C.), known for a speech protesting proposed taxation on women's property to fund a civil war begun by men.

when virtue is the basis; when acts of kindness cement the union, the Sex in many instances have set no bound to that faithful attachment which their hearts have exultingly acknowledged. Filial duty—conjugal affection—persevering constancy—these receive in the female bosom the highest perfection of which they are, in the present state, susceptible.

The young Roman, supporting her imprisoned parent by the milk of her own chaste bosom, if unparalleled in history, would yet, in like situation, obtain many imitators; and the feelings of a daughter would prompt, for the relief of the authors of her being, the noblest exertions. The celebrated Mrs. Roper,[1] eldest daughter of Sir Thomas Moore, continued his affectionate solace during his imprisonment: With heart-affecting anguish she rushed through the guards to catch, from the illustrious martyr, a last embrace. Bending under a weight of calamity, she obtained permission to pay him sepulchral honours; and, regardless of the tyrant's power, she purchased the venerable head of the meritorious sufferer: Yet, too noble to permit the consequences to fall upon another, with dauntless courage she became her own accuser; and, loaded with fetters for two crimes, "for having watched the head of her father as a relique, and for having preserved his books and writings," appeared with unconcern before her judges—justified herself with that eloquence which virtue bestows on injured merit—commanding admiration and respect—and spent the remainder of her life in solitude, in sorrow, and in study.

But women, unable to support existence, when deprived of those with whom they have exchanged the nuptial vow, have mounted the funeral pile, and hastened to rejoin their deceased partners in other worlds. Portia,[2] the daughter of Cato Uticensis, and wife of Brutus, hearing of the death of her husband, disdained to live; and when debarred access to the usual weapons of destruction, made her exit by resolutely swallowing burning coals of fire! Julia,[3] the wife of Pompey,

---

1. **Mrs. Roper:** Margaret Roper, née More (1505–1544), English translator, letter-writer.

2. **Portia:** a Roman woman (?– 42 B.C.) who was renowned for her courage and her insistence on being a confidante to her husband in affairs of state.

3. **Julia:** Julia (?–54 B.C.) negotiated peace between her father, Julius Caesar, and her husband, rulers of Rome.

expired upon seeing his robe distained with the blood which she imagined had issued from his veins. Molsa Tarquinia, rendered illustrious by genius and literature, of unblemished virtue, and possessing, also, a beautiful exterior, although one of the brightest ornaments of the Court of Ferrara,[1] and receiving from the people of Rome, that unprecedented honour, the freedom of their city, mourned, nevertheless, through a long life, until the hour of her dissolution, the husband of her youth. Artemisia,[2] wife of Mausolus, rendered herself illustrious, and obtained immortality, by her devotion to the memory of her husband. The Mausoleum, which she reared in honour of him, was considered as one of the seven wonders of the world; and it gave name to all those succeeding monuments, which were distinguished by extraordinary marks of magnificence. Artemisia expired, the victim of inconsolable regret and tender sorrow, before the Mausoleum was completed. Victoria Colonna, Marchioness of Pescaira,[3] ardently engaged in literary pursuits, while fame did ample justice to her productions; yet, separated by the stroke of death, in the morning of her days, from an illustrious and gallant husband, appropriated her remaining years to unceasing grief, lamenting, in her pathetic Essays, the long-lost hero. The celebrated Mrs. Rowe,[4] equally conspicuous for genius and virtue, continued faithful and persevering in her attachment to her deceased husband; nor could a length of years abate her regrets.

Ninthly, They are capable of supporting, with equal honour, the toils of government. Semiramis[5] appears to have associated all the virtues and vices which have received the masculine stamp—she extended her empire from Ethiopia to India, and subdued many nations—her buildings and gardens were also magnificent—and she governed, in many respects, judiciously. Artemisia, queen of Caria, and daughter of Lygdamis, possessing, during the minority of her son, sovereign authority, distinguished herself, both by her counsels and her personal valour.

---

1. **Ferrara:** a commonality in northern Italy.

2. **Artemisia:** an Asian princess (?–c.350 B.C.).

3. **Victoria Colonna:** Vittoria of Pescara (1490–1547); Italian poet.

4. **Mrs. Rowe:** Elizabeth Singer Rowe (1674–1737); "Philomela"; English poet, journalist, and member of the religious reform movement known as the Dissenters.

5. **Semiramis:** mythical Assyrian queen and founder of Babylon.

Amalasuntha governed with the greatest justice, wisdom, and prudence. Julia Mammæa educated her son, Alexander Severus,[1] implanting in his bosom the seeds of virtue, and adorning him with every princely accomplishment: He was worthy of the high rank to which he was raised, and disposed to become the father of his people: His mother presided in his councils; the era of their administration was tumultuous and hazardous, and its disastrous termination is one of the events which the student of history will not fail to deplore.

Zenobia[2] united genius and valour—she was dignified by the title of Augusta. After the demise of her husband, the supreme authority devolving upon her, she governed with rectitude, firmness, and intrepidity. She preserved the provinces in their allegiance, and added Egypt to her dominions. Moreover, when led into captivity, she knew how to *bring into subjection, her feelings; she endured misfortune with the heroism of a noble spirit, and found a solace for the loss of royalty, and the pageantry of a throne, in those rational pursuits, which solitude and freedom from care uninterruptedly permit.* Longinus[3] was her preceptor and friend; and she was worthy of his tuition and preferable attachment. Elizabeth of England[4] was endowed with energetic talents; her reign was glorious for the people over which she presided; she was undoubtedly a great politician, and governed with uniform vigour; she is characterized as possessing much penetration, and an understanding fruitful of resources; her foreign negociations were conducted with propriety and dignity; her mind was opened and polished by all the aids of an extensive education, and adversity was among her preceptors. Christina, queen of Sweden,[5] governed her subjects twenty-one years, with uniform wisdom and unimpeached prudence, when she magnanimously resigned her crown; thus giving a rare example of an elevation of intellect, which has not been surpassed.

---

1. **Julia Mammæa...Severus:** Julia Mammæa was regent of Rome during her emperor son's minority. Mother and son were assassinated in A.D. 235 by military partisans.

2. **Zenobia:** Zenobia reigned as queen of Palmyra (Syria) from A.D. 267–272.

3. **Longinus:** Greek literary critic (fl. first century A.D.).

4. **Elizabeth of England:** Elizabeth Tudor (1533–1603) became Queen Elizabeth I of England in 1558; orator, translator, poet, religious writer.

5. **Christina:** learned queen of Sweden (1626–1689), patron of the arts; reigned 1632–1654.

Tenthly, and *Lastly,* They are equally susceptible of every literary acquirement. Corinna,[1] it is said, triumphed a fifth time over the immortal Pindar,[2] who had publickly challenged her to contend with him in the poetical line. Sappho,[3] the Lesbian poetess, was admired by the ancients—she produced many poems, and was addressed as the tenth Muse. Sulpicia,[4] a Roman lady, who lived under the reign of Domitian,[5] was called the Roman Sappho. Hypatia,[6] beautiful, learned, and virtuous, the daughter of Theon, presided over the Platonic school at Alexandria, about the close of the fourth century; she was judged qualified to succeed her father in that distinguished and important office; her wisdom was held in universal esteem; and from her judgment no one thought proper to appeal: Persons cloathed in public authority, even the first magistrates, deliberated with her on the most urgent and important emergencies; this unavoidably drew around her succeeding circles of men; yet she maintained her intercourse with characters of various descriptions, without the shadow of an impeachment of her reputation, until basely traduced, in a *single instance,* by bigotted and interested calumniators. Cassandra, a Venetian lady, attained an accurate skill in languages, and made great proficiency in the learning of her times; she composed with facility, both in numbers and in prose, in the language of Homer, Virgil, and Dante; she was a proficient in the philosophy of her own and preceding ages; she rendered theology harmonious; she supported theses with brilliancy; she lectured publickly at Padua; she blended the fine arts with her serious studies; and the mild complacency of her manners constituted the completion of her character: She received homage from sovereign pontiffs, and sovereign princes; and she continued an ornament of her Sex, and of humanity, one hundred and two years.

---

1. **Corinna:** Greek poet (fifth century B.C.).

2. **Pindar:** Greek poet (ca. 518–ca. 438 B.C.)

3. **Sappho:** Greek poet from Lesbos (seventh–sixth century B.C.).

4. **Sulpicia:** Sulpicia II (first century A.D.), Roman poet.

5. **Domitian:** Emperor of Rome (first century A.D.).

6. **Hypatia:** philosopher and teacher (A.D. 370–415) whom Socrates ranked as the first among contemporary philosophers.

The daughter of Sir Thomas Moore, Mrs. Roper, already cited under the eighth article, whose virtues were polished by literary attainments, corresponded in Latin with the celebrated Erasmus,[1] and successfully appropriated many years of her life to study: Her daughter inherited her erudition, and her amiable qualifications. The Seymours,[2] sisters, and nieces of a king, wrote elegantly in Latin. Isabella of Rosera,[3] in Spain, by her substantial arguments, natural deductions, and able rhetoric, greatly augmented the number of believing Jews; the great church of Barcelona was open for the exertion of her pulpitorial abilities; and she acquired much honour by her commentaries upon the learned Scotus. France knew how to estimate the talents of the Dutchess of Retz; she pursued her studies amid the seducing pleasures of a court; and, although young and beautiful, spoke the ancient languages with propriety and elegance. Mary Stuart,[4] queen of Scotland, possessing all the advantages of exterior, and every sexual grace, assiduously cultivated her mind: Her learning was as remarkable as her beauty; she could, we are informed, write and speak six languages; her numbers enchanted the Gallic ear; and, at an early age, she pronounced before the French Court a Latin oration, calculated to convince her hearers, that literary pursuits are proper to the Female Sex. Beauty could not plead in vain; the lovely speaker exemplified, in her own character and attainments, the truth she inculcated; she was, herself, that happy combination, the practicability of which she laboured to impress; and conviction undoubtedly irradiated the minds of her audience.

In the thirteenth century, a young lady of Bologna, pursuing, with avidity, the study of the Latin language, and the legislative institutions of her country, was able, at the age of twenty-three, to deliver, in the great church of Bologna, a Latin oration, in praise of a deceased person, eminent for virtue; nor was she indebted for the admiration she

---

1. **Erasmus:** Desiderius Erasmus (1466?–1536), Dutch priest, educator, writer.

2. **The Seymours, sisters:** Anne, Jane, and Margaret Seymour, poets who composed in 1549 an elegy of 104 couplets honoring the French author Marguerite de Navarre (1492–1549).

3. **Isabella of Rosera:** Isabella I (1451–1504), Queen of Castile 1474–1504; aided Columbus's expedition.

4. **Mary Stuart:** (1542–1587), also a poet, essayist, letter-writer.

received, to the indulgence granted to her youth, or Sex. At the age of twenty-six, she took the degree of a Doctor of Laws, and commenced her career in this line, by public expositions of the doctrines of Justinian: At the age of thirty, her extraordinary merit raised her to the chair, where she taught the law to an astonishing number of pupils, collected from various nations. She joined to her profound knowledge, sexual modesty, and every feminine accomplishment; yet her personal attractions were absorbed in the magnitude and splendor of her intellectual abilities; and the charms of her exterior only commanded attention, when she ceased to speak. The fourteenth century produced, in the same city, a like example; and the fifteenth continued, and acknowledged the pretensions of the Sex, insomuch that a learned chair was appropriated to illustrious women.

Issotta Nogarolla[1] was also an ornament of the fifteenth century; and Sarochisa of Naples was deemed worthy of a comparison with Tasso.[2] Modesta Pozzo's[3] defence of her Sex did her honour; she was, herself, an example of excellence. Gabrielle, daughter of a king, found leisure to devote to her pen; and her literary pursuits contributed to her usefulness and her happiness. Mary de Gournai[4] rendered herself famous by her learning. Guyon,[5] by her writings and her sufferings, hath evinced the justice of her title to immortality. Anna Maria Schuman of Cologne, appears to have been mistress of all the useful and ornamental learning of the age which she adorned: She was born in 1607; her talents unfolded with extraordinary brilliancy: In the bud of her life, at the age of six years, she cut, with her scissors, the most strik-

---

1. **Issotta Nogarolla:** Isotta Nogarola (1420?–1466), noted for her learning and as a writer of poetry, dialogues, and letters.

2. **Tasso:** Torquato Tasso (1544–1595), Italian poet and dramatist.

3. **Modesta Pozzo:** Italian poet (1555–1592), religious author and dramatist who published under the name of Moderata Fonte.

4. **Mary de Gournai:** Marie Le Jars de Gournay (1566–1645), French editor and essayist; known especially for treatises on the equality of the sexes.

5. **Guyon:** Jeanne-Marie Bouvier de La Motte, Madame Guyon (1648–1717), French religious writer.

ing resemblances of every figure which was presented to her view, and they were finished with astonishing neatness. At ten, she was but three hours in learning to embroider. She studied music, painting, sculpture and engraving, and made an admirable proficiency in all those arts. The Hebrew, Greek and Latin languages were familiar to her; and she made some progress in the oriental tongues. She perfectly understood French, English and Italian, and expressed herself eloquently in all those languages; and she appropriated a portion of her time, to the acquirement of an extensive acquaintance with geography, astronomy, philosophy, and the other sciences: Yet she possessed so much feminine delicacy, and retiring modesty, that her talents and acquirements had been consigned to oblivion, if Vassius, and other amateurs of literature, had not ushered her, in opposition to her wishes upon the theatre of the world: But when she was once known, persons of erudition, of every description, corresponded with her; and those in the most elevated stations, assiduously sought opportunities of seeing and conversing with her.

Mademoiselle Scudery,[1] stimulated by necessity, rendered herself eminent by her writings. Anna de Parthenay[2] possessed great virtues, great talents, and great learning; she read, with facility and pleasure, authors in the Greek and Latin languages; she was a rational theologician; she was a perfect mistress of music; and was as remarkable for her vocal powers, as for her execution on the various instruments which she attempted. Catharine de Parthenay,[3] niece to Anna, married to Renatus de Rohan, signalized herself by her attention to the education of her children; and her maternal cares were crowned with abundant success: Her eldest son was the illustrious Duke of Rohan, who obtained immortal honour by his zeal and exertions in the Protestant cause; and she was also mother to Anna de Rohan, who was as

---

1. **Mademoiselle Scudery:** Marie-Madeleine du Moncel de Martinval Scudéry (1607–1701), French letter-writer and novelist.

2. **Anna de Parthenay:** sixteenth-century French poet and composer.

3. **Catharine de Parthenay:** Catherine de Parthenay (1554-1631), French poet, dramatist, satirist, translator; married Viscount Rene de Rohan, Prince of Leon, in 1575.

illustrious for her genius and piety, as for her birth. She was mistress of the Hebrew language; her numbers were beautifully elegant; and she supported, with heroic firmness, the calamities consequent upon the siege of Rochelle.

Mademoiselle le Fevre,[1] celebrated in the literary world by the name of Madame Dacier, gave early testimonies of that fine genius which her father delighted to cultivate. Her edition of Callimachus was received with much applause. At the earnest request of the Duke de Montansier, she published an edition of Florus, for the use of the dauphin; she exchanged letters with Christina, queen of Sweden; she devoted herself to the education of her son and daughter, whose progress were proportioned to the abilities of their interested preceptress: Greek and Latin were familiar to her; and she was often addressed in both those languages, by the literati of Europe. Her translation of the Iliad was much admired. She is said to have possessed great firmness, generosity, and equality of temper, and to have been remarkable for her piety. Maria de Sevigne[2] appropriated her hours to the instruction of her son and daughter; she has enriched the world with eight volumes of letters, which will be read with pleasure by every critic in the French language. The character of Mary II.[3] Queen of England, and consort to William of Nassau, is transcendently amiable. She is delineated as a princess, endowed with uncommon powers of mind, and beauty of person. She was extensively acquainted with history, was attached to poetry, and possessed a good taste in compositions of this kind. She had a considerable knowledge in architecture and gardening; and her dignified condescension, and consistent piety, were truly admirable and praiseworthy— Every reader of history, and lover of virtue, will lament her early exit.

---

1. **Mademoiselle le Fevre:** Anne Lefebvre, Madame Dacier (1647–1720), French scholar, editor, translator, pamphleteer.

2. **Maria de Sevigne:** Marie de Rabutin–Chantal, marquise de Sévigné (1626–1696), French letter-writer.

3. **Mary II:** (1662–1694). Mary Stuart, proclaimed joint sovereign with her husband William of Nassau, Prince of Orange, in 1689.

The Countess of Pembroke[1] translated from the French, a dramatic piece; she gave a metrical edition of the Book of Psalms, and supported an exalted character.

Anna Killigrew,[2] and Anna Wharton,[3] were eminent, both for poetry and painting; and their unblemished virtue, and exemplary piety, pointed and greatly enhanced the value of their other accomplishments. Catharine Phillips[4] was, from early life, a lover of the Muses; she translated Corneille's[5] Tragedy of Pompey into English; and in this, as well as the poems which she published, she was successful. Lady Burleigh, Lady Bacon, Lady Russell, and Mrs. Killigrew, daughters of Sir Anthony Cook,[6] received from their father a masculine education; and their prodigious improvement was an ample compensation for his paternal indulgence: They were eminent for genius and virtue, and obtained an accurate knowledge of the Greek and Latin languages. The writings of the Dutchess of Newcastle,[7] were voluminous; she is produced as the first English lady who attempted what has since been termed polite literature. Lady Halket[8] was remarkable for her erudition; she was well skilled, both in physic and divinity. Lady Masham,[9] and Mary Astell,[10] reasoned accurately on the most abstract particulars in

1. **Countess of Pembroke:** Mary Sidney, Countess of Pembroke (1561–1621), translated Garnier's *Antonie;* also a poet, patron, and editor.

2. **Anna Killigrew:** Anne Killigrew (c.1660–1685), English poet and painter.

3. **Anna Wharton:** Anne Wharton (1659–1685), English dramatist and poet.

4. **Catharine Phillips:** Katherine Philips, née Fowler (1631–1664), English poet, dramatist, translator, letter-writer.

5. **Corneille:** Pierre Corneille (1606–1684), French dramatist.

6. **Lady Burleigh…Cook:** Mildred Burghley; Anne Cooke, Lady Bacon (1528–1610), translator and letter-writer; Elizabeth Cooke, Lady Hoby and later Lady Russell (1529–1609), poet and translator; Katherine Killigrew; Sir Anthony Cooke (1504–1576), politician, scholar and tutor to Edward VI.

7. **Dutchess of Newcastle:** Margaret Cavendish, née Lucas (1623–1673), English philosopher, biographer, autobiographer, and poet.

8. **Lady Halket:** Lady Ann Halkett, née Murray (1623–1699), English memoirist and teacher.

9. **Lady Masham:** Damaris Masham, née Cudworth (1658–1708), English religious writer.

10. **Mary Astell:** poet, letter-writer, religious and political essayist (1666–1731), especially known for her critiques of women's social oppression.

divinity, and in metaphysics. Lady Grace Gethin[1] was happy in natural genius and a cultivated understanding; she was a woman of erudition; and we are informed that, at the age of twenty, *"she treated of life and morals, with the discernment of Socrates, and the elegance of Xenophon"*[2]— Mr. Congreve[3] has done justice to her merit. Chudleigh, Winchelsea, Monk, Bovey, Stella, Montague[4]—these all possess their respective claims. Catharine Macauley[5] wielded successfully the historic pen; nor were her exertions confined to this line—But we have already multiplied our witnesses far beyond our original design; and it is proper that we apologize to our readers, for a transgression of that brevity which we had authorized them to expect.

Nor are the modern Fair a step behind,
In the transcendent energies of mind:
Their worth conspicuous swells the ample roll,
While emulous they reach the splendid goal.

We take leave to repeat, that we are not desirous to array the Sex in martial habiliments; we do not wish to enlist our women as soldiers; and we request it may be remembered, that we only contend for the *capability* of the female mind to become possessed of any attainment within the reach of *masculine exertion*. We have produced our witnesses; their depositions have been heard; the cause is before the public; we await their verdict; and, as we entertain all possible veneration for the respectable jury, we shall not dare to appeal from their decision.

---

1. **Lady Grace Gethin:** English essayist (1676–1697).

2. **Xenophon:** Greek historian (c.430–c.355 B.C.).

3. **Mr. Congreve:** William Congreve (1670–1729), English Restoration dramatist.

4. **Chudleigh...Montague:** English authors: Mary, Lady Chudleigh, née Lee (1656–1710), poet and defender against women's oppression; Anne Finch, née Kingsmill, Countess of Winchilsea (1661–1720), poet; "Monk," Mary Molesworth (?–1715), poet; Catharina Bovey (or Boevey) (1669–1726), philanthropist; "Stella," Esther Johnson (1681-1728), friend of Jonathan Swift; Lady Mary Wortley Montagu (1689–1762), letter-writer and essayist.

5. **Catharine Macauley:** English Whig radical, historian, philosopher, and advocate of women's education (1731–1791).

But while we do homage to the women of other times, we feel happy that nature is no less bountiful to the females of the present day. We cannot, indeed, obtain a list of the names that have done honour to their Sex, and to humanity, during the period now under observation: The lustre of those minds, still enveloped in a veil of mortality, is necessarily muffled and obscure; but the curtain will be thrown back, and posterity will contemplate, with admiration, their manifold perfections. Yet, in many instances, fame has already lifted her immortalizing trump. Madame de Genlis[1] has added new effulgence to the literary annals of France. This lady unites, in an astonishing degree, both genius and application! May her indefatigable exertions be crowned with the success they so richly merit—May no illiberal prejudices obstruct the progress of her multiplied productions; but, borne along the stream of time, may they continue pleasurable vehicles of instruction, and confer on their ingenious author that celebrity to which she is indisputably entitled. France may also justly place among her list of illustrious personages, the luminous name of Roland. Madame Roland[2] comprised, in her own energetic and capacious mind, all those appropriate virtues, which are characterized as masculine and feminine. She not only dignified the Sex, but human nature in the aggregate; and her memory will be held in veneration, wherever talents, literature, patriotism, and uniform heroism, are properly appreciated.

The British Isle is at this moment distinguished by a constellation of the first magnitude. Barbauld, Seward, Cowley, Inchbald, Burney, Smith, Radcliffe, Moore, Williams, Wollstonecraft,[3] &c. &c.—these

---

1. **Madame de Genlis:** Stéphanie-Félicité du Crest de Saint-Aubin, comtesse de Genlis (1746–1830), French novelist, memoirist, educational writer and dramatist.

2. **Madame Roland:** Manon Philipon, Madame Roland de La Platière (1754–1793), French political activist, letter-writer, essayist, memoirist.

3. **Barbauld...Wollstonecraft:** English authors: Anna Laetitia Barbauld, née Aikin, (1743–1825), poet, essayist, author of children's literature; Anna Seward (1742–1809), poet, novelist, letter-writer, known as "The Swan of Lishfield"; Hannah Cowley, née Parkhouse, (1743–1809), poet and dramatist; Elizabeth Inchbald (1753–1821), actress, dramatist, essayist and novelist; Fanny (Frances) Burney (1752–1850), letter–writer, novelist, diarist, memoirist; Charlotte Smith, née Turner, (1749–1806), novelist; Ann Radcliffe (1764–1823), novelist; Jane Elizabeth Moore (1738–?), poet and memoirist; Helen Maria Williams (1762–1827), poet, novelist, letter-writer, translator; Mary Wollstonecraft (1759–1797), essayist and novelist, best known for her feminist tract *A Vindication of the Rights of Woman* (1792).

ladies, celebrated for brilliancy of genius and literary attainments, have rendered yet more illustrious the English name.

Nor is America destitute of females, whose abilities and improvements give them an indisputable claim to immortality. It is a fact, established beyond all controversy, that we are indebted for the discovery of our country, to female enterprize, decision, and generosity. The great Columbus, after having in vain solicited the aid of Genoa, France, England, Portugal, and Spain—after having combated, for a period of eight years, with every objection that a want of knowledge could propose, found, at last, his only resource in the penetration and magnanimity of Isabella of Spain, who furnished the equipment, and raised the sums necessary to defray the expenses, on the sale of her own jewels; and while we conceive an action, so honourable to the Sex, hath not been sufficiently applauded, we trust, that the equality of the female intellect to that of their brethren, who have so long usurped an unmanly and unfounded superiority, will never, in this younger world, be left without a witness. We cannot ascertain the number of ingenious women, who at present adorn our country. In the shade of solitude they perhaps cultivate their own minds, and superintend the education of their children. Our day, we know, is only dawning—But when we contemplate a Warren, a Philenia, an Antonia, a Euphelia,[1] &c. &c. we gratefully acknowledge, that genius and application, even in the female line, already gild, with effulgent radiance, our blest Aurora.

But women are calculated to shine in other characters than those adverted to, in the preceding Essays; and with proper attention to their education, and subsequent habits, they might easily attain that independence, for which a Wollstonecraft hath so energetically contended; the term, *helpless widow,* might be rendered as unfrequent and inapplicable as that of *helpless widower;* and although we should undoubtedly continue to mourn the dissolution of wedded amity, yet we should derive consolation from the knowledge, that the infant train had still a remaining prop, and that a mother could *assist* as well as *weep* over her offspring.

That women have a talent—a talent which, duly cultivated, would

---

1. **Warren...Euphelia:** American authors: Mercy Otis Warren (1728–1814), dramatist, poet, historian, and correspondent of Murray's; "Philenia," pen name of Sarah Wentworth Morton (1759–1846), poet and prose writer; "Antonia" and "Euphelia" are unidentified.

confer that independence, which is demonstrably of incalculable utility, every attentive observer will confess. The Sex should be taught to depend on their own efforts, for the procurement of an establishment in life. The chance of a matrimonial coadjutor, is no more than a probable contingency; and if they were early accustomed to regard this *uncertain* event with suitable *indifference,* they would make elections with that deliberation, which would be calculated to give a more rational prospect of tranquillity. All this we have repeatedly asserted, and all this we do invariably believe. To neglect polishing a gem, or obstinately to refuse bringing into action a treasure in our possession, when we might thus accumulate a handsome interest, is surely egregiously absurd, and the height of folly. The *united efforts of male and female* might rescue many a family from destruction, which, notwithstanding the efforts of its *individual* head, is now involved in all the calamities attendant on a dissipated fortune and augmenting debts. It is not possible to educate children in a manner which will render them *too beneficial* to society; and the more we multiply aids to a family, the greater will be the security, that its individuals will not be thrown a burden on the public.

An instance of *female capability,* this moment occurs to memory. In the State of Massachusetts, in a small town, some miles from the metropolis, resides a woman, who hath made astonishing improvements in agriculture. Her mind, in the early part of her life, was but penuriously cultivated, and she grew up almost wholly uneducated: But being suffered, during her childhood, to rove at large among her native fields, her limbs expanded, and she acquired a height of stature above the common size; her mind also became invigorated; and her understanding snatched sufficient information, to produce a consciousness of the injury she sustained in the want of those aids, which should have been furnished in the beginning of her years. She however applied herself diligently to remedy the evil, and soon made great proficiency in writing, and in arithmetic. She read every thing she could procure; but the impressions adventitiously made on her infant mind still obtained the ascendency. A few rough acres constituted her patrimonial inheritance; these she has brought into a state of high cultivation; their productions are every year both useful and ornamental; she is mistress of agricolation, and is at once a botanist and a florist. The most approved authors in the English language, on these subjects, are in her hands, and she studies them with industry and success.

She has obtained such a considerable knowledge in the nature of soils, the precise manure which they require, and their particular adaption to the various fruits of the earth, that she is become the oracle of all the farmers in her vicinity; and when laying out, or appropriating their grounds, they uniformly submit them to her inspection. Her gardens are the resort of all strangers who happen to visit her village; and she is particularly remarkable for a growth of trees, from which, gentlemen, solicitous to enrich their fruit-gardens, or ornament their parterres, are in the habit of supplying themselves; and those trees are, to their ingenious cultivator, a considerable income. Carefully attentive to her nursery, she knows when to transplant, and when to prune; and she perfectly understands the various methods of inoculating and ingrafting. In short, she is a complete *husbandwoman;* and she has, besides, acquired a vast stock of general knowledge, while her judgment has attained such a degree of maturity, as to justify the confidence of the villagers, who are accustomed to consult her on every perplexing emergency.

In the constant use of exercise, she is not corpulent; and she is extremely active, and wonderfully athletic. Instances, almost incredible, are produced of her strength. Indeed, it is not surprising that she is the idol and standing theme of the village, since, with all her uncommon qualifications, she combines a tenderness of disposition not to be exceeded. Her extensive acquaintance with herbs, contributes to render her a skilful and truly valuable nurse; and the world never produced a more affectionate, attentive, or faithful woman: Yet, while she feelingly sympathizes with every invalid, she is not herself subject to imaginary complaints; nor does she easily yield to real illness. She has lately been indisposed—and a life so valuable, when endangered, embodied a host of fears for its safety: With difficulty she was persuaded to lie down upon her bed; and the young woman who attended her, and to whom she had endeared herself by a thousand good offices, after softly closing the shutters and door of her apartment, privately summoned the aid of a physician; and when the medical gentleman made his appearance, she accompanied him to the apartment of her friend; but behold, the bird was flown! and when pursued, she was found at a distance from her habitation, directing some labourers, who were employed in her service, and who, she was fearful, were not sufficiently attentive to her previous instructions. The event proved she had acted judiciously; for, braced by the fresh air, her nerves new strung, assumed their usual tone, her sickness vanished, and her native vigour returned.

Although far advanced in years, without a matrimonial connexion, yet, constantly engaged in useful and interesting pursuits, she manifests not that peevishness and discontent, so frequently attendant on *old maids;* she realizes all that independence which is proper to humanity; and she knows how to set a just value on the blessings she enjoys.

From my treasury of facts, I produce a second instance, equally in point. I have seen letters, written by a lady, an inhabitant of St. Sebastian (a Spanish emporium), that breathed the true spirit of commerce, and evinced the writer to possess all the integrity, punctuality and dispatch, which are such capital requisites in the mercantile career. This lady is at the head of a firm, of which herself and daughters make up the individuals—Her name is *Birmingham*. She is, I imagine, well known to the commercial part of the United States. She was left a widow in the infancy of her children, who were numerous; and she immediately adopted the most vigorous measures for their emolument. Being a woman of a magnanimous mind, she devoted her sons to the profession of arms; and they were expeditiously disposed of, in a way the best calculated to bring them acquainted with the art of war. Her daughters were educated for business; and, arriving at womanhood, they have long since established themselves into a capital trading-house, of which, as has been observed, their respectable mother is the head. She is, in the hours of business, invariably to be found in her compting-house;[1] there she takes her morning repast; her daughters act as clerks, (and they are adepts in their office) regularly preparing the papers and letters, which pass in order under her inspection. She signs herself, in all accounts and

---

1. **compting-house:** counting-house; a room in which account books are kept and business is transacted.

letters, *Widow Birmingham;* and this is the address by which she is designated. I have conversed with one of our captains, who has often nego-
ciated with her the disposal of large and valuable cargoes. Her
consignments, I am told, are to a great amount; and one of the principal
merchants in the town of Boston asserts, that he receives from no house
in Europe more satisfactory returns. Upright in their dealings, and
unwearied in their application, these ladies possess a right to prosperity;
and we trust that their circumstances are as easy, as their conduct is meritorious.

"Would you, good Mr. Gleaner, station us in the compting-house?"
No, my fair country-women, except circumstances unavoidably pointed
the way. Again I say, I do but hold up to your view, the *capability* of
your Sex; thus stimulating you to cultivate your talents, to endeavour to
acquire general knowledge, and to aim at making yourselves so far
acquainted with some particular branch of business, as that it may, if
occasion requires, assist in establishing you above that kind of depen-
dence, against which the freeborn mind so naturally revolts. Far be it
from me, to wish to *unsex* you—I am desirous of preserving, by all
means, those amiable traits that are considered as characteristic—I reverence the modesty and gentleness of your dispositions—I would not
annihilate a single virtue; but I would assiduously augment the faithfulness and affection of your bosoms. An elegant panegyrist[1] of your Sex,
hath assigned you the superiority in the feelings of the heart; and I cannot more emphatically conclude my subject, than in his beautifully
pathetic language:

"The pleasures of women must arise from their virtues. It is by the
cradle of their children, and in viewing the smiles of their daughters, or
the sports of their sons, that mothers find their happiness. Where are
the powerful emotions of nature? Where is the sentiment, at once sublime and pathetic, that carries every feeling to excess? Is it to be found in
the frosty indifference, and the sour severity of some fathers? No—but
in the warm and affectionate bosom of a *mother*. It is she, who, by an
impulse as quick as involuntary, rushes into the flood to preserve a boy,

---

1. **panegyrist**: creator of eulogies or elaborate praise.

whose imprudence had betrayed him into the waves—It is she, who, in the middle of a conflagration, throws herself across the flames to save a sleeping infant—It is she, who, with dishevelled locks, pale and distracted, embraces with transport, the body of a dead child, pressing its cold lips to her's, as if she would reanimate, by her tears and her caresses, the insensible clay. These great expressions of nature—these heart-rending emotions, which fill us at once with wonder, compassion and terror, always have belonged, and always will belong, only to Women. They possess, in those moments, an inexpressible something, which carries them beyond themselves; and they seem to discover to us new souls, above the standard of humanity."

Desultory Thoughts upon the Utility of Encouraging a Degree of Self-Complacency, Especially in Female Bosoms.

Self-estimation, kept within due bounds,
However oddly the assertion sounds,
May, of the fairest efforts be the root,
May yield the embow'ring shade—the mellow fruit;
May stimulate to most exalted deeds,   5
Direct the soul where blooming honor leads;
May give her there, to act a noble part,
To virtuous pleasures yield the willing heart.
Self-estimation will debasement shun,
And, in the path of wisdom, joy to run;   10
An unbecoming act in fears to do,
And still, its exaltation keeps in view.
"To rev'rence self," a Bard long since directed,
And, on each moral truth he well reflected;
But, lost to conscious worth, to decent pride,   15
Compass nor helm there is, our course to guide:
Nor may we anchor cast, for rudely tost
In an unfathom'd sea, each motive's lost,
Wildly amid contending waves we're beat,
And rocks and quick sands, shoals and depths we meet; 20
'Till, dash'd in pieces, or, till found'ring, we
One common wreck of all our prospects see!
   Nor, do we mourn, for we were lost to fame,
And never hap'd to reach a tow'ring name;

Title. This essay was originally published in *The Gentleman and Lady's Town and Country Magazine: or, Repository of Instruction and Entertainment* 6 (October 1784): 251–53.

Ne'er taught to "rev'rence self," or to aspire,   25
Our bosoms never caught ambition's fire;
An indolence of virtue still prevail'd,
Nor the sweet gale of praise was e'er inhal'd;
Rous'd by a new stimulus, no kindling glow.
No soothing emulations gentle flow,   30
We judg'd that nature, not to us inclin'd,
In narrow bounds our progress had confin'd,
And, that our forms, to say the very best,
Only, not frightful, were by all confest.

I think, to teach young minds to aspire, ought to be the ground work of education: many a laudable achievement is lost, from a persuasion that our efforts are unequal to the arduous attainment. Ambition is a noble principle, which properly directed, may be productive of the most valuable consequences. It is amazing to what heights the mind by exertion may tow'r: I would, therefore, have my pupils believe, that every thing in the compass of mortality, was placed within their grasp, and that, the avidity of application, the intenseness of study, were only requisite to endow them with every external grace, and mental accomplishment. Thus I should impel them to progress on, if I could not lead them to the heights I would wish them to attain. It is too common with parents to expatiate in their hearing, upon all the foibles of their children, and to let their virtues pass, in appearance, unregarded: this they do, least they should, (were they to commend) swell their little hearts to pride, and implant in their tender minds, undue conceptions of their own importance. Those, for example, who have the care of a beautiful female, they assiduously guard every avenue, they arrest the stream of due admiration, and endeavour to divest her of all idea of the bounties of nature: what is the consequence? She grows up, and of course mixes with those who are less interested: strangers will be sincere; she encounters the tongue of the flatterer, he will exaggerate, she finds herself possessed of accomplishments which have been studiously concealed from her, she throws the reins upon the neck of fancy, and gives every

encomiast[1] full credit for his most extravagant eulogy. Her natural connexions, her home is rendered disagreeable, and she hastes to the scenes,
whence arise the sweet perfume of adulation, and when she can obtain
the regard due to a merit, which she supposes altogether uncommon.
Those who have made her acquainted with the dear secret, she considers as her best friends; and it is more than probable, that she will soon
fall a sacrifice to some worthless character, whose interest may lead him
to the most hyperbolical lengths in the round of flattery. Now, I should
be solicitous that my daughter should possess for me the fondest love, as
well as that respect which gives birth to duty; in order to promote this
wish of my soul, from my lips she should be accustomed to hear the
most pleasing truths, and, as in the course of my instructions, I should
doubtless find myself but too often impelled to wound the delicacy of
youthful sensibility. I would therefore, be careful to avail myself of this
exuberating balance: I would, from the early dawn of reason, address
her as a rational being; hence, I apprehend, the most valuable consequences would result: in some such language as this, she might from
time to time be accosted. A pleasing form is undoubtedly advantageous,
nature, my dear, hath furnished you with an agreeable person, your
glass, was I to be silent, would inform you that you are pretty, your
appearance will sufficiently recommend you to a stranger, the flatterer
will give a more than mortal finishing to every feature; but, it must be
your part, my sweet girl, to render yourself worthy respect from higher
motives: you must learn "to reverence yourself," that is, your intellectual existance; you must join my efforts, in endeavouring to adorn your
mind, for, it is from the proper furnishing of that, you will become
indeed a valuable person, you will, as I said, give birth to the most
favorable impressions at first sight: but, how mortifying should this be
all, if, upon a more extensive knowledge you should be discovered to
possess no one mental charm, to be fit only at best, to be hung up as a
pleasing picture among the paintings of some spacious hall. The flatterer, indeed, will still pursue you, but it will be from interested views,
and he will smile at your undoing! Now, then, my best Love, is the time

---

1. **encomiast:** person known for giving formal, lavish praise.

for you to lay in such a fund of useful knowledge, as shall continue, and augment every kind sentiment in regard to you, as shall set you above the snares of the artful betrayer.

Thus, that sweet form, shall serve but as a polished casket, which will contain a most beautiful gem, highly finished, and calculated for advantage, as well as ornament. Was she, I say, habituated thus to reflect, she would be taught to aspire; she would learn to estimate every accomplishment, according to its proper value; and, when the voice of adulation should assail her ear, as she had early been initiated into its true meaning, and from youth been accustomed to the language of praise; her attention would not be captivated, the Siren's song[1] would not borrow the aid of novelty, her young mind would not be enervated or intoxicated, by a delicious surprise, she would possess her soul in serenity, and by that means, rise superior to the deep-laid schemes which, too commonly, encompass the steps of beauty.

Neither should those to whom nature had been parsimonious, be tortured by me with degrading comparisons; every advantage I would expatiate upon, and there are few who possess not some personal charms; I would teach them to gloss over their imperfections, inasmuch as, I do think, an agreeable form, a very necessary introduction to society, and of course it behoves us to render our appearance as pleasing as possible: I would, I must repeat, by all means guard them against a low estimation of self. I would leave no charm undiscovered or unmarked, for the penetrating eye of the pretended admirer, to make unto himself a merit by holding up to her view; thus, I would destroy the weapons of flattery, or render them useless, by leaving not the least room for their operation.

A young lady, growing up with the idea, that she possesses few, or no personal attractions, and that her mental abilities are of an inferior kind, imbibing at the same time, a most melancholly idea of a female, descending down the vale of life in an unprotected state; taught also to regard her character ridiculously contemptible, will, too probably,

---

1. **Siren's song:** In general, the term refers to anything that distracts the attention from the correct path or action; in classical mythology, the Siren was a sea nymph that lured mariners to destruction with her seductive singing.

throw herself away upon the first who approaches her with tenders of love, however indifferent may be her chance for happiness, least if she omits the present day of grace, she may never be so happy as to meet a second offer, and must then inevitably be stigmatized with that dreaded title, an Old Maid, must rank with a class whom she has been accustomed to regard as burthens upon society, and objects whom she might with impunity turn into ridicule! Certainly love, friendship and esteem, ought to take place of marriage, but, the woman thus circumstanced, will seldom regard these previous requisites to felicity, if she can but insure the honors, which she, in idea, associates with a matrimonial connection—to prevent which great evil, I would early impress under proper regulations, a reverence of self; I would endeavour to rear to worth, and a consciousness thereof: I would be solicitous to inspire the glow of virtue, with that elevation of soul, that dignity, which is ever attendant upon self-approbation, arising from the genuine source of innate rectitude. I must be excused for thus insisting upon my hypothesis, as I am, from observation, persuaded, that many have suffered materially all their life long, from a depression of soul, early inculcated, in compliance to a false maxim, which hath supposed pride would thereby be eradicated. I know there is a contrary extreme, and I would, in almost all cases, prefer the happy medium. However, if these fugitive hints may induce some abler pen to improve thereon, the exemplification will give pleasure to the heart of

CONSTANTIA. October 22, 1784.

Sketch of the Present Situation of America, 1794
[Written April, 1794.]

Now, by my manhood, my full soul disdains
These dark'ning glooms, which suddenly pervade;
True dignity an equal part sustains,
Lending its calm and persevering aid.

That melancholy pause, and *extreme* dejection, which at this present so apparently pervades every order of citizens among us, is, methinks, rather derogatory to the American character. The question, relative to opening the temple of Janus,[1] seems to be agitated with unbecoming warmth; and a zeal, not properly tempered by knowledge, is, I conceive, strikingly exemplified by every party.

That our country hath, during a most auspicious period, been borne forward upon the full tide of prosperity, no one but the embittered, the cynical, or the interested incendiary, will deny. Peace, with her olive wreath, was to us the celestial harbinger of unexampled felicity; agriculture hath flourished in primeval beauty, fostered on the bosom of liberty, and fanned by the genial airs of the meek-eyed goddess, it is rapidly approximating the highest perfection of which it is susceptible. Our manufactures have surprisingly advanced. Our navigation is extensive; almost every stream conveys the well freighted bark; and our commerce, wafted by the breezy gale, hath accumulated riches upon the far distant shore. Whether trade ought not to partake in *some degree* the nature of its favourite elements; and whether under the general regulations of rectitude, it would not find its own *advantageous* and *equal* balance, may be considered as problematical: at any rate, unaided by

---

Title. The bracketed notation is Murray's. This essay appeared in *The Gleaner,* 1:26-27.

1. **Janus:** in Roman mythology, the god of beginnings and endings.

treaties of commerce, our merchants, obtaining the object of their wishes, have, in many instances, found their enterprizes crowned with uncommon success.

The arts and sciences are also attaining naturalization in our soil; and *literature, blest source of rational elevation,* literature hath enlisted its votaries: The extensive and energetic movements of the soul are afloat; the sciences and the virtues love the venerable shades and sequestered haunts of liberty; and, cultivated successfully in this new world, we had hoped they would become patrons of frugality, temperance, and that holy religion, which smootheth the bed of death.

Our citizens, intuitively, as it should seem, had become sensible of that *indiscriminate* advantage, derived to the *community* in general, where *each individual receives from the common fund,* and *where every member contributes his quota, for the benefit of the whole;* in one word, every one seemed sensible of the blessings of a good government, and *federalism* was the basis, on which we were successfully building the superstructure of every thing useful, every thing virtuous, every thing ornamental. What a fearful and destructive hydra[1] is faction! War is its eldest born, and with the eye of the basilisk it seeketh to annihilate the cherub peace. Dreadful is the progress of war; it is retrograde to almost every virtue; the duties of benevolence it inverteth; it enjoineth upon every individual to afflict and harass by every possible means. Cultivation is no more. Destruction, with shocking exultation, exerciseth in every goodly walk its fatally blasting influence. Population laments its murdered millions; the earth is humectated[2] by the blood of our fellow creatures; and those infernal demons, discord and malice, are glutted by the calamities of the human species. A late elegant writer inimitably pourtrays the consequences even of *successful war;* perhaps a review of the picture may be of use.—"We must fix our eyes not on the hero returning with conquest, nor yet on the gallant officer dying on the bed of honour, the subject of picture and of song; but on the private soldier, forced into the service; exhausted by camp sickness and fatigue; pale,

---

1. **hydra:** in Greek mythology, a nine-headed monster; when one head was cut off, two heads would replace it. One of the twelve labors of Hercules was to destroy the hydra.

2. **humectated:** moistened, saturated.

emaciated, crawling to an hospital with the prospect of life, perhaps a long life, blasted, useless, and suffering. We must think of the uncounted tears of her who weeps alone, because the only being who shared her sentiments is taken from her; no martial music sounds in unison with her feelings; the long day passes, and he returns not! She does not shed her sorrows over his grave, for she has never learnt whether he ever had one. If he had returned, his exertions would not have been remembered individually, for he only made a small imperceptible part of a human machine, called a regiment. We must take in the long sickness which no glory soothes, occasioned by distress of mind, anxiety, and ruined fortune. These are not fancy pictures; and if you please to heighten them, you can every one of you do it for yourselves. We take in the consequences, felt perhaps for ages, before a country which has been completely desolated, lifts its head again; like a torrent of lays, its worst mischief is not the first, overwhelming in ruin towns and palaces, but the long sterility to which it condemns the track it hath covered with its stream. Add the danger to regular governments which are changed by war, sometimes to anarchy, and sometimes to despotism. Add all these, and then let us think when a General performing these exploits is saluted with *Well done, good and faithful servant,* whether the plaudit is likely to be echoed in another place." But however deplorable the calamities of war, such is the nature of the present scene of things, that there *are circumstances* which fully involve the *necessity of appealing to the sword.* When our dearest, essential, and most important interests are invaded, when our existence, as a nation, is put to the hazard, *when negociations fail,* when we are subjected to contumelious[1] indignities, when we are despoiled of our property, and stripped of the hopes of redress—in emergencies thus pressing, every sentiment of *self-defence* will throw the gauntlet for the battle. That it is precisely upon these evil times we have fallen, many *resentfully* and *vehemently* pronounce; and, not yet freed from the jealousies and entanglements of European politics, while the hemisphere of the elder world is thus dreadfully tempested, nothing but an overweening self-partiality, could lead us to expect escaping at least the outskirts of the hurricane;

---

1. **contumelious**: insolently abusive and humiliating.

but if we have been unwarrantably and unnecessarily injured, and if our abilities are adequate to the contention, let every American play the man for his country. Let not our faces thus gather paleness; but, when properly authorised by the authority which we have conferred, let us combine, hand and heart, to work out our own political salvation; and if our cause is thus righteous, the God of armies will again lead us forth, and doubtless the palm of victory will be ours.

But deliberation here maketh a pause—Against whom shall we commence hostilities? So many are the wrongs which we are said to have suffered from the maritime belligerent powers, that an unprejudiced American will hesitate against which to prefer the loudest complaints; and the investigations made in the general council of our nation, so nearly poizeth the scale of depredation, that the closest observer, uninfluenced by party, is at a loss to decide upon the question. Yet, it is said, our obligations to France, furnishing a balance in her favour, ought in equity to destroy the equipoise; and indeed it is greatly to be wished the conduct of that nation had been such, as to have sanctioned the most unlimited election of her interests. If, when emerging from the benighted clouds of despotism; if, when exonerating herself from the intolerable oppression of unlimited authority, she had known where to erect the barriers; if she had not outraged every feeling of humanity, most atrociously committing acts, at which even the bosom of stoism agonizes at every pore, over which rectitude must pour the never failing tear, and at which fortitude hath learned to weep; if she had supported the constitution which she swore to maintain, we should doubtless have felt for her like veneration, as when the gallant and virtuous La Fayette,[1] directing her councils, led forth her armies, and, pointing her steps to victory and fame, extorted the mingling and unhesitating applause of an admiring world. But alas! France exhibits, at this period, a spectacle, from which lacerated truth indignantly hastes, at which reason stands aghast, while morality and holy religion have received from base and murderous hands a fatal stab.

---

1. **La Fayette:** Marie-Joseph-Paul-Yves-Roch-Gilbert du Motier, marquis de La Fayette (1757–1834), French general and statesman who aided the Patriots during the American Revolution.

Perhaps the only advantage which the revolutionary tribunal can boast over the *lettre de cachet,*[1] or the justly *execrated Bastile,*[2] is, that not prolonging the sufferings of its victims, it hasteth to bestow upon them, through the instrumentality of the executioner, a speedy emancipation from its tyranny. Whole hecatombs[3] have been immolated; every person who differeth in opinion from the ruling faction is arrested, tried, and executed. The *federalist* findeth no mercy; and even an *avowed wish* to qualify their *boasted indivisibility,* by a single feature of the American government, is estimated as treasonable. With regard to our obligations to France, it ought surely to be considered, whether gratitude can ever teach us to abet, even the most *liberal* and *disinterested* benefactor, in *deeds* of *darkness and of death:* And, when it is remembered, that the well-timed aid, from which we derived advantages so indisputably beneficial, was procured through the instrumentality of him, *whom we then hailed as our magnanimous ally—which ally* hath, by the most sanguinary men and measures, been, by violent hands, arrested in the middle of his days! when these circumstances are adverted to, they may possibly be regarded as an *extenuation of our crime,* although barely for the sake of evincing our *loyalty to the Gallic name,* we should not conceive ourselves obligated to leap the bounds of rectitude.

Yet, strange as it may seem, faction hath introduced its cloven foot among us; with astonishing effrontery it hath dared to lift its baleful head; and, drawing the sword of discord, it is preparing to sheath it in the vitals of that *infant constitution, whose budding life expands so fair to view,* and whose *docile texture,* yielding ample *hope* to *cultivation,* ensures the mellowing growth to every *desired improvement.* Is not the idea of murdering in the very cradle so promising an offspring, a conception which can have received a form only in the maddening

---

1. **lettre de cachet:** letter with an official seal (French), usually signifying authority to imprison a named person without benefit of trial; often used during the French Revolution as a means of secretly imprisoning a political opponent.

2. **Bastile:** the Bastille, a Parisian fortress, long used as a prison for criminals and political prisoners. On 14 July 1789, Parisian citizens stormed the Bastille in an attempt to free prisoners and gain ammunition; this date is usually denoted as the beginning of the French Revolution.

3. **hecatombs:** the slaughter of hundreds.

pericranium[1] of *hell-born* anarchy? Is there an individual who will not devoutly say—May the Parent of the universe shield our country from the progress of that Tartarean[2] fiend which hath so long desolated France! Yea, we confidently pronounce that every patriotic bosom hath glowed with indignation, and every virtuous sentiment hath recoiled from the frenzy of that parricide, which so licentiously suspended over the head of our matchless Chief, the execrable guillotine! over the head of that venerable patriot whose bosom is the seat of every virtue; whose disinterested efforts for the public weal, stand unrivalled in the records of immortal fame; whose superior talents, and whose revolving hours are invariably appropriated to the general good; whose unyielding magnanimity, hath gleamed athwart the darkest and most distressing moments, the luminous rays of manly hope; who, far from bending beneath the load of national depression, hath considered every event, with the firmness of inflexible virtue; who, like another Atlas, hath still supported the mighty fabric of a various and complicated government; whose penetrating genius, and expanding resources, unravelleth the intricacies of duplicity, and presenteth the extricating hand of wisdom; who glows with the rapture of the hero upon every instance of national elevation—in one word, who was the illustrious leader, the boast, and the very soul of our armies, and who continues the brightest gem in the enfolding robes of peace.

Will ye not veil to the father of your country, ye associated declaimers? Is it your element to arraign, to cavil, to censure, and to exercise a kind of fanciful despotism? Why will you thus pervert talents capable of rendering you, to this younger world, the richest blessing? Yet, if ye will still pertinaciously proceed, the hand of freemen can never arrest your course; for still ye are cherished by the genial influence of that liberty, whose equal ray, in imitation of its great prototype, invigorateth the poisonous as well as the salutary germe.

But, suffer a fellow-citizen to make the inquiry—What is your object? Why are you thus studious to create divisions? Why are you ambitious of forming an *aristocracy* in the midst of your brethren?

---

1. **pericranium**: the external membrane of the skull.
2. **Tartarean**: referring to the regions in Hades reserved for punishment of the wicked.

Ought not the nation at large to constitute one vast society of people, bound by common ties, common wishes, and common hopes? Hath any part of the Union *constitutionally* delegated their powers to you? To whom will you appeal? The late envoy of France, *in effect, at least,* threatened an appeal to the people! But surely, neither the quondam[1] ambassador or his adherents have sufficiently attended to the origin, nature and completion of our happy constitution.

If ever any government might, strictly speaking, be characterized, in a rationally republican sense, *the government of the people,* the regulations made for the administration of order, in these States, is indubitably that government. This is an axiom which I should imagine could never be controverted. Perhaps, the manner of obtaining and establishing our government, hath not, in every respect, a parallel. Delegates appointed by the *free, unsolicited, uncorrupted,* and *unanimous voice of the people,* were, *by the people,* invested with authority to weigh, ponder, and reflect; they assembled, they deliberated, examined, compared, and finally arranged. To the consideration of the *sovereign people,* the result of the collected wisdom of our Continent was presented; every article, every sentiment was examined, in every possible view; it was analyzed and scrutinized, in the completest, most uncontrolled, and rigorous manner. Orators embodied the whole force of their eloquence; writers exercised their most energetic talents, and in the strict examination the best productions of the press were engaged: Every member of the community had an undoubted right to investigate; public bodies lent their luminous aid; and, in the momentous research and expected decision, friends and enemies alike combined. Behold the catastrophe—how loudly doth it pronounce the eulogy of our constitution—how doth it dignify and eternize the American system! One State and another, time after time, gradually and *deliberately,* adopt and ratify a plan, which so evidently embraceth the interests of *the people* at large. In some of our governments, the sanction yielded is unanimous, and, in every part of the Union, the large and respectable majority of *the people,* is unexampled in the annals of legislation.

Surely, I say, a government thus originating, thus sanctioned, and

---

1. **quondam**: former, sometime.

thus established, may be unequivocally pronounced, in every *proper sense, the government of the people.* To whom then, from such a government, can we appeal? The answer is obvious; but, may our political Hercules crush the Hydra faction, however multifarious may be its powers of mischief, or however widely diffused its poisonous influence.

In this era of general consternation and perturbed suspense, it is undoubtedly our wisdom to abide the result of those investigations and debates, which properly constitute the department of gentlemen, whom we have commissioned to take upon them the administration of public affairs. If the Gleaner might be permitted to breathe a wish, it would be for the general observance and establishment of order, and that every citizen would learn, *habitually,* to venerate *offices* and *characters* devoted to, and engaged in, the administration of justice, and to which every *good and worthy member of the community is alike eligible.*

The Gleaner, from a series of accurate and unimpassioned observations, is induced earnestly to hope, that the general government will still continue to preclude all *illegal interference,* all *foreign, unconstitutional,* and *unbecoming influence.* And he confesses, that he experienced the enthusiasm of approbation, when he observed in the public prints, that dignified movement of Congress, which directed the galleries to be vacated, upon an indecent attempt made, to approbate men and measures, by *testimonies, proper* only to mark the merit of the votaries of the sock and buskin.[1] Yea, verily, this new world is the heritage of liberty; but it is of that liberty which decidedly avoweth her *system,* her *regulations,* her *laws,* her *subordination;* to all of which she exacteth the most scrupulous obedience. I am not ignorant, that *licentiousness* too often assumes the sacred name of liberty: Licentiousness, engendered by darkness, nursed by ignorance, and led forth by impudence; murder and devastation are her ministers; hell-born ambition is her incentive; and the most confirmed and rigorous despotism remaineth her invariable object.

Liberty! heaven descended goddess, rational and refined—No, she hath not a single feature of the audacious impostor, who, with such

---

1. **buskin:** a laced boot. Socks and buskins were worn by actors in ancient theater productions; socks represented comedy, and boots represented tragedy.

astonishing effrontery, artfully arrogateth her character and offices, and who, by a series of execrable machinations, after clothing herself in the sky-wrought robes of the bright celestial, demandeth her honours, procureth against her the most shocking and libellous declamations, and woundeth her in the upright exercise of those pure and wholesome institutions, which are replete with the most salutary and benign influence, upon the morals and happiness of our species. Nay, the blighting and contagious breath of licentiousness, stigmatizeth *decent* and *corrected* liberty, as the most degenerate and servile traitor! and, denounced by anarchy, the terms, usurper, despot, and tyrant, with every other frightful appellation which the black catalogue can produce, is liberally and indiscriminately bestowed upon her. Between liberty and licentiousness we cannot trace the smallest analogy; they have been strikingly and beautifully contrasted. Liberty has been compared to an informed, elevated, and well regulated mind; her movements are authorized by reason; knowledge is her harbinger; wisdom administereth unto her; and all her interpositions are mildly beneficent: Tranquillity results from her arrangements; and a serene and equal kind of contentment is her eldest born. Licentiousness is said to resemble the unbridled and tumultuous career of him, who, intoxicated by the inebriating draught, and having renounced his understanding, would invert the order of nature; eager to pour the inundation which shall level every virtue, and annihilate every distinction, he exulteth in his fancied prowess, riots amid the confusion which he creates, and unduly exalting himself, he posteth full speed to destruction.

But my subject unexpectedly growing upon me, the fear of exceeding my limits induces me to postpone its termination to a future Gleaner.

Necessity her various grades designs,
And with subordination *peace* combines.

I said that genuine liberty recognized her systems, her laws, and her regular chain of subordination; to all of which she exacted the most scrupulous obedience; and, if this were not true, I confess that I, for one, should be inclined to deprecate her domination. Surely, that state must be fruitful of calamities, which admitteth not an acknowledged superior; where every person hath, in every respect, an absolute and uncontrollable right to consult his own feelings, submitting himself to no other empire than that of his wayward passions.

It is not, in every sense, that Nature is equal in her productions. The same plastic hand that formed a Newton,[1] lends existence to an oyster. Nature levels and diversifies her wide extended lawns, winds her serpentine walks, and spreads her ample fields; but she also erects her mounds, fashions her knolls, elevates her acclivities, and piles together her stupendous mountains. The ocean rolls one vast world of waters; but the little stream murmurs gently and pleasingly along. The huge leviathan and the polypus,[2] are alike inhabitants of the sea. The elephant and the tatou,[3] the ostrich and the humming bird, respire in our world, while naturalists are at a loss even to name the numerous grades, which make up and complete the shades between these extremes. A various growth of flowers please the eye; vegetables sustain and nourish; fruits regale the palate; and poisonous plants, obtaining a luxuriant growth, rear their baleful heads. To trace the varieties of nature, is indeed a fruitful avocation; the region of fancy is stocked with reflections, while, to the curious observer, engaged in the pursuit, hardly an hour revolves, which produces not an accession of ideas.

Light and shade are productive of the finest effect; the eye is offended by a continuity of the same objects; hills and vallies, succeeding each other, furnish the most enchanting views; the interjacent plain is pleasingly terminated by the sequestered grove; the glade beautifully diversifies the forest; and yonder tall majestic eminence is gracefully skirted by the enamelled meadow which is outspread beneath. The seasons succeed each other, and the revolutions of day and night, possessing their peculiar charms, are salutary and grateful. Nor is this multiformity observable only in the less nobler parts of the creation: The human being has varieties, which may almost be pronounced endless. The

---

1. **Newton:** Sir Isaac Newton (1642–1727), English philosopher and mathematician.

2. **leviathan…polypus:** large, formidable sea animals.

3. **tatou:** armadillo.

degrees of intellect, if we may judge by effects, are very unequally proportioned. Now a luminous genius darts through the complicated arrangements of nature; its pervading ken[1] is subtil and energetic; its powers are adequate to researches the most profound; it investigates, and obscurity is no more; the arcana[2] of ages, yielding to its animated and elucidating progress, relinquisheth the impenetrable veil; its versatility, and the depth of its observations are astonishing; and, amid the blaze of refulgent[3] day, it lifts its aspiring head. But the natal place of this luminary, the same village, perhaps the same family, ushered into being the unfortunate idiot, whose faculties are scarcely adequate to the absolute calls of existence. Some dignified minds, born to all the energy of being, devote their time and talents to inform, to rectify, to improve, and in every sense to benefit mankind; others again, are so *absorbed in self,* that were it not for the catalogue of their individual wants and wishes, we should not know that they continued to vegetate. If persons of this description have any principles but that of self love, they are so completely under the direction of, and assimilated by this their *ruling passion,* that it is difficult to trace, in their actions, the smallest vestige of a foreign influence. Is it just to refuse to merit its unquestionable dues? Is it equitable to deny to virtue the palm of honour? Or, ought we to hesitate in doing reverence to a superiority indubitable and decided?

Where is *unvaried equality to be found?* Not in heaven, *for there are principalities and powers:* Not, certainly, in any of the distributions which we have traced on earth; for it is unquestionable, that *variety* constitutes one of the principal beauties in the arrangements of nature. Nor is it the growth of the Tartarean regions; for there the *arch fiend* exerciseth those powers, which proclaim his regality; and, even *Licentiousness* hath her chosen favourite whom she constituteth chief of the savage band of murderers. I do not say, that my reading and observation are sufficiently extensive to decide; but were I to hazard a conjecture, I would suggest, that, from the days of that first murderer who slew his

---

1. **ken:** knowledge.
2. **arcana:** secret or mysterious knowledge.
3. **refulgent:** radiant.

brother, the levelling scheme hath, strictly speaking, continued a chimera,[1] floating only in the brain of the speculatist, or figuring splendidly in the theories, which his fertile imagination hath commissioned to issue from the press.

Perhaps the late Doctor *Johnson,*[2] who may be styled the monarch of literature, however rich in resources, could not have hit on an argument more effectually calculated to slash conviction upon the feelings of a certain *female historian* (of no inconsiderable merit, notwithstanding) than when waiting upon her, in her decent apartments in the city of London, and assuming the humble and serious features of conviction, he addressed her to the following effect:—"Madam, influenced by your good sense, and the irrefragable strength of your arguments, you at this moment behold before you, the proselyte[3] of your opinions. I am at length confident, that the children of men are all upon an equal footing; and, madam, to give you proof positive that I am indeed a convert, here is a very sensible, civil, worthy, well-behaved citizen, your footman; I make it my request that he may be permitted to sit down and dine with us." Doctor Johnson, upon this, or some similar occasion, made a remark, which, agreeable to the general tenor of his observations, carrieth its evidence along with it, and which the experience of every day may serve to corroborate. "Your *levellers,*" said the Doctor, "wish to *level down* as far as themselves, but they cannot bear levelling *up* to themselves; they would all have some people under them; why not then have *some people* above them? I would not more deprive certain characters of their respect, than of their money. I consider myself as acting a part in the great system of society, and I do to others as I would have them do to me. There would be a perpetual struggle for precedence, were there no rules to discriminate rank."

There is no calculating the disorders which may result from relaxing the series of subordination; if conviction is suspended, we need but make the trial. I am surrounded by a family of men and maid servants. I am placed upon extensive grounds, which call for the regular aid of cul-

---

1. **chimera:** an illusion, especially an unrealizable dream.
2. **Doctor Johnson:** Samuel Johnson (1709–1784), English lexicographer and author.
3. **proselyte:** new convert.

tivation, for all the various routine of agricultural attention. The vernal season is hasting forward—the morning is delightful. On a day so propitious much business may be accomplished: With the early dawn I quit my pillow, I supplicate Mary to direct her woman to prepare me an immediate breakfast; she, carelessly, pronounces me quite as eligible to that task myself. I apply to Abigail, who refers me to another, and another; and, as *equality* admitteth no distinctions, the probability is, that I am finally brought back again to Mary herself. Possibly, after many entreaties, the females may all combine; one bears a cup, another a saucer; a table is dragged from that apartment, and a tea-kettle from this; ignorant of each other's plans, and having no one to direct, the process is impeded and confused, and when at length the motley assemblage is completed, and the refection presented, the spoiled tea, coffee, chocolate, and bread and butter, all evince the opposite hands employed in their manufacture. But this is the fair side of the business; they might have engaged in a tumultuous *fracas,*[1] and, consigning the whole apparatus to destruction, they might have left me no other consolation, than that of soothing my vexation, by singing, in Homeric numbers, the dismal crash of that eventful morning.

Well, but to proceed. Breakfast over, I sally forth. I *advise* that the cattle be yoked, and that such a parcel of manure be conveyed to yonder sterile spot. Jonathan insists that the horse-cart is sufficient to drag it. Thomas is of his opinion. William sides with me, and we prepare for a trial of strength; equally divided, our opposition bars our purpose; from words we proceed to blows; the females are alarmed; they take their sides; the plot thickens; appearances grow formidable; a doughty battle ensues; bloody noses are the consequence; and the day is sacrificed to discord. Every morning is thus ushered in; every portion of time is marked by opposition. Now the land shall be hedged with bushes, anon the ready rock shall present the barrier, and again the wooden enclosure is all the rage. To-day we will plough, to-morrow we will sow. Nay, you are too early, you are too late; this is sufficient, that is not enough; we will go hither and thither, every where, and no where.

Thus roll on the days, weeks and months. Autumn is at the door, the

---

1. **fracas:** noisy quarrel or brawl.

lands are uncultivated, and famine, with its meagre stride, is rapidly advancing to our borders. Meanwhile, even in this tumultuous era, my house, my estate confesseth a potentate.[1] Anarchy reigneth supreme, and desolation administereth her commands. To prevent, or to guard against consequences, which every sober sentiment must deprecate, becomes impossible; no member of the family hath authority to interpose the dictatorial document, and the commands of the fiend are perforce obeyed. Who shall prevent the spreading evil? If licentiousness is successful in her imposture; if, assuming the mask of liberty, she completeth her deception; if we prostrate before this baleful destroyer, where, I demand, is my safety? What security can I have, that my neighbour, whose sinewy arm can bear away the prize of strength, will not snatch from me that patrimony, which, descending from a virtuous line of ancestors, I have preserved, at the expense of laborious days, and many a self-denying conflict? Surely, language, in attempting an enumeration of the calamities of licentiousness, is baffled in the description! and even *conception* must fall short of the mischiefs which she produceth.

But if the *theory* of equality is not *practicable* in the contracted circle of domestic life, much less will that experiment succeed which would realize it, in regard to the heterogeneous[2] collection of beings which constitute a nation. Doth not Liberty associate her laws, her regulations, and her distinctions? Is not good government the basis on which she erecteth the superstructure of all those operations so beneficial to mankind? Yes, Liberty, sacred and genuine Liberty, draweth with precision the line, nor will she permit a litigation of the inherent Rights of Man. She alloweth no imaginary claims; she is fearful of disturbing the regular succession of order; she is fond of the necessary arrangement of civil subordination; and she dreadeth that tumultuous and up-rooting hurricane, which, inmingling the various classes of mankind, destroyeth the beautiful gradation and series of harmony, again restoring all that wild uproar, resulting from the rude and mishapen domination of

---

1. **potentate:** ruler, one who wields great power.

2. **heterogeneous:** consisting of diverse ingredients or constituents.

chaos. Yes, we repeat it, that people, that nation, that tribe or family, which is destitute of legislation, regulation, and officers of government, must unquestionably be in a deplorable situation. The strong will invariably oppress the weak; to the lusty arm of athletic guilt, imbecile innocence will fall a prey, and there is no power to redress! hence the time registered axiom, *"It is necessary to relinquish a part, for the preservation of the whole."* Liberty delegates her powers, and to this effulgent[1] goddess, her anointed ministers, with that integrity and patriotic firmness which becometh the servants of a patroness, who still regards the children of men with an eye of benignity, fail not to render up their accounts.

Let us suppose a people in a state of nature, and let us suppose them made up of all those varieties of constitution, intellect, passions, and corporeal strength, which are commonly found in a community. Experience hath convinced them, that anarchy is pregnant with every evil; and they finally combine to form the league of government. What is the mode for the administration of justice, which we would recommend to such a people? Possessed by a wish to render permanent, and give the requisite dignity, energy, execution, and obedience to the social order which we should aim at establishing, we should be solicitous to adopt in our form of polity, that graduatory junction which would cement and bind together, in an amicable and mutual exchange of good offices, the various classes of citizens. Fancy, for a moment, invests me with the venerable and honorary character of a legislator; and, for the purpose of forming, for a set of well disposed men, a code of regulations, I imagine myself seated, with the pen of inquiry in my fingers, and my design being to compile a government of *laws,* rather than of *individuals,* I am naturally solicitous to promulgate institutions, which shall be at once salutary, efficacious and pleasing. With a view of tracing and combining an eligible plan, I might turn over huge folios[2] of information, and, pursuing a science of such vast importance to mankind, which in its operations is capable of the highest public utility, or which may become

---

1. **effulgent:** radiant.

2. **folios:** leaves of a manuscript book.

the root of every evil, investigation can hardly be too scrupulously exact. But what would be the result of an application to various writers? Doubtless we should find ourselves involved in a labyrinth of opposite testimonies; and, confused by a multiplicity of contradictory and perhaps fallacious opinions, reflection would be absorbed, and decision at a stand.

The ancients have remarked, that, cultivated by the hand of liberty in the dwellings of freedom, the arts and sciences flourished with invigorated charms; that neither the Persians or Egyptians understood their beauties; that from the Greeks, although too often engaged in hostilities, and struggling in the toils of poverty, they obtained maturation; that they declined with that freedom, once the glory of the Grecian republics, and that, with their august patroness, winging their etherial way to celebrious Rome, they there continued their splendid career, until the immolation of liberty, in that imperial city, muffled in dark and portentous clouds those intellectual luminaries; and hence, from these incontrovertible facts, it is confidently asserted, that the arts and sciences can never flourish but in the soil of freedom. Yet, in opposition to a conclusion which may have been too hastily formed, we are told, that *modern Rome* and Florence have enwreathed with perfection, sculpture, painting, music and poetry; and that Florence, after the usurpations of the family of Medici,[1] made the most rapid proficiency in those arts. Ariosto, Tasso, Galileo, Raphael, and Michael Angelio;[2] these illustrious painters, poets and mathematicians, it is observed, were not born in republics. Reubens,[3] it is said, collected and established his school at Antwerp, and not at Amsterdam; and in Germany, the true polish of manners is rather to be found at Dresden than at Hamburgh.

France hath undoubtedly furnished a striking example of the prosperity of literature in an absolute government. Philosophy, poetry, dra-

---

1. **Medici:** family that controlled Florence from the fifteenth century until 1737.

2. **Ariosto…Michael Angelio:** Ludovico Ariosto (1474–1533), Italian epic and lyric poet; Torquato Tasso (1544–1594), Italian poet; Galileo Galilei (1564–1642), Italian astronomer, mathematician, and physicist; Raphael Santi (1483–1520), Italian Renaissance painter; Michelangelo Buonarotti (1475–1564), Italian Renaissance painter.

3. **Reubens:** Peter Paul Rubens (1577–1640), Flemish painter.

matic eminence, oratory, history, painting, architecture, sculpture, music—these have received the most extensive cultivation, and the highest honours in the *kingdom* of France: And we are moreover assured, that the *cidevant* subjects had astonishingly meliorated that most grateful and beneficial of all arts, *l'Art de Vivre,*[1] the necessary and social art, which involves a mutual interchange of sentiments.

Thus *contradictory* are those streams of information, which yet may have originated in the fountain of wisdom. The superstructures of governments have generally been raised upon apprehension and compulsion; in such circumstances, error hath been almost unavoidable, and it can never be matter of wonder, that human systems are susceptible of improvement.

In the novelties of Lycurgus,[2] the features of artifice and fraud are but too prevalent. Solon,[3] although the votary of wisdom, and undoubtedly the mild and beneficent friend of mankind, yet even Solon entertained despotic ideas of the powers vested in him, and we cannot forbear observing, that he considered himself as possessing an *optional* authority, to implant the germe of despotism, or to emit the rays of bland and corrected freedom. Numa, by virtue of the goddess Egeria,[4] might have originated the grossest impositions; and it is an indubitable truth, that the rights of man are irreconcileable with a relinquishment of that privilege of inquiry, which may erect a barrier to the inundation of evil. Turning, for a moment, from all those reservoirs of knowledge, which, nevertheless, I must ever unceasingly venerate, I wave the occupation of a Gleaner, and simply lighting the torch of reason at the flame of experience, I will, for the organization of my sketch of immunities, consult those sentiments and conclusions, which are the natural growth of a plain mind.

Common sense pronounces, that a people destitute of a leader, and

---

1. **l'Art de Vivre:** the art of living (French).

2. **Lycurgus:** Spartan lawgiver (ninth century B.C.).

3. **Solon:** lawgiver (ca. 638–559 B.C.).

4. **Numa…Egeria:** The legendary Roman king Numa Pompilius was advised by the goddess-nymph Egeria.

destitute of legislation, loudly demand the *protecting hand of a guardian power;* and, liberty adds, that a chief should be obtained by the joint suffrages of the people at large. To this end, they must be convened in their several districts, where, uninfluenced by party or by passion, let them commission him, whom they esteem most worthy, to assume that august title—*The Father of his Country;* and, after reciprocating the most solemn engagements, after consecrating him by their joint affections and benedictions, let them invest him with authority to lead them against their combined enemies, to fight their battles, and, by the wisdom of his regulations, to procure them victory, and to guarantee their just immunities. Let this their chosen patriot be aided by a general council, consisting of delegates according to the number of the people. Let these delegates be appointed by a decision, influenced only by the intrinsic worth of the candidates. Let them form two distinct deliberative bodies, or houses, properly qualified and authorized to ACT AS CHECKS upon each other; and, let these three branches be invested with powers, fully adequate to all the purposes of legislation. To the *departments* thus appointed to these *high offices* of trust, let the utmost veneration be annexed; but I would ordain, that the individuals who filled them, should, after a stated time, be removable at the pleasure of the people. Even the First Magistrate should hold his place but in consequence of frequent re-elections; and for high crimes and misdemeanors, he should be considered as amenable to the laws. Upon legislative acts he should possess only a conditional negative; and while his fellow-citizens were aided by his counsels, they should be secured from his encroachments. He should always be considered as the Chief Warrior of the people; but in the formation of treaties, he should call in, at least, one branch of the legislature, and the same concurrence should be necessary to the appointment to offices. The commerce or currency of the nation should not be subjected to the prescriptions of its Executive, nor should he arrogate, in matters of conscience, even the shadow of jurisdiction. As a faithful and vigilant friend of the people, he should be unwearied in his informations, recommendations, and all such constitutional measures, as he should conceive would conduce to the public weal;[1] and, during his administration, he should be careful to exact a faithful obedience to the laws. If in any single instance I entrusted him with discretionary or absolute power, it shall be in granting reprieves, or remission of offences; for, as I would always give the scale to preponderate on the side of mercy, so I would arm the Executive with the lenity of clemency, while I debarred him the exercise of measures unduly sanguinary.[2]

Yet with the dignified and honorary distinctions of government, I would be careful to invest the Man of the people. Ambassadors, and other public ministers, should mingle in his train, and every rational insignia of respect should ornament his *department*. His *office* should ensure the highest respect; and I would yield obedience to the *individual* as long as he was entitled to *public confidence* and respect.

The judicial power should be separate from the executive, and I would invest it with as large a share of *independence* as could consist with *reciprocality* and *union;* while the degree of guilt involved in crimes of almost every description, should be determined by the empannelled peers of the culprit. "But all this is only collecting the instruments, while the code of institutions are yet unfashioned." True, but as legislative acts should be the result of the most mature deliberation, we will search in the great volume of nature, we will turn over the leaves of experience, and thus selecting the gems, and from time to time accumulating our system, we will finally present the luminous compendium to the consideration, and, as we hope, to the acceptation of unprejudiced reason. Meanwhile, skimming the surface of my subject, I present only the rudiments of a system, which fancy hath pleasingly contemplated.

Doth the reader exclaim— *"Surely these hints are nothing more than the lineaments of the constitution of the United States!"* Well, honest friend, they are the *lineaments of nature*—the *lineaments of liberty*—they make a part of that contract to which she consents; and, without entering into the complex and admirable intertexture of those united and separate

---

1. **weal:** well-being.

2. **sanguinary:** bloodthirsty, murderous.

governments, which constitute our federalism, we pronounce, that these are the leading features of that subordination, without which, GENUINE LIBERTY would no longer irradiate our hemisphere.

May the parties which are originated, stimulate the exertions of her real votaries; may no description among us ever assume the gorgon head of faction; and, may the mutual jealousies, dissentions and ambition, which pervade, serve as antidotes to each other. Parties, in a state of civil and political liberty, have been compared to the passions of an individual; and, as the passions are said to be the elements of life, so the animated and resuscitating spirit of party is observed to be essential to the existence of genuine freedom. Be it so; and may the public weal, the public tranquillity, be, by every means, promoted.

Necessity of Religion, Especially in Adversity

Turn how we may, avoid it how we will,
Innate conviction must attend us still;
Religion follows as our guardian shade,
Ardent to bless, though impiously betray'd.
Our every breath Omnipotence proclaims;   5
A God Omnific varied nature names;
The breeze is his—the uprooting whirlwind's roar—
The gentle rill—the waves of every shore;
'Tis God directs the day—and God the night,
As erst he spake, and Nature sprang to light.   10

No—Atheism will never do. The prime procurer and minister of the French arrangements, at length accedes to this axiom; and Gallia, having guillotined her sovereign, and blasphemously sought to dethrone and annihilate the Monarch of Heaven, becomes, in her present resolutions, solicitous to re-establish the Deity in her systems, to invest the Supreme with those divine honours, which the language of nature hasteth to bestow, which the dictates of reason invariably award.

Opposed, from principle, to those sanguinary decrees, which, pronouncing the death-warrant of whole hecatombs of my species, fail not to let loose the dogs of war, I will confess, that I have not felt for the name of Robespierre[1] any of those cordialities which constitute the aggregate of amity. The anarchy and consequent enormities, prevalent in France, together with those licentious principles, which have apparently been so generally embraced, I have considered as replete with

---

Title. This essay appeared in *The Gleaner,* 1:31.

1. **Robespierre:** Maximilien-François-Marie-Isidore de Robespierre (1758–1794), a leader of the French Revolution.

incalculable evils, as the baleful precursors of every ill which can afflict humanity! Such my sentiments, I expected not from the report of Robespierre, those strong and glowing sensations, which, whenever I attend to the voice of truth, most delightfully expand my soul—But I have read—and, charmed with the prevalent contour of the composition, the energy and beauty of the diction, and the demonstrative propriety and sublimity of the observations—while I do homage to the translator, I cannot but join my suffrage to those applauses, by which America has marked the *new-born* piety of the French politician.

It is true that, as being a member of the protestant community, I am necessitated, by my creed, to renounce all supplications made to saints, whatever eclat may have attended their canonization. I may not feel at liberty to cry out, "Oh! *Sancta Robespierre, ora pro nobis;* "[1] yet if he, *in reality,* shall at length pursue the *mild dictates of truth* and *reason,* every sentiment of my soul will combine to wish him God speed. An admirer of the report in the gross, I yet conceive that the following extracts can hardly be too often repeated, can scarcely be too strongly inculcated, or too deeply engraven upon the tablets of reflection. "What was the wish of those, who, in the bosom of the conspiracies with which we were surrounded, in the midst of the embarrassments of such a war, at the moment while the torch of civil discord was still smoking, suddenly attacked all kinds of worship by violence, to establish themselves as the furious apostles of annihilation, and as the fanatic missionaries of atheism? Attend only to the happiness of your country and the interests of humanity; *cherish all opinions and institutions which console and elevate the mind;* reject those which tend to degrade and corrupt them; *revive* and exalt all those generous sentiments and those great moral ideas which they have wished to extinguish; *reconcile by the charms of friendship, and the bonds of virtue, those citizens whom they have wished to divide. Who has given thee the mission of announcing to the people, that the Deity does not exist?* To you who are attached to this barren doctrine, and who are not animated in the cause of your country, *what advantage do you derive* from *persuading man that a blind force presides in his destiny,*

---

1. **Sancta Robespierre...nobis:** Holy Robespierre, pray for us (Latin).

and strikes by chance his virtues or his vices; and that his soul is only a transient breath which is extinguished at the tomb? Will the idea of his annihilation inspire him with more pure or more elevated sentiments than that of his immortality? Will it inspire him with more respect for his fellow men, or for himself; more attachment to his country; more firmness in braving tyranny; more *contempt for death* or pleasure? *You who regret a virtuous friend, do you not delight to reflect that the most valuable part of him has escaped decease?* You who weep over the corpse of a son or a wife, *are you consoled by him who tells you that nothing more of them remains than a vile heap of dust?* Unfortunate men, who expire under the stroke of an assassin! your last sigh is an appeal to eternal justice! Innocence, on the scaffold, makes the tyrant turn pale in his triumphal car: Would it have this ascendancy if the tomb put upon a level the oppressor and the oppressed? Miserable sophist![1] from whence do you derive this right of rending from innocence the sceptre of reason, and of placing it again in the hands of vice; *to throw a melancholy veil over nature, to drive misfortune to despair;* to encourage vice, to afflict virtue, to degrade humanity? *The more a man is endowed with sensibility and genius, the more is he attached to those ideas which aggrandize his being, and which elevate his mind; and the doctrine of men of this character should become that of the universe.*

"Ah! how can those ideas differ from truth? At least I cannot conceive how nature could have suggested to man any *fictions* more useful than these *realities;* and if the existence of a God, if the immortality of the soul, were only dreams, they would still remain the most splendid of all the conceptions of the human mind.

"The idea of the Supreme Being, and the immortality of the soul, is a continual invitation to justice: It is then social and republican. He who can replace the Deity in the system of social life, is, in my opinion, a prodigy of genius; and he, who without having replaced him, only endeavours to banish him from the mind of man, appears to me a prodigy of stupidity or perversity. If the principles I have hitherto developed are errors, I am deceived in what the world unite to revere. Observe

---

1. **sophist:** false reasoner.

with what art Cesar, pleading in the Roman senate in favour of the accomplices of Cataline,[1] lost himself in digression against the doctrine of the immortality of the soul; so well calculated did these ideas appear to him, to distinguish in the hearts of the judges the energy of virtue; so closely did the cause of vice appear to him, connected with that of Atheism. Cicero,[2] on the contrary invoked against the traitors both the sword of the law and the thunder of the gods. Socrates, when dying, conversed with his friends on the immortality of the soul. Leonidas,[3] at Thermopyles, supping with his companions in arms, at the moment of executing the most heroic design that human virtue ever conceived, invited them for the next day to another banquet in a new life.

"A great man, a real hero, esteems himself too much to be pleased with the idea of his annihilation. A villain, contemptible in his own eyes, and horrible in those of other men, perceives that nature cannot afford him a more splendid boon than that of his annihilation. Religion collects mankind together, and by collecting them together you will render them better; for when men are thus assembled, they endeavour to please each other, which can only be effected by those things that render them estimable. Give to their reunion a great moral and political motive, and the love of virtuous things will, with pleasure, enter their hearts; for mankind do not see each other without pleasure."

I had but recently perused the whole of this very excellent moral report, when one of the best informed, and most sentimental of my friends, put into my hands a piece selected from the London Morning Chronicle of November 29, 1793.

To the matured judgment of this friend I am in the habit of paying high deference; and he conceived, that whether we regarded the little narration as a fact, or an ingenious reproof of the conduct of the predominant party in France, it contained a sufficient quantum of good

---

1. **Cataline:** Lucius Sergius Catilina (ca. 108–62 B.C.), a Roman politician who plotted to overthrow the Roman consuls. Julius Caesar argued for moderation when the conspirators were condemned to death by the Roman Senate.

2. **Cicero:** Roman philosopher and orator (106–43 B.C.).

3. **Leonidas:** Spartan king, fifth century B.C., who blocked the Persian army at Thermopylae; but the battle turned and all of the Spartan soldiers were slain.

sense to merit preservation. It is a proper supplement for the celebrated report of Robespierre, and in my office of caterer for my readers, perhaps I could not do better than to offer it to their acceptance. I subjoin it, therefore, with an added wish, that it may contribute as largely to their pleasures, as it did to the satisfaction of the Gleaner.

"A few days after the bishop of Paris and his vicars had set the example of renouncing their clerical character, a curi[1] from a village on the banks of the Rhone, followed by some of his parishioners, with an offering of gold, silver, saints' chalices, rich vestments, &c. presented himself at the bar of the house. The sight of the gold put the Convention in very good humour, and the curi, a thin venerable looking man, with grey hair, was ordered to speak. I came, said he, from the village of—, where the only good building standing (for the chateau has been pulled down) is a very fine church; my parishioners beg you will take it to make a hospital for the sick and wounded of both parties, they being equally our countrymen; the gold and silver, part of which we have brought you, they entreat you will devote to the service of the State; and that you will cast the bells into cannon, to drive away its foreign invaders. For myself I am come with great pleasure to resign my letters of ordination, of induction, and every deed of title, by which I have been constituted a member of your ecclesiastical polity. I am still able to support myself with the labour of my hands, and I beg you to believe that I never felt sincerer joy than I now do in making this renunciation—I have longed to see this day; I see it, and am glad.

"When the old man had done speaking, the applauses were immoderate. You are an honest man, said they all at once; a brave fellow, you do not believe in God; and the President advanced to give him the fraternal embrace. The curi did not seem greatly elated with these tokens of approbation; he retired back a few steps, and thus resumed his discourse:

"Before you applaud my sentiments, it is fit you understand them; perhaps they may not entirely coincide with your own. I rejoice in this day, not because I wish to see religion degraded, but because I wish to

---

1. **curi**: curé; parish priest (French).

see it exalted and purified. By dissolving its alliance with the State, you give it dignity and independence; you have done it a piece of service which its well-wishers would never have had courage to render it, but which is the only thing wanted to make it appear in its genuine lustre and beauty. Nobody will now say of me, when I am performing the offices of my religion—It is his trade—he is paid for telling the people such and such things—he is hired to keep up a useful piece of mummery. They cannot now say this; and therefore I feel myself raised in my own esteem, and shall speak to them with a confidence and frankness, which before this I never durst venture to assume.

"We resign, without reluctance, our gold and silver images and embroidered vestments, because that we have never found, that looking upon gold or silver made the heart more pure, or the affections more heavenly: We can also spare our churches; for the heart that wishes to lift itself up to God, will never be at a loss for room to do it in;—but we cannot spare our religion, because, to tell you the truth, we never had so much occasion for it. I understand that you accuse us priests of having told the people a great many falsehoods. I suppose this may have been the case; but till this day we have never been allowed to inquire, whether the things which we taught them were true or not. You required us formerly to receive them all without proof, and you now would have us reject them all without discrimination. Neither of these modes of conduct become philosophers, such as you would be thought to be. I am going to employ myself diligently, along with my parishioners, to sift the wheat from the bran, the true from the false: If we are not successful, we shall be at least sincere.

"I do fear, indeed, that while I wore those vestments which we have brought you, and spoke in the large gloomy building which we have given up to you, I told my poor flock many idle stories. I cannot but hope, however, that the errors we have fallen into have not been very material, since the village has in general been sober and good; the peasants are honest, docile, and laborious; the husbands love their wives, and the wives their husbands; they are fortunately not too rich to be compassionate, and they have constantly relieved the sick and fugitives of all parties, whenever it has lain in their way. I think, therefore, what I have taught them cannot be so very much amiss. You want to extirpate priests; but will you hinder the ignorant from applying for instruction, the unhappy for comfort and hope, the unlearned from looking up to the learned? If you do not, you will have priests, by whatever name you will order them to be called; but it is certainly not necessary they should wear a particular dress, or be appointed by state letters of ordination. My letters of ordination are, my zeal, my charity, my ardent love for my dear children of the village—if I were more learned, I should add my knowledge; but, alas! we all know very little; to man every error is pardonable, but want of humility.

"We have a public walk, with a spreading elm tree at one end of it, and a circle of green round it, with a convenient bench. Here I shall draw together the children as they are playing round me. I shall point to the vines laden with fruit, to the orchard, to the herds of cattle lowing round us, to the distant hills stretching one behind another, and they will ask me how these things came? I shall tell them all I know or have heard from wise men who have lived before me; they will be penetrated with love and veneration; they will kneel, I shall kneel with them; they will not be at my feet, but all of us at the feet of that good Being, whom we shall worship together; and thus they will receive within their tender minds, *a religion*. The old men will come sometimes from having deposited under the green sod one of their companions, and place themselves by my side; they will look wishfully at the turf, and anxiously inquire—*Is he gone forever? Shall we be soon like him? Will no morning break over the tomb?* When the *wicked cease from troubling, will the good cease from doing good?* We will talk of these things; I will comfort them; I will tell them of the goodness of God; I will speak to them of a life to come; I will bid them hope for a state of retribution.

"In a clear night, when the stars slide over our head, they will ask what those bright bodies are, and by what rules they rise and set? And we will converse about different forms of being, and distant worlds, in the immensity of space, governed by the same laws, till we feel our minds raised from what is grovelling, and refined from what is sordid.

"You talk of Nature—this is Nature; and if you could at this moment extinguish religion in the minds of all the world, thus would it be kindled again. You have changed our holy days; you have an undoubted right, as our civil governors, so to do; it is very immaterial whether they are kept once in seven days, or once in ten; some, however, you will leave us, and when they occur, I shall tell those who choose to hear me, of the beauty and utility of virtue, and of the dignity of upright conduct. We shall talk of good men who have lived in the world, and of the doctrines they have taught; and if any of them have been persecuted and put to death for their virtue, we shall reverence their memories the more—I hope in all this there is no harm. There is a book, out of which I have sometimes taught my people: It says, we are to love those who do us hurt, and to pour oil and wine into the wounds of a stranger; it has enabled my children to bear patiently the spoiling of their goods, and to give up their own interest to the general welfare. I think it cannot be a very bad book. I wish more of it had been read in your town; perhaps you would not have had so many assassinations and massacres. In this book we hear of a person called JESUS; some worship him as a God; others, as I am told, say it is wrong to do so;—some teach that he existed before the beginning of ages; others, that he was born of Joseph and Mary. I cannot tell whether these controversies will ever be decided; but in the mean time, I think we cannot do otherwise than well in imitating him; for I learn that he *loved the poor, and went about doing good.*

"Fellow citizens, as I travelled hither from my own village, I saw peasants setting amongst the smoking ruins of their cottages; rich men and women reduced to deplorable poverty; fathers lamenting their children in the bloom and pride of youth; and I said to myself—*these people cannot afford to part with their religion.* But indeed you cannot take it away; if, contrary to your first declaration, you choose to try the experiment of persecuting it, you will only make us prize it the more, and love it the better. Religion, *true* or *false,* is so necessary to the mind of man, that you have already begun to make yourselves a new one. You are sowing the seeds of superstition at the moment you fancy you are destroying superstition; and in two or three generations your posterity will be worshipping some clumsy idol, with the rights perhaps of a bloody Moloch,[1] or a lascivious Thamusar.[2] It was not worth while to have been philosophers, and destroyed the images of our saints for this; but let every one choose the religion that pleases him: I and my parishioners are content with ours; it teaches us to bear the evils your childish or sanguinary decrees have helped to bring upon the country.

"The curi turned his footsteps homeward; and the Convention looked for some minutes on one another, before *they resumed their work of blood.*"

The Gleaner is aware, that the republishing of the foregoing, cannot fail of unveiling him to the gentleman, from whom he received the manuscript; but he has such perfect confidence in the indulgence and honour of the disposition of his respected friend, and in that of those with whom he stands immediately connected, as to rest assured that they will not betray a secret, which he, the Gleaner, hath delayed to reveal to the dearest of his associates.

---

1. **Moloch:** Ammonite god of fire associated with sacrifices of children.

2. **Thamusar:** probably Thammuz, a Syrian nature deity worshipped, especially by women, in a yearly resurrection rite.

Spirit Independent of Matter

I love to trace the independent mind;
Her beamy path, and radiant way to find:
I love to mark her where disrob'd she stands,
While with new life each faculty expands:
I love the reasoning which new proofs supplies,   5
That I shall soar to worlds beyond the skies;
The sage who tells me, spirit ever lives,
New motives to a life of virtue gives.
  Blest immortality!—ennobling thought!
With reason, truth and honour, richly fraught—   10
Rise to my view—thy sweet incentives bring,
And round my haunts thy deathless perfumes fling;
Glow in my breast—my purposes create,
And to each proper action stimulate.

As there is no idea, by which I am so exquisitely tortured, as that of annihilation, I naturally turn, with disgust and horror, from the reasonings of him, who, laying impious hands on that principle of animation which originates in Deity, would confound it with the common mass of matter; and who, with grub like industry, having enveloped himself in his earthy cone, entertains as little expectation of breaking his sepulchral enclosure, as the reptile who thus mechanically encrusts itself.

"Mamma," said my little grand-daughter to Margaretta, "Mamma, where do butterflies go?" I repeat, that a child may ask a question which would puzzle a Sir Isaac Newton to resolve. But although neither the wise nor the untaught may be able to descant *learnedly* on the destination of butterflies, yet do we take inexpressible pleasure in tracing their

---

Title. This essay appeared in *The Gleaner,* 2:62.

various and surprising transmutations, and in dwelling with eager attention on their eventful career, until, borne on the gentle zephyr, they become tenants of the aërial world.

May not the butterfly be considered as a humble figure of the creature Man? In its reptile state it seems fastened to the earth; it is indefatigable in its attempts to obtain that subsistence it will need but a little while. At length it is evidently on the decay; it sets about preparing for its departure; it makes ready the filaments in which it enwrappeth itself; it enfolds and contracts them; gradually they become a sepulchral crust, in which securely enveloped, the deceased insect *apparently bids a final adieu* to the busy scenes in which it hath taken so laborious a part. But mark the astonishing change: These habiliments of death are thrown off—the hideously disgusting form is no more—its newly acquired wings are expanded—they assume a variety of hues, and look as if designed in the gayest moments of a fertile and brilliant imagination. Hardly will the little flutterer deign to rest on the bosom of that earth, to which it formerly so closely adhered; and, perched on some beauteously fragrant flower, and indulging in all the rich variety of ambrosial food, it sips the embosomed sweets. With what astonishing celerity its movements are performed—lightly it pursues its elevated path, and we gaze with admiration upon its wonderful improvements. Was not the whole process submitted to our observation, we should call in question its reality; and cold philosophy would teach us, first, to reason—secondly, to doubt—and, finally, to embrace the creed of infidelity.

Man, in his present state of being, moves heavily on this opaque globe—he is principally solicitous, respecting matters which appertain wholly to this life—he is often anxiously oppressed, while every accession to that property he is carefully seeking to augment, does but increase his burdens. But whatever impediments may seem to bar his way, he, however, advances onward—he attains the period when his quick sense of earth-born joys is no more—he verges on the days on which he can say he hath no pleasure—for a little moment he abides, and his open grave is prepared—he is inclosed in the narrow house, and the green turf clothes, with undistinguishing verdure, the hallowed spot where he reposes. Do we say that we have bid him an eternal adieu? we do not speak correctly; for, in the morning of the resurrection, he shall burst the barriers of the grave—he shall issue from the chambers of the tomb. Behold how mortality hath put on immortality—he is beautiful as the inhabitants of the celestial world—he hath become as a winged seraph—he mounts, he soars on high—he pursues his trackless way— he attains the heaven of heavens, and he mingles with the angels who surround the throne of Deity.

Is my figure exceptionable?—I shall not contend—I did not expect it would answer in all its parts. I think, however, some of its features will be acknowledged striking; and I could as easily, had I not ocular demonstration, believe the resurrection of the body, inclosed in yonder tomb, as I could lend my credence to the egg, the worm, the cone, the aurelia, and the butterfly.

Yet, I do not vehemently insist on the resuscitation of this time-worn tenement. In the bloom of youth, and vigour of my days, my reluctance to a final separation from organs so incomparably well adapted to my exigencies, was extreme; but a length of years have revolved—the fine machine is going to decay—I begin to detect its inconveniences—it is a heavy clog upon my purposes—and, when I am bounding forward with all the celerity of thought, I am retarded and pulled back by its unwieldy properties. I naturally wish for a vehicle more agile; and imagination, darting into futurity, anticipates accommodations more consonant with my wishes. Hardly a day passes, in which I do not discover, in my present residence, new instances to prove that the building is greatly impaired; nor is this a circumstance of regret. My glass informs me, that time hath furrowed my face; that my eyes no longer sparkle with the vivacity of youth; that the glossy ornaments of my head are rapidly giving place; that my form is bent; that I hobble in my gait, &c. &c. No matter—my attachment to this earthly residence is also on the decline, and I will support, with fortitude, the sufferings which may be necessary to its dissolution. Whether my all-wise and omnific Father will raise it again on a nobler principle, is a question that cannot greatly agitate my mind, since I know that his paternal goodness will ordain for me, precisely that habitation, which shall be the best calculated for the full enjoyment of all my faculties. If I—if my best self can escape from this wreck of nature, I am then sure to be as *"blest as I can bear;"* and, the *superiority* and *inferred durability* of spirit, is beyond a doubt.

"Certainly not," cries the opposer, *"for the mental* faculties decay with the corporeal; *thus evincing the truth of the hypothesis, which describes them as both perishing together."*

But against such a comfortless and derogatory sentiment I enter my protest. The immortal principle of life, retaining, *in this debilitated body,* its pristine vigour, glows indignant at the humiliating idea; and, notwithstanding the *decaying organs by which it operates,* it still asserts its own inherent fervours. *Age* cannot, in *reality,* curtail the inborn powers of the soul; their elasticity, for want of use, may be abridged, but their *native energies* can never depreciate. From the moment in which the immortal mind becomes a sojourner in mortality, certain organs, by which it is to operate, are assigned to the celestial resident, and these organs become the medium of its manifestations. In infancy the mental faculties are under a necessity of awaiting the acquirements of that progressing machine, in which they are enveloped; and the reason is obvious; the most skilful artist must be furnished with instruments proper to his occupation. In the vigour of manhood the soul still finds many a laudable wish ungratified—its habitation is not in every respect accommodated to its views—it would move with all the rapidity of motion—it would take the wings of the morning, and compass the globe in a day—it would design and execute in one and the same moment—and the restless anxiety it experienceth is a presumptive proof, that it is appointed to a higher and more perfect state. Old age arrives—and the *bodily organs, ordained for dissolution, experienceth the imbecility that marked the state of childhood*—the imprisoned spirit assays to quicken the sluggish stream—it endeavours to rouse the torpid pulse—it would render flexile the stiffening sinews—with tremulous anxiety it searches every compartment, throws its inquiring glance through each avenue, and would act upon the complicated machine as in those days when it appeared so much under its command—but it will not be—and it is in vain to struggle against a statute which hath passed the great seal of Heaven. The retiring immortal at length becomes conscious that it is on the eve of its departure; it collects its scattered faculties, and, submitting to that state which bears a strong resemblance to inactivity, and which is imposed by necessity, it awaits, with more or less resignation, the approaching moment of its final emancipation. But shall we for this expatiate on its diminished lustre, strip it of its immortality, prepare its funeral dirge, and consign it to the gulph of oblivion? Strange perversion of ideas! most illogical conclusion! and truly unworthy sacrifice of all those commanding incentives to virtue and splendid hopes, that originate in an expectation of future existence.

That it is highly irrational to characterize the immortal mind, from the *demonstration* it maketh of its faculties by the medium of *decaying bodily organs,* is apparent from a variety of considerations. An illustrative figure this moment presents. I take my seat in the midst of a respectable company—a musician is introduced—I have heard much of this performer—he is very eminent, understands every branch of music, is unequalled in the line of his profession, and particularly excels upon the piano-forte—the instrument is opened, and he commences his efforts with a favourite piece of music. But what a futile attempt!—sounds the most discordant issue from the piano—not a single note is in unison—the flats and sharps are confounded—he is out of time—*a child, practising his lesson,* would have produced better tones. O horrid! I exclaim; surely, the artist is either grossly deficient, or he has *lost those exquisite powers of execution, for which he has been so highly celebrated; his faculties, probably, are on the decay.*

"Mistaken man," replies the master of the house, "your conjecture is erroneous; nothing can be further from the truth. *The instrument, my good Sir, is out of tune; nay, more, an accident hath despoiled it of its principal keys; the complicated machinery is obstructed in its most capital parts; in short, it is worn out by time, disastrous removals, and unskilful usage."* Ought I not to feel conscious of my injurious estimation of the musician? Does not the circumstance of the *decayed instrument* restore my high raised ideas of *his abilities?* and will it not be proper, that I henceforward render him the homage which must ever be due to superior acquirements?

I confess, I take a superior pleasure in tracing, improving and cherishing, every idea which establishes the *pre-eminence, independence* and

immortality of the mind; and, in the multifarious reflections I have anxiously made on this subject, I have derived much consolation, from
recurring to the surprising activity the spirit often evinces, when the
bodily organs are fast locked in the embraces of the *image* of *death.* I
have thought, that the action of the spirit is in no moment *entirely suspended;* and although I have passed many nights without a *consciousness*
of having dreamed, yet it does not therefore follow, that the mental faculties have been unemployed. The most pleasing visions have sometimes gathered round my sleeping hours; method and propriety have
been in full exercise; but when the re-action of the corporeal organs has
re-called the vagrant spirit, only disjointed images have remained, and it
has been beyond my power to recover a single connected idea. Again, I
have only been able to recollect that I *have dreamed,* without the vestige
of an impression, by which I could trace the nature of the vision. From
these facts I gather, that I may dream without being at all conscious,
after the shadows of the night have fled, that my mind has been thus
occupied. It appears to me of consequence, to establish the *constant
activity* of the soul; for, if it can, for a single moment, be divested of its
consciousness and the appendages of animation; if it can *slumber with
the body,* it may slumber for ages, it may lose its identity, it may sink
into oblivion; and we are, by consequence, conducted to the comfortless verge of materialism! But having expressed myself freely on this subject in an Essay, which may in future be submitted to the public eye, I
wave it for the present.

I know that dreams are whimsical, perplexing and fallacious; yet we
do not always understand their origin or tendency; and, I conceive,
there may be analogies in nature, of which we are entirely ignorant.
One thing appears to me certain, that dreams furnish no inconsiderable
evidence of that *pre-eminence, independence* and *immortality,* which I am
solicitous to confirm. A person far advanced in years, and entering on
the winter of life, every day accumulates infirmities. Suffering under a
severe paroxysm of the gout, after a succession of hours marked by
anguish, nature, quite exhausted, forgets itself in the arms of sleep; to
the couch of misery the pain-worn body is still confined; but the gladdened spirit, as if felicitating itself on its momentary exemption,

indulges the full career of fancy. The scene is instantly changed—a surprising revolution succeeds—youth again blooms on the cheek—the nerves are new strung—the sinews resume their wonted agility—the blood flows briskly through the veins—health braces the frame—hope glows in the bosom—the heart leaps for joy—all is enchantment, the enchantment of the morning of life—he contemplates the tenderest attachment—he forms new connexions—he becomes impassioned—and he feels over again the ardours of youth. But alas! the fleeting vision is on the wing—a creaking door—an impertinent footstep—the charm is broken—and the mind is again embodied by age, infirmity, and consequent suffering. Yet, I ask, has it not thus produced a proof of its *pre-eminence* and *independence;* and may not its *immortality* be fairly inferred?

But it is said, that we vainly deduce a proof of the immortality of the soul from dreams, since there are existing many strong reasons to suppose, that dogs and several other animals dream. And let them dream—they have my cheerful permission; nor have I any objection to those *faithful creatures bearing me company in my native sky.* I should be charmed with a treatise which should prove, beyond the shadow of a doubt, the future and immortal existence of every animated being. I should be right happy to witness the era predicted by the prophet Isaiah, who tells us, that the lion and the lamb shall lie down together; and should they be led by the hand of blooming innocence, the scene would be still more highly wrought. In one word, could I answer my little Margaretta's question, *"Where do butterflies go?"* it would become to me a new source of pleasure.

SELECTED LETTERS

The letters in this volume are from The Letterbooks, Judith Sargent Murray Papers (Z/1827), Manuscript Collection, Mississippi Department of Archives and History, and are included here with the permission of the Mississippi Department of Archives and History, Jackson, Mississippi. The numbering is Murray's; the transcriptions are by the editor. Many of Murray's letters have been water-soaked, some are deteriorating at the edges, and a few are extant only in fragmentary pieces; for these reasons, certain words and occasionally phrases are illegible. Excerpts of letters have been used to allow broader representation of the more than two thousand letters in the Mississippi collection.

LETTER 14 TO MR MURRAY

My Dear Sir   *Gloucester November 14 1774*

   If I am not mistaken in the character of the person I have the pleasure to address, it will be most agreeable to him, that I should lay aside all that awe, and reverence, which his unquestionable superiority demands, and approach him with the freedom of a sister, conversing with a brother whom she entirely esteems—I am not much accustomed to writing letters, especially to your sex, but if there be neither male nor female in the Emmanuel[1] you promulgate, we may surely, and with the strictest propriety, mingle souls upon paper—I acknowledge a high sense of obligation to you, Sir. I have been instructed by your scriptural investigations, and I have a grateful heart—Your revered friend, Mr. Relly,[2] has taught me, by his writings, the rudiments of the redeeming plan, but you have enlarged my views, expanded my ideas, dissipated my doubts, and led me to anticipate, and with sublime and solemn pleasure, the morning of the resurrection...

Letter 14. **Murray:** John Murray, the author's future husband.

1. **Emmanuel:** usually "Immanuel," a name referring to Christ in his incarnation (Isa. 7:14).

2. **Relly:** James Relly (1722–1778), a leading proponent of Universalism in eighteenth-century England. His preaching and writings were instrumental in converting John Murray to Universalism.

LETTER 22 TO THE SAME

Gloucester October 1ˢᵗ 1775

Take now, my dear Sir, an account which will, I have no doubt, interest your humanity. My Mother being in want of a domestic, concurred that it would be beneficial to the Community, were she to receive a female, from the house which stands among us, a shelter for the indigent and unfortunate people—and for the purpose of selecting a proper person, she commissioned me to pay a visit to this temporary prison of Penury.[1]

Our Almshouse is occupied by unsuccessful industry, destitute vice, miserable Old Age, and helpless infancy—This miscellaneous receptacle of suffering, is romantically situated at the foot of a steep declivity— Huge rocks form a semicircle, enclosing every part of the house except the front which is washed by a copious view. Its appearance was in no sort descriptive of the wretched life it sheltered—A peregrination[2] through the several apartments cannot fail of encircling the heart— Here deformed childhood, and there decrepid years—on one hand the forlorn infant whose mingled hairs betray the aggravated crime of its miserable parents, on the other, the degenerate female, her pasty coloured rags seeming fit emblems of her guilt.

I passed through many divisions of this abode of wretchedness, in pursuit of an ancient Woman, from whom I received the rudiments of reading, and who I had lately learned had fled to this last resort of wretchedness—I sought and at length found her—As I was formerly a favourite, she rejoiced to see me. I went prepared, not like the son of Jacob[3] with a little balm, and a little honey—but with what was much better calculated to exhilarate the fleeting spirits such as a bottle of wine, and many &c's, to which the good Woman believed she had bid a final adieu—How unconcerned are the children of opulence—How

---

Letter 22. **the same:** John Murray.

1. **Penury:** extreme poverty.

2. **peregrination:** a walk or journey, especially by foot.

3. **the son of Jacob:** In Gen. 43:11, Judah, son of Jacob and Leah, is travelling to Egypt with balm and honey for his long-lost brother, Joseph.

scant is the provision which is made for the suffering part of our species—Penitence, it should seem, is fled from our globe, and compassion no more inhabits the breast of Man.

The present unnatural contest hath augmented the miseries of our little Town, to an almost incredible degree—Persons formerly in easy circumstances, are now greatly depressed, while the poor are involved in every species of suffering, to which the sons and daughters of indigence can possibly be subjected—Say, Dear Sir, you who are at the fountain head of intelligence, is there no hope of an accommodation, will not the rich blessing of peace again illumine our Land? Or is the peerless Goddess fled forever from our borders?—...

LETTER 48 TO MY SISTER

Boston July 1ˢᵗ 1776

You will, my dearest Girl, account for my silence when you are informed that I have been extremely ill, and that, with a disorder which rendered it presumptuous to address any of my friends—After this you will not need to be told, that I have passed through the Small Pox—Yes, my dear, I have submitted to innoculation, and have, not withstanding, suffered severely—No less than one hundred pustules in my face, so that you will judge what a fright I am—But, no matter, I am now qualified to render any service in my power, to those friends who may in future suffer in this way. My Physician assures me that I should not run the least risk, in returning home this day. I have taken every precaution that the most scrupulous timidity could suggest—Yet the fear of alarming my connexions, will keep me here another week, or ten days when I may surely return—Say, my Love, may I not safely meet you at that period? I believe I shall venture—I am impatient to see you once more—it seems a little age since I left Gloucester, and although I have been cruelly treated in that place, yet recollection is constantly reminding me that in Gloucester, my dearest connexions still inhale the vital air—Fancy often presents you in my sleeping moments, and I dream myself once more among you—Yet the fleeting vision is too soon dissolved, and waking I exclaim—Beloved and most precious Circle, do you indeed exist, or are you only <u>ideas</u> floating athwart the disk of imagination, which, however

I may heretofore have realized, I shall not again be permitted to embody?—See, my sweet Girl, how you have erred, I have not figured splendidly in the Beau monde, but I have been constantly confined by illness, although had your conjectures been correct, you have yet to learn the heart of your sister, if you suppose she would prefer any enjoyment, which the round of dissipation can bestow, to the pleasures which result from friendship. Often, and often, since I left home, hath my bosom sighed for the kind soothings of an amiable sister, for the dear presence of an affectionate Mother—Indeed Home hath ever been to me a word possessing most potent charms... May Peace, uninterrupted Peace be with you.

LETTER 54 TO [MISS GOLDTHWAIT]

Gloucester June 6th 1777

Your last letter, my dear, came to hand only a few hours since—Its date announces that it was long since designed for me. Yet, believe me, dear Girl, I neither condemned, nor ever arraigned you; and, although far from being indifferent, I was fully convinced that I had in my Cousin an obliging Correspondent—Many circumstances, I well knew, might have induced you to postpone writing, but I cannot so easily forgive you, for omitting an account of my Aunt, and her little Maria—Do you not know, my dear Girl, that every Man is not an Adam—"True" you reply "but surely they ought to be [unto?] their own Eves" Perhaps they ought—yet I might confess that my aspiring soul, would hang with more rapturous delight upon the seraphic sounds which we may suppose we may suppose [sic] would be attained by an angel of the Most High, than upon the tongue of any mortal, however dignified, however beloved, and this, I imagine, would more especially be my choice, were my senses divested of that density, in which our first Parents, by their heedless wondering, hath so wrapped them about...I fancy, however, that the next to divine female,[1] recently passing from the hands of her creating God, considering the many opportunities which she hourly

---

Letter 54. Murray's title to this letter was "Letter 54 to the Same." It referred to Letter 53, also addressed to Miss Goldthwait, who was Murray's cousin.

1. **next to divine female:** Eve.

enjoyed with her Cara Spose[1] would, upon the occasion supposed [?] by Milton, have preferred the conversation of the bright [Celestial?]—But be this as it may, surely, if indeed she were so humble, so meek, so docile her good Man might easily have resisted her blandishments, when she so successfully solicited leave to quit his protecting side, and thus the wretched progeny of this deluded pair, had been saved from the count-less evils, which have encompassed them—That Eve was indeed the weaker Vessel, I boldly take upon me to deny—Nay, it should seem she was abundantly the stronger vessel since all the deep laid Art of the most subtle fiend that inhabited the infernal regions, was requisite to draw her from her allegiance, while Adam was overcome by the influence of the softer passions, <u>merely by his attachment to a female—a fallen female</u>—in whose cheek "<u>Distemper flushing glowed</u>"[2] and you know, my dear, that by resisting the aberrating[3] Fair One, Adam would have given the highest proof of manly firmness—...

LETTER 159 TO MRS SAYWARD OF OLD YORK

Madam   *Gloucester September 8 1781*

The contents of this letter will, I am persuaded, be a sufficient apol-ogy for its abruptness. You may remember when you were last at Gloucester, you proposed placing one of the children of your late brother, with me. I should detest my own heart, if I did not read there, a disposition to do all the good within the compass of my power—My then expressed reluctance, did not proceed from want of inclination, but from <u>positive</u> want of ability. Some acquisitions have recently rendered our circumstances easy, and we flatter ourselves, we have now a prospect of providing for one of the orphans[4] in question—but upon Mary, both Mr Stevens and myself, have ever placed our election—It would, on many accounts, be highly inconvenient to admit a younger child into our family—you know, dear Madam, that my various commissions,

---

1. **Cara Spose:** dear spouse (Italian).

2. **"Distemper flushing glowed":** *Paradise Lost,* book 9, line 887.

3. **aberrating:** deviating from what is common or normal.

4. **the orphans:** Judith and John Stevens took in two orphaned girls, Mary and Hannah ("Anna"). See also Letter 235.

necessitate me to be much from home—The residence of Hannah under this roof, would involve a weight of care, besides. I repeat, that I feel for Mary uncommon partiality—Your own experience hath no doubt convinced you, that it asks a large stock of affection, to encounter, with becoming calmness, the various caprices commonly found in the early part of life, you must be sensible, that the superintendence of the little Girl's education, would be wholly in my department, and you know, that as I am not bound by the ties of Nature, it is indispensable that I should fortify my heart, by previous tenderness...

LETTER 235 TO ANNA

Boston June 16th 1782

My good little Girl, once requested me to inform her how she should address me—If, my dear, your feelings will allow you to style me your maternal friend, I shall be both honoured and gratified by the appella-tion, and uniformly solicitous for your well being, I flatter myself, my pretensions to a distinction so respectable, are not altogether fanciful, while to discharge toward you the duties of a Mother, will be not only my pride, but my pleasure. You are, my Love, apprized that your pros-pects in life, are not the most eligible—An Orphan, and destitute of those advantages, to be derived from fortune it is incumbent upon you to seize every opportunity which presents for improvement. I do not, my dear Girl, speak thus to wound your feelings, but merely to stimu-late your efforts—...Let it then be your ambition, to lay an early foun-dation for independance. Make yourself mistress of every kind of needle work—You are already acquainted with plain sewing, but this is not enough, you must use dispatch and neatness in all its branches, or it will not answer the desired purpose—On my return home, I shall introduce you into the varieties of this truly feminine occupation, embroidery, tambour, knotting, flowering, &c. &c.—You must carefully attend at best to the <u>theory</u> of every kind of family work—Thus you will be able to <u>direct</u>, and if [ever?] adversity impels—even to <u>practice</u>. These my Anna are, in female life, indispensable requisites, <u>useful</u> attainments,

---

Letter 235. See note on *the orphans* in Letter 159, above.

without which, we are incapable of sustaining with propriety, the character we are called to sustain—But you must not stop here—A diamond taken from the Mine, cannot exhibit the brilliancy which distinguishes it when received from the hand of the Lapidary. Nay, more, this invaluable gem, would probably attract as little notice as the earth by which it is [illegible] were it continued in its native habiliments—I have made writing a part of your education, your efforts must be persevering, nor stop short of perfection—You can [illegible] your grammar verbatim, be not as the parrot who simply chatters what he never <u>feels</u> but let <u>sense</u> as well as <u>sound</u> be your object, or your labour in committing any thing to memory, will be to little purpose. The study of figures is <u>pleasant</u>, as well as useful. So when I again take my place, as preceptress to my beloved Girl, we will, by way of remuneration for the attention she hath already paid to those pursuits, which hath been recommended to her, attempt, at least the rudiments of geography, geometry, and astronomy, we will together enter those flowery paths of science, so productive of instruction of the highest kind and of sentimental entertainment—But although you should chance to possess a genuinely cultivated intellect, you must not allow your acquirements, unduly to elate your spirit—shun every measure of fancied superiority. We are generally indebted to others for information, and intrinsic knowledge is never the parent of exaltation…. There is a dignity of comportment proper to our sex—Young calls upon us to "<u>Reverence ourselves</u>"[1]—… that genuine delicacy which should always distinguish the conduct of young Ladies. One little circumstance, to be found in that excellent work, I have dwelt upon with unabating pleasure: I will give you its outlines, it will serve to explain what I mean, by wishing to cultivate that tenderness of disposition, and feelings, which is shocked at the idea of censuring the actions of an absent person. Upon some occasion, a young Lady who was upon terms of intimacy with Miss Harlowe,[2] was in a large party, to which by her presence, she gave dignity, and importance not only arraigned but condemned. Miss Harlowe listened, with silent concern, to a number of

---

1. **Reverence ourselves:** *Conjectures on Original Composition* (1759), by Edward Young (1683–1765).

2. **Miss Harlowe:** the title character in *Clarissa Harlowe* (1748), a novel by the English author Samuel Richardson (1689–1761).

deviations, which indeed, as represented, partook an uncommon degree of folly—When, quitting her seat, and rising in the midst of the loudly accusing company, she thus earnestly petitioned—"Let me entreat you, my young friends, to consider me as Miss Fanny Darlington—Here I stand, unworthy of a place in this assembly, except I can acquit myself of the highly censurable charges brought against me—allow me to examine, scrupulously to examine, every circumstance, and if I have indeed, thus reprehensibly accumulated indiscretions, banish me from your Circle, or if it shall appear that I have been most unfeelingly defamed, restore me to your good opinion—to your wonted indulgence"—The attempt was worthy of a Clarissa, and conducting the trial with consummate wisdom, and judgment, she perfectly exculpated the injured absent individual, and bringing her off triumphant, was unanimously applauded: even the censorious were pleased with her unaffected candour...and by general consent, she was led to her chair and voted—universally—[the?] double rank in this well distinguishing Circle, as Miss Fanny Darlington and Miss Clarissa Harlowe—Your good sense will teach you to admire, and to profit by this little story[.] I expect you will copy all the letters you receive from me—I have taken pains to write them fair that you may find no difficulty in decyphering them—copying will impress them upon your mind and you must acquaint yourself with the precise meaning of every word[.] This you will do, if you love your maternal friend.

LETTER 408 TO MY BROTHER

Gloucester May 18—1785

My Cousin, departing for Boston at an early hour in the morning leaves me only a moment to say, that I most sincerely congratulate you, on your arrival in Boston—My heart, I do assure you, beats with no common pleasure—Your letter conveyed the first authentic intelligence: Yesterday it was reported, but I have been too often deceived by the breath of common fame...I have not been inattentive to your interest, believe me, my dear, I did not wait to be thus called upon, in order to [enact] an

---

Letter 408. **my brother:** Winthrop Sargent, Jr.

interference respecting your black boy. No effort in my power hath been wanting, I have repeatedly solicited the masters of our fishing vessels to employ him, I knew it was a matter of consequence to you, and it could not therefore be regarded with indifference by me[.] I expatiated upon the capacity of the Boy, for the business for which he was proposed, with many etceteras—But these kind of people are very obstinate, and very ignorant, as well as very proud—To all I could urge, a single objection was, in their opinion, sufficient—He was a <u>Negro</u>[.] Their crews unified together and they were determined never to make a companion of a black Man. The same reason operates in regard to foreign voyages, and I am assured, that had the matter been insisted upon, by any of our owners, the ship's company would immediately have left the vessel…

LETTER 564 TO MRS PILGRIM OF LONDON

Gloucester August 1—1787

Almost twelve months, revolving in their respective circles, have completed their destined events, since my last address to Mrs Pilgrim—It hath been to me a desolating period[1]—the days of sorrow have been multiplied, the sigh of agony hath burst from my bosom, and the tear of woe hath descended upon my cheek—High were my expectations raised—but the voice of decision pronounced against me, and my regrets were proportioned to my hopes—The mournful tale hath already reached your ears My venerable friend hath transmitted the particulars of my sad story, and I assay not the melancholy repetition—No, let me rather draw a veil over the gloomy past, and illume the night of sorrows, by anticipating the cloudless morning of immortality—When your last favour was handed me, I was incapable of breaking the seal, but I embraced the first calm moment, to attend to its contents, and I have now, my dear Madam, to acknowledge your unmerited kindness, to express my gratitude, and to supplicate a continuation of your distinguishing esteem—from that warm attachment which seems to glow, in the first paragraph of your letter, I persuade myself you will receive pleasure from the information, that my health is in a good measure

---

1. **desolating period:** John Stevens died in late 1786.

restored, and that in circumstances the most adverse, the God of my life
hath arrested the course of sickness, new strung my nerves, and given
fresh elasticity to the whole system—Mysterious procedure!—but thus
it is, however we struggle in the toils, resignation ultimately becomes a
mother of necessity—Mrs Hayley alias Jeffries, residing chiefly in our
Metropolis, from which my abode is distant, I have not had frequent
opportunities of making those observations, which might, perhaps,
have gratified me to give a decisive answer to your questions: yet, having
near relations in Boston, I am often a visitor there, in one of those excur-
sions, I was introduced to the Lady, while Mrs Hayley, and I confess I
was entertained, and edified by her conversation—If her exterior be not
altogether prepossessing, if her dress partakes too much the juvenility of
youth, yet in her manners (at least such was my impression, through the
day which I passed with her) there is sufficient propriety—her mind
seems in a great degree informed—she has, I am told much mercantile
knowledge. The sentiments she uttered were striking, and dignified, her
language was elevated and her occasional remarks highly judicious—
Common fame, however, ascribes to Mrs Jeffries a <u>mixed</u> character, but
while I accustom myself to give full credit to every anecdote, which is
calculated to do honour to its subject, I reject, at least one half of the
reports, borne upon the wings of detraction—My reason is obvious,
such is the depravity of human Nature, and so general the influence of
envy, that we are much more sedulously employed, in collecting the
blighting tale, with the malicious comments of slander, than in holding
up to view the productions of rectitude, or in yielding that applause,
which is due to the good and honourable character—My dear Mrs Pilgrim will recollect, that I [advert?] solely to goodness merely human; if I
err in this rule, which I have established from the earliest period of my
life, I am consoled by the reflection, that my mistake cannot possibly be
productive of mischevious consequences A very extraordinary instance
of Mrs Hayley's munificence, was, in the days of my Tranquility, wafted
to my ear—I seized the pen of panegyric, painting in [energetic?] language, feelings which were deeply impressed upon my soul—Some
steps, since taken by the subject of my encomium,[1] might in the opin-

---

1. **encomium:** high praise.

ion of many, call upon me to suppress sentiments, which even at the time, were deemed sufficiently glowing. But the action which I aimed at celebrating was <u>true</u>—It was <u>benign</u> in its origin and most salutary in its consequences, and, in my opinion, it could scarcely be too highly praised. Of Mrs Hayley's motive for her third marriage, I am ignorant, but I presume she was stimulated by that universal principle[:] a wish to augment the share of happiness she enjoyed—It caused great speculation for a time, but it shared the fate of all other novelties—familiarity destroyed its consequence—Balloons would in truth become very valuable, could they safely transport us over the broad Atlantic—With what inexpressible pleasure might I then set my tea table, and allow my heart to flutter, with the expectation of seeing my little Circle graced, by the presence of a friend so condescending as Mrs Pilgrim, and after we had sipped the cheering beverage together, taking my place beside you in the aerial machine, I would hie me to the Metropolis of the World, and not contented with an afternoon, I would gratify my admiration of whatever is excellent among men, by days, weeks, months and years of wonder…Very liberal sentiments, as they respect religion, seem more and more prevalent in America—The free born soul, conscious of its native rights, demands emancipation[—] sweet equality is taking place in the mental world, and every one resumes the prerogative with which nature hath invested him—to think for himself—Surely this is precisely the point to which every effort should tend—Capital offenders are amenable to the Legislator—This the order, the necessary subordination of a well regulated government, will always ensure—but with matters of faith, with religious codes or doctrines—let not human authority intermeddle…

LETTER 615 TO MRS SARGENT

Gloucester April 15—1788

I received your letter with much pleasure—It contained many communications which were productive of the truest satisfaction. But, shall I, to my dear, my sympathising friend, confess the truth, the letter from my brother, by which it was accompanied, gave me the most exquisite pain—"Strange"—you exclaim: "Passing strange"—Yet it is but too true—Doth not a friendship like ours demand the most unbounded confidence? "Surely it doth." I have been more explicit to you, than to any other person—and I will henceforth bid adieu to reserve—I will open the door of my heart, and my candid, my indulgent friend, entering the most secret avenue shall freely expatiate there…Allow me then to take a cursory view of my past life—I was early, very early, united in marriage to a worthy Man—His virtues were many, and I justly esteemed the husband which fate had given me—Among his good qualities, probity and undeviating integrity, were not the least conspicuous, he possessed also a gentle, and conceding nature, which were the more to be valued as they are so rarely the growth of the manly bosom—Yet, although greatly sensible of his worth, my ungovernable heart, refused to acknowledge the softer emotions—I believed myself incapable of love, as traced by the pencil of the Poet—and far from indifferent, I was rendered happy, by the consideration, that the purest fires of friendship, irradiated my bosom, and that I felt for no other la belle passion.[1] I determined, in the strictest sense, to discharge every obligation, and my perseverance in the path of duty, more than tranquilized my soul—In the misfortunes which involved Mr Stevens, I took my full share, and I lamented with the deepest agony, the melancholy catastrophe of his life—. But my serenity returned, and, as I had often thought, and frequently expressed my sentiments, that after having once worn the nuptial chain, and providence had sundered the bond, a subsequent life of retirement, and freedom, was most proper, most ornamental, and most dignifying to the female character, so the demise of Mr Stevens, made no change in my ideas, and I still say, if the heart be at ease, a single life is the most eligible. Nay, I conceive, if the tender affections were in a first Choice grafted upon esteem, the delicacy of a woman's mind, if it be indeed cast in a feminine mould, will not admit a second election—I did not, however, imagine, I was debarred the pleasure to be derived, from a sentimental intercourse, from sentimental, virtuous friendship, and my bosom glowed with an attachment for Mr Murray, which impelled it to recoil from every idea, of relinquishing his valuable society—The World it seems will not allow to a single Woman, an intellectual connexion with an individual of the other sex—but I had

---

1. **la belle passion:** the tender passion (French).

determined to brave the world, and conscious of innate rectitude, that my every action, my every thought, relative to Mr Murray would abide the test of the nicest honour, I believed I might be allowed to pursue my course, with tolerable tranquility—I will, however, own, that during the past twelve months, my sentiments partook rather too great a degree of tenderness, and although I became alarmed, yet having marked out to myself a path, pride assisted my perseverance, and I carefully suppressed every rebellious thought—But the event which banished Mr Murray from America, effectively removed the vale. I was solicitous to yield <u>in person</u> that relief, which the balm of sacred friendship might supply, and that I was denied the privilege of sympathizing with a Man, whom I so much esteemed, and revered, was to me an agonizing consideration—Discretion, however, erected her barriers and prudence bound me a fast prisoner in this dreary apartment—In short, I could no longer deceive myself, my soul became a scene of tumult, and upon every rising thought, was stamped too sure a confirmation, that I had in fact become a slave, to the most impetuous of all passions, of which I had, erroneously considered myself incapable—Just at this juncture I received a letter from Mr Murray—It informed me that delicate attention to my honour, and feelings, had kept him silent, but driven, by the malice of his enemies, from the Continent; he could not depart, without disclosing to me the treasured secret of his soul, since he might thus risque the happiness of his life—he could not but indulge a hope, that domestic felicity might yet be his—he acknowledged he had long loved me, even from the commencement of our acquaintance, with ardour loved me, but that he would have sacrificed his life, rather than admitted a thought in regard to me, which my own guardian angel would blush to own, but that, as I had now for many months, been released from my early vows, he presumed to calculate upon a favourable hearing, and to supplicate, at least for a continuation of my esteem. I was now, you will allow, furnished with a fresh motive for admiration of him, who had at length avowed himself my Lover. How assiduous, and how honourable, through the course of a number of years, had been his deportment, how unwearied, and how disinterested his exertions—preferring, in every instance, the interest of Mr Stevens to his own, and pointing him out to me, in the most amiable light—How indefatigable were his endeavors to extricate us from our embarrassments, to <u>liberate Mr Stevens, and to continue him in his native place</u>, and, after the departure of that unfortunate Man, how zealous to procure the suffrage of his Creditors, for his <u>return</u>—How just, how generous, how next to divine, was this procedure—who would have believed him activated by the passion which he now confesses—Influenced by grateful remembrance, rendered energetic by the then situation of Mr Murray, while the softest sentiments blended with every tender, and grateful recollection, my answer to the letter, which contained a declaration of his attachment, was conceived in terms, as indulgent to the hopes he had formed, as female reserve and observation due to my character would allow—and now, why should I hesitate, since the laws of God, nor my country, oppose my union—...

Now then, my beloved friend, is the period for you to exert yourself in my favour and I call upon that friendship, which I have never yet questioned[,] to espouse my cause, to engage warmly on my side, to plead for me, and surely, an advocate so lovely, cannot sue in vain—If you can so far succeed, in conciliating my brother, as to induce him to continue to me his accustomed complacency, I will acknowledge that if I had received from you, no other instance of kindness, this alone, would be sufficient to bind me eternally yours—...Allow me to be importunate, to urge you to expedition in the arduous task, which emboldened by your tender friendship, I have presumed to enjoin—To your experienced, and often exercised feelings, it would be superfluous to add, that those sensations which are excited by suspense, are indeed truly corroding—Pity me then, and delay not the remedy which your interference, and influence may furnish.

LETTER 422 TO MRS P[ILGRIM] OF LONDON

Gloucester, November 8 1791

...Yes my honored friend, to my Maria I owe as much, as one mortal can to another, and her name and innate worth, will be ever engraven upon my heart—But upon this subject, for the above reason, I expatiate

---

Letter 422. The numbering of the letters in the letter books varied after the late 1780s.

not—it shall suffice to say, that my domestic felicity is confirmed, and that I am in truth a happy creature—What though my prospects for my daughter are not as eligible as those which upon a like occasion I might once have indulged—yet if the health of her Father is continued, we shall not want the necessaries of life—the means of informing her mind may be furnished us, and she may become a valuable member of society—A candidate for immortality she is certainly born, and that she is designed to add a lustre too, and to gem the crown of her Redeemer, at some period or other she will assuredly know—since in the day when he maketh up his jewals, the word of Jehovah is pledged, that she shall not be wanting—This then is enough—and with this the best feelings of my soul are satisfied.

May you, Madam, still be able to say that your complaints are few—still for you may the vale of life be sloped—May you descend it with the partner of your days—May your sons—your daughters—with their blooming progeny flourish round you—May you still permit your American adopted, a place in your bosom, and may you often transmit to her the epistles of your love—These dear Lady, range themselves among the first wishes of your truly affectionate friend—

LETTER 423 TO MARIA

Glocester [sic] *December 28th 1791*

...For thus pouring into the patient ear of my Maria my hopes, and my fears, accustomed as I am to unbosom my self to her, I make no apology—for the Brother and for the Sister, she hath long felt, and her native benevolence called into action, and augmented by the energetic dispositions of amity, will give her in our affairs a very deep interest.[1]

...Your letter by my Father was carefully handed—To make friends

---

Letter 423. **Maria:** Maria's identity is unknown. Murray had a cousin named Maria, but the several letters to Maria suggest by content that she was a friend and not a relative. Maria is the only correspondent with whom Murray signed her letters "Constantia."

1. **interest:** The beginning of the letter recounts Murray's fears when she learned that her eldest brother had been wounded in battle; the wound was minor and he accompanied General Arthur St. Clair to Fort Washington. St. Clair (1743–1818) was the first general of the Northwest Territory and was defeated by Native American forces in the Territory in 1792.

for my little Sojourner[1] is now the first object of my life, and should she be continued in existence, my means to attain them will be an effort to endow her with those qualities, which will lay claim to the esteem of the worthy—From the embraces of our common friend if instinct is any thing more then a name, she will never shrink for intuitively she will know that in the breast of her honored patroness tenderness exhaustless flows—Yes, certainly, I will avail myself of the privilege which you so condescendingly grant, and our gratitude to her maternal friend, her infant tongue shall early learn to lisp—My heart beats with the most pleased sensations as I hear you express your attachment to her and again pronounce her right happy, thus in the dawn of her being to have secured unto herself a Patroness—a Mother and a friend…

The inclosed lines[2]—which a knowledge of your partiality for me, and my productions, induceth me to transmit, and which were scratched out while sitting by the cradle of our daughter, will inform you how I am, and how employed—with the duties of my new department I am highly pleased, and in my individual character I can truly say I never enjoyed life so well—…Farewel—Remember me to the individuals of your family, and believe me ever—ever most affectionately, and truly   Your CONSTANTIA—

---

1. **my little Sojourner:** Murray's daughter, Julia Maria.

2. **inclosed lines:** No enclosure is extant.

THE TRAVELLER RETURNED

Title. The play was first performed at the Federal Street Theatre in Boston on 9 March 1796. *The Traveller Returned* ran in *The Gleaner*, 3:80-84.

PERSONS of the DRAMA

MEN	*WOMEN*
MR. RAMBLETON	MRS. MONTAGUE
MAJOR CAMDEN	HARRIOT MONTAGUE
MR. STANHOPE	EMILY LOVEGROVE
ALBERTO STANHOPE	MRS. VANSITTART
MR. VANSITTART	BRIDGET
PATRICK O'NEAL	
OBADIAH	

Members of the Committee of Public Safety—Officer, Soldiers, Sailors, and Servants.

ACT FIRST.

SCENE—A Parade—Sea Prospect—Ship discovered at a Distance.

Enter Mr. Rambleton.

RAMBLETON. 'Tis well—auspicious morn, I hail thy gladsome rays—
once more I breathe again my native air—once more I tread that earth,
now doubly dear, for having given birth to such a race of heroes, as
Rome, in all her pride of greatness, could never boast. [*Hallooing
without.*]

Enter Patrick, with Sailors bearing Trunks.

PATRICK. Ow, may I never see my own sweet country again, if I did not
think this *land* of America had been all *salt water,* d'ye see, we were so
long in finding it. Arrah now, *while we are standing here,* by my soul
we may as *well be looking after a place to rest our-shelves* in, so we may.

RAMB. Here, friends deposit your burdens in this niche. Your ship is
under sail; it will be prudent for you to get on board as soon as
possible. Farewell, comrades. [*Gives them money.*]

SAILORS. [*all vociferate*] God bless your honour; you are a gentleman.
God bless your honour!

Exeunt Sailors.

RAMB. Now, Patrick, you must keep guard here, while I proceed to
reconnoitre.

PATR. Ow, that I shall master; but did you not say now, that you should
be after taking your land tacks on board?

RAMB. I did, Patrick; twelve miles from this city, nineteen years since, I
left my family.

PATR. Twelve miles, do you say? Ow then, that is but a trifle, my dear:
It is only *six miles a-piece*, master; and who would grudge that, I
wonder, for the sake of seeing the sweet faces of wife and children. But
did not you say now, how that you had *written them word you was
dead, or the like of that?*

105

RAMB. I said, Patrick, that they probably supposed me dead, for they have not heard from me since I left them. A friend whom I commissioned for that purpose has informed me in general terms of their welfare; I forbad particulars.

PATR. Arrah, is not that strange, now?

RAMB. I have very powerful reasons for my conduct; and remember, Patrick, you must be secret.

PATR. Ow, never fear Patrick O'Neal, Sir; an Irishman shall hang, drown, and quarter for you, Sir, and afterwards serve you every bit as well as if *nothing at all at all* had happened.

RAMB. I had an estate in this city. I am not sure that I shall not find my family here; but my present purpose is to take lodgings.

PATR. Arrah, get out with that, now. If Patrick O'Neal was *three thousand miles separated* from his bit of an Irish girl, he shall swing his hammock *close along side of her for all that, Honey.* Give me *lave* to say, Sir, would it not be better if you went right home to your own wife, now?

RAMB. All in good time, Patrick. But hist! who have we here? Stand a one side.

Enter Major Camden.

MAJOR C. This sea breeze is very refreshing during this sultry season; I will enjoy it a little. Hah! a ship under sail, and without colours, too! this looks suspicious. Bless me! a stranger of dignified mien and prepossessing aspect; I will accost him—It is a divine morning, Sir.

RAMB. It is so, young man; and I feel enough interested in you to wish you may enjoy it.

MAJOR C. Thank you, Sir. Can you tell from whence came yonder ship, that now crowds every sail to quit our coast?

RAMB. I can, Sir. You wear your country's uniform, and it is a fair presumption that you will emulate her virtues. That ship, Sir, is British property, hired by me to transport myself, my baggage, and my servant, across the vast Atlantic.

MAJOR C. But are you not apprized that our guardian legislators have recommended to the good people of the United States a suspension of all intercourse with the subjects of his Britannic majesty, during the war?

RAMB. Yes, Sir; but I presume they have not proscribed the true-born sons of America?

MAJOR C. Certainly not, Sir.

RAMB. Well, Sir, in this land of liberty I commenced my being. Some years previous to the present struggle, private motives induced me to quit it; and, perhaps, I should not yet have returned, had not fame's shrill clarion so loudly sounding my country's honours, have given to ambition the fleetest wings, and thus accelerated my suspended purpose.

MAJOR C. Your words involve conviction: And yet, perhaps, I should not trust.

RAMB. The morn of life is seldom found suspicious —I come prepared to aid a struggling people—My purse, my counsel, they shall both be their's; and, if need be, my sword shall fight their battles.

MAJOR C. [*pausing.*] What is the line of conduct which Camden should pursue?

RAMB. *Camden!—hah! that name awakens in my soul the strongest passions.* [*Aside.*] If you have doubts, examine well my baggage—my person—I dare the strictest scrutiny.

MAJOR C. Pshaw! I disdain suspicion, and venerate your frankness.

RAMB. Only direct me for a single night to some convenient lodging.

MAJOR C. I am at present here on duty; will you accept apartments under the same roof with me?

RAMB. Most gladly.

MAJOR C. Then, Sir, I will conduct you.

RAMB. I will speak to my servant, and accompany you immediately. Here, Patrick—

Patrick comes forward.

PATR. Sir.

RAMB. I shall send persons, who will assist in conveying my trunks to my lodgings.

PATR. So do then—and, by the body of St. Patrick, my *shelf* shall be able to carry them like nothing *at all at all.*

Exeunt.

SCENE changes to an Apartment in an Inn.
Mr. and Mrs. Vansittart at breakfast.

MRS. V. Why husband, at this rate we shall certainly starve!

VANS. *Vife, vife!* I *to vish* you *woult* eat your *preat ant putter,* and let that content you at *this present time.*

MRS. V. Content me! Lord, how can I be contented? no *jonteel* people are contented: Besides, are we not over head and ears in debt, and not a single dollar to help ourselves? I thought, when I married a Dutchman, who, they say, can make land out of water, that I should at least have been above so low a thing as poverty.

VANS. *Lort, Lort!* Mrs. Vansittart, you are quite *unreasonaple* now—Have not I *tolt* you a *thousant* times, that I *coult* not *vork* without tools? Suppose I *pe* a *Tutchman*—*vhy* my *creat* ancestor, Van Tromp himself, *coult* never fleet his ships *vithout vater.* You are as *pat* as the Egyptian task-masters; for you are *alvays* expecting *preak vithout shtraw.*

MRS. V. I say, husband, there is straw enough; and you miss many a *jonteel* opportunity. Major Camden for instance—he could not appear so *alegunt* without a power of money. I warrant you, his trunks contain many a good pound; and, as he is in such haste to get rid of his cash, as to part with it to every shameless beggar, no one could say, it would not be doing a *perlite* thing, to assist him in the disposal of it.

VANS. *Torothy, Torothy!* how are we to come at it, *at this present time?*

MRS. V. Get every thing in readiness, force the trunks, make off before we are discovered, and thus give all our creditors the slip at once.

They rise from table.

VANS. Mercy on us! mercy on us!

MRS. V. In the general confusion into which the great people are thrown, it would be easy to retire *indignantly* with our money, and nobody would be the wiser.

VANS. *Torothy, Torothy! tost* thou never reflect? [*Screams in her ear.*] *Tost* never think of the *callows, chilt? Cot a'* mercy! it *voult* make my very *ploot* chill, to see my poor *tear Torothy* swinging in the air! [*Affects to weep ludicrously.*]

MRS. V. Lord! Mr. Vansittart, how could you fright a body so?

[*Knocking at the door.*] I sha'n't get the odious figure out of my head to-day—you are as *unperlite* as a *Heartentot.*[1] [*Knocking at the door repeated.*] Do see who is at the door; for pity's sake, how came it fastened? [*Vansittart opens the door.*]

Enter Major Camden, introducing Mr. Rambleton.

MAJOR C. Landlord, I have brought you a new lodger, and I recommend him to your best attention.

VANS. [*Bowing.*] *Ve shalt pe prout* to *vait* on the *shentleman, at this present time.*

MAJOR C. Mrs. Vansittart, be so obliging as to order breakfast in your little parlour.

MRS. V. You shall be obeyed, Sir. [*affectedly.*]

MAJOR C. I will show you into the parlour, Mr. Rambleton.

Exeunt Major Camden and Mr. Rambleton.

MRS. V. Rambleton—Rambleton—Who can this same Rambleton be?

VANS. *Rampleton, Rampleton*—and *vat* the plague is that to you?— Now, *vhy ton't* you set *apout* getting *preakfast* for the *shentlemen,* I say?

MRS. V. Lord! man, it is already got; I have only to order it in.

Exit Mrs. Vansittart.

VANS. *Vicket jate! vicket jate!* it *vill pe* a *vonter* if she *toes* not *prink* me to shame; *ant* yet, *Cot* knows, I have *creat* occasions. If I *coult* safely come at a *coot hantsome rount* sum, I *pelieves* I *shoult* not stick at pocketing it, any more than poor *Torothy.* [*Loud knocking at the door.*]

Mrs. Vansittart passes hastily over the stage, and throws open the door. Enter Patrick, with Porters bearing trunks.

PATR. Arrah now, good people, can you tell me if one Mr. Rambleton has cast anchor hereabouts?

MRS. V. O yes, Sir; and he is now at breakfast in the parlour.

---

1. **Heartentot:** Hottentot; a name Caucasians used in reference to what they considered the primitive culture of the people of South Africa.

PATR. Arrah, then, Patrick O'Neal did not care if my *shelf* had a little of that same breakfast, *after Master Rambleton has eaten it, Honey.* By my soul, I am quite *wary*—so I am; and if you shall *be after* showing me where I will stow this rich cargo, I will be for stepping into your cabin a bit, and *trating* myself with *breakfast, dinner and supper, all at one meal*—so I shall.

MRS. V. Here, Mr. Patrick—this way, this way, if you please; I will show you Mr. Rambleton's chamber.

PATR. Mr. Patrick! How the *jeuce* could the sweet *crature* find out my name, now?

Patrick and the Porters follow Mrs. Vansittart with the baggage.

VANS. So, so—Mrs. Vansittart is likely to get into *pusiness,* I *fint, at this present time.*

Exeunt.

SCENE—A Parlour in the Inn.
Mr. Rambleton and Major Camden just rising from the breakfast table.

RAMB. Well—I would travel many a rood[1] to see this wonder of a man: I have never doubted his intrepid valour and inborn patriotism; but, are his military talents so great as you describe?

MAJOR C. I hold them to be unequalled, Sir. Having the happiness to be born in the neighbourhood of Mount Vernon, I have enjoyed the patronage of the General, and I have been an eye-witness of the most glorious achievements.

RAMB. Cannot you furnish me with some examples? I should dwell with singular pleasure on a recital so interesting.

MAJOR C. Fame early marked the steps of the youthful Warrior; and his political address, undaunted bravery, and military talents, were all evinced in his journey from Winchester, his defence of Fort Necessity, and his judicious arrangements after Braddock's[2] defeat.

---

1. **rood:** typically, seven or eight yards.

2. **Braddock:** Edward Braddock (1695–1755), British general who participated in the French and Indian Wars.

RAMB. His conduct would indeed have done honour to a veteran.

MAJOR C. And, Sir, were there no other proofs of his uncommon military abilities, but the victorious actions of Trenton and Princeton, (both of which were the result of his superintending genius) they were alone sufficient to place him on the highest summit of martial glory!

RAMB. Young man, I admire thy generous warmth.

MAJOR C. O, Sir! had you seen him in an hour of the greatest public depression—his noble bosom torn with apprehensions for his oppressed country—hazarding his person in front of the enemy's line—animating his followers by example, as well as precept—and, with intrepid valour, pressing on *to death or victory!*

RAMB. May eternal blessings crown his honoured head!

MAJOR C. Various are the scenes which have witnessed his undaunted bravery; while his unyielding fortitude and equanimity, under the pressure of complicated evils, authorize the most elevated ideas of the firmness and magnanimity of his mind.

RAMB. It is hardly possible to reverence his virtues too highly; and yet, the ignominious death of Major Andre[1] has taught some people to question his sensibility.

MAJOR C. Gracious God! Had they witnessed the struggles, which the fate of that interesting, brave, and truly accomplished man occasioned in the bosom of the Warrior, they would have learned to venerate the sorrows of a martial spirit. But, Sir, there are periods, when *sacrifices on the altar of public opinion become absolutely indispensable.*

RAMB. Undoubtedly there are.

MAJOR C. Question his sensibility, Sir! he deeply laments the calamities of the war! and, while his soul bleeds for his country, the delicacy of his feelings acknowledges a suitable sympathy with the unfortunate of every description.

RAMB. This finishing of his character gives me inexpressible satisfaction.

MAJOR C. I glory in my country, Sir; and, while I do reverence to Warriors, Philosophers and Statesmen, whose fame shall reach the utmost verge of polished humanity, I forget not to estimate, as they

1. **Major Andre:** John André (1751–1780), British spy who collaborated with the American turncoat Benedict Arnold during the American Revolution.

deserve, the merits of those matchless soldiers, whose hardships have been incredible—who have withstood the most splendid offers of the enemy, when, at the same moment, their footsteps over the frozen ground were tracked by their blood!

RAMB. Heroic men! they merit more than language can express! How long have you served in this unequalled army, Sir?

MAJOR C. My father had designed me for mercantile life; but, on the commencement of hostilities, he received letters from a friend abroad, which determined him to arm me in my country's cause.

RAMB. *Little does he suspect the hand which penned those letters; but, though my bounding heart would leap into his bosom, I will not yet disclose myself.* [*Aside.*] To bear arms in defence of the invaded Rights of Man,[1] is truly honourable, Sir.

MAJOR C. It is so, Sir; and many brave citizens have lately joined our standards. Some hours hence, the noble volunteers will rendezvous on that parade where first we met: Should your curiosity lead you thither, you may observe a specimen of that spirit which actuates the bosoms of FREE AMERICANS!

RAMB. I will not lose the opportunity, Sir.

MAJOR C. Engagements unavoidable command me hence.

RAMB. Do not hesitate—we are both at home.

Exit Major Camden.

I will attend to my baggage, and then prepare for observation.

Exeunt.

SCENE—A Bed-Chamber in the Inn.

Enter Mr. Rambleton, preceded by Patrick.

RAMB. Patrick, I have business abroad, and I wish you to tarry within during my absence.

---

1. **Rights of Man:** the international philosophy behind the American and French Revolutions and articulated in Thomas Paine's *Rights of Man* (1791–92), in defense of the French Revolution.

PATR. *Juring* your absence? Ow! that I shall, Sir? and, *although I wander all over the city, I shall not stir a bit.* Never fear Patrick O'Neal, Sir.

RAMB. Well, good Patrick, leave me for the present.

PATR. Ow! that I shall now, with the *biggest pleasure in life.*

Exit Patrick.

RAMB. So far is well. [*Takes out a box, from which he produces a miniature picture, richly set, on which he gazes impassioned.*] Angelic loveliness! and could such a form become the receptacle of deliberate vice? Yet she was grossly wanting, both to herself and me, if not absolutely guilty; and this day must decide, whether the portrait or the original shall ever again resume their seat in my bosom. [*Puts up the miniature in the box, and places it on the toilette.*] My agitation, so near the scene of action, is extreme. Perhaps—But I'll think no more—It is full time that I commence my operations.

Exit.

END OF THE FIRST ACT.

ACT SECOND.

SCENE—An Apartment in Mrs. Montague's House.
Emily Lovegrove is seated in a contemplative attitude—she rises and
advances forward.

EMILY. Misfortune upon misfortune! The loss of my dear and tender parents! my patrimony, reduced by the ruinous paper currency almost to nothing; and, as if these repeated strokes were not sufficient, I am no sooner adopted by the sister of my mother, from whom I receive even maternal tenderness, than my wayward heart becomes ungratefully attached to the very man who is on the point of marriage with her daughter! Gracious Heaven! was ever unfortunate girl so cruelly circumstanced! But here comes my unsuspecting cousin, as happy as youth, innocence and vivacity can render her.

Enter Harriot Montague.

HARRIOT. Dear Emily, where have you hid yourself; why I have had the most divine ramble imaginable, and have been searching the house over to make you a partaker of my felicity; but tell me, dear, has not this straw hat and lilach ribbons a most fascinating effect? O I have been so enchantingly flattered—But I protest you look as if you had been in tears! you are melancholy, my dear.

EMILY. No, Harriot, not melancholy, only tranquil; but where have you been, my love?

HARRIOT. Been! why, you shall hear: I just looked in on Mrs. Fallacy, and found her exercising her talents at ridicule, by describing to neighbour Chitchat in a manner truly ludicrous, the party she last night entertained, in such a high style of elegance, and with such apparent affection—Ha, ha, ha.

EMILY. And could this give you pleasure, Harriot? it has, I assure you, a contrary effect on me; *I shall henceforth, never enjoy myself in her society.*

HARRIOT. Never enjoy yourself in her society, Emily? why she is the most *sprightly and agreeable woman in the world.*

EMILY. It may be so; *but I should be confident that I, in my turn, should be served up as the subject of her unwarrantable mirth:* And, indeed, Harriot it is an eternal truth, *that whoever will divert you at the expense of any one with whom they are apparently in the habits of friendship, will not hesitate to sacrifice you, whenever occasion offers.*

HARRIOT. Ah, this may do well enough for you plodding, sentimental girls; but I, who resolve to enjoy the present moment, am determined to laugh where I can, and not be so grossly absurd as to throw myself into the horrors by anticipated evil—ha, ha, ha! laughing, my dear, is absolutely necessary to my existence—ha, ha, ha.

EMILY. You are a happy girl, cousin.

HARRIOT. Why, so I think, Emily; for who should I meet at Mrs. Fallacy's but Miss Worthy, Arrabella Clermont, and Eliza Meanwell; so, gallanted by Alberto Stanhope, away we scampered, and had the most delectably romantic promenade that can be conceived of.

EMILY. Had *Major Camden* been of the party, the pleasure you seem to have derived therefrom, might have been accounted for.

HARRIOT. For pity's sake, Emily, be quiet, or you will absolutely make me as melancholy as yourself.

EMILY. Will the name of Major Camden make you melancholy, cousin?

HARRIOT. O yes, it is a perfect antidote to every mirthful idea.

EMILY. Amazing! I had thought you regarded him as your future husband.

HARRIOT. So mamma would have me, Emily; but if ever I do marry, child, it will be a distant day; and I pray Heaven that Major Camden may not be the man.

EMILY. What can be your objection to Major Camden? he is young, rich, handsome, gay, generous, informed, and polished.

HARRIOT. Bless me! Emily—why, you have given him qualities enough for a line of high sounding Alexandrine measure;[1] and, if you had but arranged them musically, I should have set you down as a most excellent poet: Could you not transpose them, my dear?

EMILY. How agreeably a heart at ease can trifle.

---

1. **Alexandrine measure:** a line of twelve syllables, popular in medieval French poetry.

HARRIOT. Well then, my dear girl, seriously, and in your own way, I allow Major Camden every attribute which you have so liberally bestowed upon him: I sincerely esteem him; but for love, [*courtesying humourously*] I must beg your pardon for that, my dear.

EMILY. Is my aunt acquainted with your sentiments?

HARRIOT. Why, child, I do not *often* keep *secrets* from my mother; she has the most contemptible idea of love—but *entre nous*[1]—I believe she has been cruelly wounded by the little archer; this, however, is conjecture; for there is a mystery in the story of my good mother, which, although my curiosity is wound up to the highest pitch, I could never yet unravel.

EMILY. But it is strange she should wish you to enter into engagements at which your heart relucts.

HARRIOT. It is not more strange than true, Emily. Major Camden commenced his acquaintance with my mother by saving her from imminent danger: She was taking an airing on a very rough road—her horses took fright—the driver was thrown from his seat—a precipice was in view—and her destruction had been inevitable, had not Providence sent Camden to her assistance, who saved her life at the risque of his own!

EMILY. I shudder at her danger! It was indeed an heroic action.

HARRIOT. The gratitude of my mother was unbounded; mine also was powerfully engaged—for a time it deceived me: Camden declared himself my lover; but although I have long since understood the situation of my own heart, I am not permitted to deal explicitly with Major Camden.

EMILY. But on what principle can my aunt proceed?

HARRIOT. She has a most exalted opinion of Major Camden—tenderly loves her daughter—and thinks the passions should always be under the government of reason.

EMILY. Heigh ho!

HARRIOT. And heigh ho! say I—but, hang it, your glooms are contagious, I believe: I'll never stir a single step in pursuit of cross

---

1. **entre nous:** between us (French).

accidents, I'm resolv'd: [*hums a tune.*] "The world, my dear Mira, is full of deceit." [*Swims gracefully in a minuet; strikes suddenly into a cotillion[1] step; and warbles a gay air.*]

EMILY. Amiable vivacity!

HARRIOT. I protest, Emily, you shall not be so grave: I have half persuaded my mother to consent to our *hop* this evening; and if you will join me, I shall be sure of success. Come, let us renew our petition in concert.

She chants a sprightly air, and runs off with Emily. Enter Obadiah, followed by Bridget—Obadiah making a clamourous out-cry.

OB. Ouns! blood and thunder! what will become of poor Obadiah!

BRIDGET. What's the matter, Obadiah?

OB. Oh! the maple log, the maple log was in me! Oh, oh, oh! what shall I do? what shall I do?

BRIDGET. What is the matter, I say, Obadiah?

OB. Oh! tarnation, tarnation, tarnation!

BRIDGET. Are you mad? [*shaking him violently.*] Tell me what ails you, I say?

OB. Oh! I have broke—I have broke—I can't speak it—

BRIDGET. Broke what?

OB. I have broke—I have broke th-th-the—what d'ye call it—I have broke th-th-the—what d'ye call it.

BRIDGET. Th-th-the—what d'ye call it—Now what the plague do you mean, Obadiah?

OB. Why that there glass thing, Bridget, by which folks finds out *when we should be cold and when we should be warm.*

BRIDGET. I'll be hang'd, Obadiah, if you don't mean the thermometer.

OB. Yes, Bridget, it is the *mormeter*, the *mormeter*; the worse luck mine! yes, yes, it is the *mormeter* sure enough—oh, oh, oh!

BRIDGET. Why, don't take on so, man; my mistress is a good kind lady, and never faults people for trifles and accidents, and the like of that.

OB. Does not she, Bridget? ha, ha, ha! [*jumps about upon the stage.*] ha,

---

1. **cotillion:** a ballroom dance.

ha, ha! Well—but, Bridget, I'll tell you a story, Bridget; I once lived with a lady—she looked as mild as a lamb, and she was not bigger than a good stout yearling; but, for all that, she had *spurits* to the back bone, as a body may *zay;* and so, as I was *zaying,* I lived with she, and I only broke a China tea-cup—it is true it belonged to a *zet;* but my little mistress was in such a bloody passion, that she flew at me, tooth and nail, as a body may *zay;* and I swamp it, if she did not fetch blood of me, Bridget.

BRIDGET. Well, well, we are no boxers here; and so do you go along about your business, and ask your mistress what we shall get for dinner.

Exeunt Bridget and Obadiah.

SCENE—A Library—Table covered with Books—Mrs. Montague making Extracts—She rises and comes forward.

MRS. M. I often think in this life of solitude, to which my errors have condemned me, it is a very fortunate circumstance that I am able to turn my attention to pursuits which are at once replete with amusement and instruction; but what says my extracts? [*reads a paper on which she has been writing.*] "*Some modern philosophers are of opinion, that the sun is the great fountain from which the earth and other planets derive all the phlogiston*[1]—"

Enter Miss Montague and Miss Lovegrove.

HARRIOT. Do, dear mamma, consent to the violin and dancing this evening, and I will be the best girl in the world.

MRS. M. Daughter, my commands were, that I would not be interrupted; let me see—where did I leave off? O, here it is; [*reads*] "*which they possess, and that this is formed from the combination of the solar rays—*"

---

1. **phlogiston:** theorized as a colorless, odorless, tasteless, weightless substance emitted in burning. In the seventeenth century, Johann Becher postulated the combustion theory that all flammable materials gave off phlogiston. The theory remained popular until the late eighteenth century when physicist Antoine Lavoisier (1743–1794) refuted the theory with the oxygen theory of combustion.

HARRIOT. O, mamma, what a combination of reasons I shall have to love and honour you, if you will but oblige me; it will amuse my cousin Emily too.

MRS. M. Peace, Harriot; your cousin has not expressed a wish of this kind. [*reads*] *"with all the opaque bodies, but particularly with the leaves of vegetables, which they suppose to be organs adapted to absorb them, and that as animals receive their nourishment from vegetables, they also obtain in a secondary manner their phlogiston from the sun."*

HARRIOT. Dear mamma, exercise is as necessary for girls, as phlogiston is for vegetables: you are our sun, mamma, and pray now beam forth thy sweet consenting rays, and we shall become the most grateful creatures in the universe.

MRS. M. [*Smiling.*] Why do'nt you speak, Emily?

EMILY. Madam, my wishes are in unison with those of my cousin.

MRS. M. You know, girls, that I am not fond of these convivial parties; my time of life and situation render them improper for me; but for this once I will indulge you.

HARRIOT. [*courtesying low.*] Dear mamma, we thank you—Emily we will be as gay as—as—but hang it, I'll not study for a simile.

EMILY. You are perfectly right, cousin, we will express our gratitude by our hilarity rather than our wit.

Harriot and Emily seem to confer apart.

MRS. M. [*resumes her reading*] *"And lastly, as great masses of the mineral kingdom, which have been found in the crust of the earth, which human nature has penetrated, has evidently been formed from the recrements of animal and vegetable bodies."*

HARRIOT. May I send to Mrs. Shapely to put the silver trimmings upon my white sattin, mamma?

MRS. M. Yes, child—[*reads*] *"These also are supposed thus to have derived their phlogiston from the sun."*

Enter Obadiah.

OB. There's Mr. Major Camden *zays* how that he wants Miss Montague.

MRS. M. Go, my dear.

HARRIOT. Heigh ho! Will you go, cousin?

EMILY. I will join you presently, my dear.

Exit Harriot.

MRS. M. [*reads*] *"Another opinion concerning the sun's rays, is, that they are not luminous till they arrive at our atmosphere, and that there uniting with some part of the air, they produce combustion."* Be so good, my dear Miss Lovegrove, to step and desire Major Camden to tarry and dine with us.

EMILY. I obey you with pleasure, Madam.

Exit Miss Lovegrove.

MRS. M. [*reads.*] *"And light is emitted, and that an etherial acid, yet undiscovered, is formed from this combustion. The more probable opinion perhaps is, that the sun is a phlogistic mass of matter, whose surface is in a state of combustion, which, like other burning bodies, emits light—"*

Enter Obadiah.

OB. Bridget wants to know as how, Madam, would you have the partridges roasted, with the pudding?

MRS. M. Yes, Obadiah.

Exit Obadiah.

[*Reads.*] *"With immense velocity in all directions; that these rays of light act upon all opaque bodies; and, combining with them, either displace or produce their elementary heat, and become chemically combined with the phlogistic part of them; for light is given out when phlogistic bodies unite with the oxygenous principle of the air. As in combustion or in the reduction of metallic calxes:*[1] *Thus in presenting to the flame of a candle, a letter wafer, if it be coloured with red lead, at the time the red lead becomes a metallic drop, a flash of light is perceived. Doctor Alexander Wilson—"*

Enter Obadiah.

---

1. **calxes:** residues left when a mineral has been subjected to combustion.

OB. There is a dreadful accident come to pass, Madam! [*Looks ruefully.*]

MRS. M. For pity's sake, what is it?

OB. Fraid to *zay,* Ma'am.

MRS. M. I command you to speak.

OB. Won't you be angry, tho'?

MRS. M. You will make me more angry if you disobey me.

OB. Well, then—adds rat me if I can speak.

MRS. M. I order you, as you value my favour, to tell what is the matter.

OB. Well, then, if I must speak, matter enow' of conscience—why, I *thinks* every thing is going to ruin—*Wauns!* I *does* not think you'll stand it long; but, *ods bodikins,* I was not to blame for this neither, for the matter of that, as a body may *zay.*

MRS. M. You would weary even patience itself, Obadiah—come to the point immediately.

OB. Well, well—point enough, in conscience. Why, you must know, Ma'am, that the cook has left open the door of the larder, and the grey cat has helped herzelf to the partridges—There, Ma'am, there is point enough, zaving your presence.

MRS. M. Is that all, Obadiah?—well, I rejoice that it is no worse—here, take this bill, and see what dispatch you can make in furnishing more.

OB. Yes, that I will, Mistress—ho, ho, ho! I swamp it, a good milk's cow this. [*Aside.*]

Exit Obadiah.

MRS. M. [*reads.*] "*Doctor Alexander Wilson ingeniously endeavours to prove, that the sun is only in a state of combustion on its surface, and that the dark spots seen on its disk, are excavations, or caverns, through the luminous crust, some of which are four thousand miles in diameter.*" [*Throws the paper on the table.*] One is really lost in the immensity of these speculations—perhaps, books engross too much of my time. I thought my daughter sighed deeply at the name of Camden; indeed, she has lately given me to understand, that she can never be his! If I cannot reward the deserving Camden by her hand, I shall regard the disappointment as the seal of my misfortunes.

Exit.

SCENE—A Parlour.
Major Camden and Miss Montague seated.

HARRIOT. Why, Major, you always make me grave; you are too serious, a great deal too serious for me.

MAJOR C. I have long, Madam, been fully convinced, that it is out of my power to render myself agreeable to you.

HARRIOT. Ha, ha, ha! That collected countenance becomes you infinitely, I protest; look always thus captivating, and I shall be half mad with love.

MAJOR C. If you knew my heart, Miss Montague—

HARRIOT. O! for heaven's sake, Camden, throw aside that lullaby tone, or I shall absolutely, [*yawns*] or I shall absolutely fall asleep.

MAJOR C. Madam, Madam, you do not use me well: [*rising*] You would not use Stanhope thus.

HARRIOT. How well he reads my heart. [*Aside.*] Stanhope is as gay as a butterfly; we have laughed in concert a full hour; I protest, I think we were made for each other—But here comes my sentimental cousin; *she is always to your taste, Major.*

Enter Miss Lovegrove.

EMILY. My aunt, Sir, requests you would dine with her to-day.

MAJOR C. She does me honour, Miss Lovegrove; and I am infinitely obliged to her charming messenger.

HARRIOT. Well, I see, by your features, you are disposed to be charming company; and so I'll take the opportunity of giving orders to Shapely, respecting my dress for the evening.

Exit Harriot.

MAJOR C. Say, Miss Lovegrove, is not extreme gaiety, and uninterrupted frivolity, strong marks of indifference?

EMILY. My cousin has a fund of vivacity, Sir; but, as it never transgresses the bounds of discretion, it would be criminal even to wish it lessened.

MAJOR C. Would, that she could combine those rational and sentimental charms, which so eminently distinguish Miss Lovegrove.

EMILY. Sir, Miss Montague is amiable and good; and innocence and gaiety are frequently associates.

MAJOR C. Would, I had known Miss Lovegrove sooner!

EMILY. [*hesitating and alarmed.*] Sir, you may assure yourself, that my interest in the heart of Miss Montague shall be wholly employed in your favour.

MAJOR C. In the heart of Miss Montague! [*takes her hand.*] Charming Emily!—But what am I about—I stand on a precipice, down which a single movement may plunge me! Oh, Miss Lovegrove! could you witness the conflict in this devoted bosom, your heavenly sensibility, enchanting woman! would extort from your mild eye the tear of gentle pity.

EMILY. [*blushing and trembling.*] Sir, you are in full possession of all my commiseration; my most arduous efforts shall be wholly your's! and I will this moment seek my cousin, and endeavour to persuade her to become every thing a man of honour can desire.

Exit precipitately.

MAJOR C. She either affects ignorance, or she does not understand me—Were I more explicit, I should be a villain. I esteem Harriot Montague; but Emily Lovegrove enchants my reason, and triumphs over my dearest sentiments! Yet, the accusation of broken faith shall not entwine a soldier's laurels—Indeed, these struggles do not well suit with my profession! America, now weeping over her desolated plains and warriors slain in battle, should be my sovereign lady. It is not thus her heroes—it is not thus that WASHINGTON inglorious wastes his hours! Well, well—I'll haste to yon parade, and there forget my weakness.

Exit.

END OF THE SECOND ACT.

ACT THIRD.

SCENE—The Parade—Sea Prospect.

*Mr. Rambleton discovered at a corner of the stage, in a
convenient position for viewing the recruits—Major Camden
enters, followed by Soldiers, clad in the American uniform, drums
beating, fifes playing, and colours flying—they perform military
evolutions, marching and countermarching—after which
Major Camden addresses them:*

MAJOR C. Well, my brave fellow-soldiers, it is a glorious cause in which we have engaged: My glowing spirit, with congenial ardours, marks your glad alacrity: Your promptness and your order far exceed my utmost expectations! but Liberty can animate to deeds that far exceed all common credibility! The Rights of Man, my friends—auspicious Liberty!—these are our objects.

SOLDIERS. Huzza for Liberty! huzza for Liberty!

MAJOR C. We have a Leader, my brave friends—the Patriot WASHINGTON—who, for the Rights of Freemen, hazards his valued life and all his dearest hopes, greatly refusing every compensation!

SOLDIERS. Long live the glorious WASHINGTON! Long live our noble General! Huzza for WASHINGTON and Liberty!

MAJOR C. When power oppressive shall be crush'd before him, and Independence on firm base establish'd, then will our General, like another Quintus,[1] gladly put off the robes of power, and seek, amid his lov'd Vernonian[2] haunts, those calm enjoyments which attend on virtue!

SOLDIERS. Huzza for WASHINGTON and Independence!

MAJOR C. Frenchmen espouse our cause—Frenchmen have joined our battles; and, fighting by our side, the brave Fayette[3] their leader, they will augment our triumphs!

---

1. **Quintus:** Lucius Quinctius Cincinnatus (519?–439? B.C.), Roman dictator; called from his farm to save the state, he returned to the plow rather than remain in power.

2. **Vernonian:** a reference to George Washington's plantation, Mount Vernon.

3. **Fayette:** Marie-Joseph-Paul-Yves-Roch-Gilbert du Motier, marquis de La Fayette (1757-1834); French general and statesman who aided the patriots during the American Revolution.

SOLDIERS. Long live the gallant French!

MAJOR C. Our guardian Legislators issue their wise decrees—their utmost efforts ardently combining, up to their best abilities they will reward us. The Congress, fellow-soldiers, are our protecting Fathers!

SOLDIERS. [*Throw up their hats.*] God protect the Congress! We will fight and die for the Congress!

MAJOR C. Lastly, my friends; remember, though 'tis an arduous struggle, yet your best interests are all at stake—your wives—your children—your liberties—THE PEOPLE OF AMERICA! If we are subjugated, we are no more a Nation!

SOLDIERS. We will defend our Liberties!—we will defend the People! Long live America! Long live our free-born Nation!

Drums beat—fifes play Washington's March—Soldiers form a procession, and, headed by Major Camden, pass off the stage. Mr. Rambleton comes forward.

RAMB. My soul is wrought up to a degree of extacy! my brave, brave boy! I glory in my son! How regular the movements of the soldiers! their evolutions would have done honour to the best disciplined troops in Europe! Thank Heaven, my inquiries relative to Louisa have hitherto proved very satisfactory, and I hasten to complete my investigation.

Exit.

SCENE—*A Parlour at Mrs. Montague's.*

Enter Harriot, followed by Obadiah.

HARRIOT. Well, Obadiah, and how did you manage?

OB. Odds flesh! why, I thought as how I should never have found *un,* Miss.

HARRIOT. You should have gone directly to Mr. Stanhope's.

OB. Adds wauns! Miss Harriot, and *zo* I did; but you *zaid* I must *zee un* myself; and *zo* I could *na* find *un*—Adds rabit it, if I did not chase all over the town.

HARRIOT. And so, then, you have not seen Mr. Stanhope?

OB. O yes, Miss—yes, yes, I have *zeed un.*

HARRIOT. And you told him I would comply with his request?

OB. Yes, Miss; but a murrain[1] deal of trouble I had first, tho'.

HARRIOT. Well—and come, what did he say?

OB. Wauns! Miss, he was nation glad.

HARRIOT. But what did he say?

OB. Why, Miss, he *zaid*—he *zaid*—*why, he did not zay nothing*, Miss.

HARRIOT. Said nothing!

OB. No, Miss, nothing—he, he, he!

HARRIOT. What do you laugh at, Impertinence?

OB. Do'ont be angry, Miss Harriot; but I *canna* help laughing; *zee!* he gave me all this money for my good news, and *something else for somebody else*, besides all this here.

HARRIOT. What is it, in the name of goodness?

OB. But won't mistress blame I, now, Miss Harriot?

HARRIOT. Fear nothing, Obadiah.

OB. But I fears mortally.

HARRIOT. Fiddlestick! Obadiah, I will take care you shall not be blamed; and, if you have any thing further to say, pr'ythee let's have it.

OB. I have nothing to *zay*, Miss; but, if I was sure I should not be turned out of doors, [*takes a letter, with gestures expressive of awkward fear, from his pocket*] I would give you this here letter.

HARRIOT. [*Snatches the paper and reads.*] Um, um, um!

OB. Addsniggers! Miss Harriot, you are nation strong.

HARRIOT. You have acquitted yourself admirably, Obadiah—reach me my scarf—do you be secret, [*gives him money*] and expect my future favour.

OB. All this for me, Miss Harriot? what a power of money it is! Adds rabbit me, if I blab—he, he, he! *Well, I vows, now, I'll zee the Panorama, and the lion*, and all the wild *beastes—ay, and I'll zee a play, too.*

HARRIOT. You may go, Obadiah—remember your word.

OB. Yes, that I wull. [*Looks at the money.*] Why, what a lucky house I have got into! Wauns! what a marvellous lucky whelp I be!

Exit, bowing and scraping his feet.

---

1. **murrain:** literally, a plague; that is, a great deal of trouble.

HARRIOT. That I am not, strictly speaking, within the line of discretion, I am fully sensible—Alberto himself will set me down as a mad girl, although I do but comply with his pressing entreaties—But what with mothers and cousins, there is no such thing as getting a moment to one's self, here; and so, for this once, I'll e'en sally forth.

Exit Harriot.

SCENE—The Inn.
Mr. and Mrs. Vansittart—Mrs. Vansittart discovered, holding a
miniature picture.

MRS. V. O the dear pretty creature! set all round with rose diamonds of the first water! I vow, husband, it is the *jonteelest* thing I ever saw.

VANS. Rose *tiamonts* of the first *vater!* I say, *Torothy,* you *hat petter* put it on the *shentleman's* toilet again—you *petter* not *pe mettleing*—I tell you, *Torothy,* you *petter* not *pe mettleing.*

MRS. V. Why, Mr. Vansittart, I would not do an *unperlite* thing, any more than another; but this Mr. Rambleton is most *pertinaciously* a *spyington* from the British. You see he has not a paper dollar in the world! nothing but good hard English crowns and guineas—his Irish servant has his pockets lined with money; and he says that his master's trunks are as rich as the mines of *Poteldo.*

VANS. *Vel,* and *vat* then?

MRS. V. Why, as sure as you are alive, Major Camden is his *accomplishment.*

VANS. *Vel,* and *vat* then?

MRS. V. Why, then it is just such another case as Arnold and Andre.

VANS. *Vel,* and *vat* then?

MRS. V. Why, then it would be doing a *jonteel* thing, and a *patrolitical* thing, to inform against them to the Committee of Safety.

VANS. And *vat shoult ve* get *py* that?

MRS. V. Every thing, husband; for, while our gentlemen were had before the Committee, we could ply the Irishman with his favourite liquor, and, when he was secured, break open the locks, seize the cash, and make the best of our way to New-York, which is at no great distance;

and there remain concealed, until opportunity offered to quit this *Freetonian* land altogether.

VANS. Cot a' mercy! *I smell a rat, at this present time.*

MRS. V. And then no one could say, black is the white of our eye; for we have but served ourselves at the expense of *abomination* tories, and thus done a *jonteel* thing for our country.

VANS. Why, *Torothy, Torothy!* thou hast *creat vistoms, ant* I have *creat* occasions, *at this present time.*

MRS. V. Well, husband, do you give information instantly; and, as soon as his toryship is secured, you shall take this picture to the jeweller's, and pretend that it belonged to one of the rich relations, of which you have so often boasted, and that you are obliged to part with it; and thus we shall find money to supply ourselves with cloaks, masks, &c. &c. in which we shall be so disguised, that our own natural-born fathers would not know us.

VANS. *Vel, vel, Torothy—put* I *tremple* all over like an aspin leaf; *ant* I have *creat* fears *ve* shall *pring* ourselves to shame!

MRS. V. What ails you, husband?—the goods of a tory are free plunder!—why, we are doing the *most handsomest* thing in the world; and, as we shall not break the trunks until the last moment, we are perfectly secure. Away to the Committee of Safety—away! I say. [*pushing him off.*]

VANS. O mercy on us! mercy on us! I *to* think there *pe creat tangers ant creat tifficulties.*

Exeunt.

SCENE—A sequestered Walk, beautifully shaded.
Alberto Stanhope and Harriot Montague are discovered, sitting on the turfed seats, and engaged in close conversation.

HARRIOT. Well, Alberto, I can only repeat, that I do most sincerely regret this clandestine intercourse; in compliance with your importunities, I have given you this meeting. The world considers me as a gay, unthinking girl; yet I have my moments of reflection. My preference of you I will not deny; but the, if possible, *augmented indulgence* of my mother, hath roused to action every proper sentiment, and the highest sense of the duty which I owe her.

ALBERTO. Perhaps, Harriot, your heart now decides in favour of Camden! but let him take care——

They rise.

HARRIOT. Pshaw, pshaw! Stanhope, this is exactly in his style. [*Throws herself into a fencing attitude.*] Yet, don't put yourself in a passion, man; for I protest, I begin to think he has absolutely thrown off his allegiance, and that he is, at this very moment, fomenting a rebellion against his sovereign lady!

ALBERTO. What means my Harriot?

HARRIOT. Why, *entre nous*, I suspect he has conceived a most violent *penchant* for Emily Lovegrove.

ALBERTO. Heaven grant it.

HARRIOT. It would be delectable! they would make the most charming sentimental pair in the world! and I take every opportunity of leaving them together, not doubting but their *private interviews* will wonderfully increase their *tendresse.*[1]

ALBERTO. Does my Harriot draw this conclusion from her own experience?

HARRIOT. [*Striking the powder out of his hair with her fan.*] Yes, villain; and hence she resolves to make no more assignations.

ALBERTO. Charming vivacity! [*seizing her hand.*]

HARRIOT. Unhand me, wretch!

ALBERTO. But what are we to do, my angel?

HARRIOT. Do! why, sit down, like the babes in the wood, and cry ourselves to sleep, and see what little robin red-breast will prepare our leafy covering.

ALBERTO. Pr'ythee, do not thus trifle with my feelings—You have forbid my application to your mother.

---

1. **tendresse:** tenderness, affection (French).

HARRIOT. Because I knew it would be ineffectual.

ALBERTO. [*Again taking her hand.*] In the name of Heaven, how shall I proceed? Shall I engage my father to intercede for me?

HARRIOT. Why, ah! these managing people understand each other best; and it is as well to proceed in the good old fashion way: [*looks at her watch.*] But it is time for me to scamper. Adieu—you will make one of our dancers this evening?

ALBERTO. Enchanting girl! I shall attend you with rapture!

Exeunt.

SCENE—An Apartment at Mrs. Montague's.

Enter Mrs. Montague and Emily.

MRS. M. Emily, where is Harriot?

EMILY. I cannot tell, Madam; but she is fond of walking, and, I suppose, is improving this fine day, by indulging in her favourite exercise.

MRS. M. Emily, young people generally understand each other. There was a time, when I conceived the heart of my girl entirely devoted to Major Camden; but she has of late given me reason to regard her attachment as problematical. Am I to impute this apparent change to caprice, or to a growing disgust?

EMILY. [*Confused and hesitating.*] Why, really, Madam, it is not for me to say.

MRS. M. Your *looks*, Emily, and your *manner*, convince me that you *could* say a great deal! I am engaged in gratitude, in honour, to Major Camden—my promise is irrevocable. I had the full consent of Harriot; and the world expects their speedy union. Tell me, Emily, if you know aught which can militate against my plans?

EMILY. [*Trembling and blushing excessively.*] Pray, Madam, excuse me! pray do!

Enter Harriot.

EMILY. What a fortunate relief! [*Aside.*]

MRS. M. Harriot, where have you been rambling?

HARRIOT. *Rambling, sure enough, mamma!* why, half the town over; and I am so delightfully fatigued—

MRS. M. Well, my love, take off your scarf, and let us have a little serious chit-chat.

EMILY. Have I your leave to retire, Madam?

MRS. M. Go, my good girl.

Exit Emily.

Tell me, Harriot—Have you ceased to love Major Camden?

HARRIOT. *To love him, mamma!* why, that is a business I have never yet begun.

MRS. M. My dear Harriot, I am serious.

HARRIOT. Well then, mamma, seriously, although I esteem Major Camden, I can never marry him; for I can never *love him, mamma.*

MRS. M. If you *esteem him, my dear, it is sufficient.*

HARRIOT. God bless you, Madam! you would not surely insist that my hand should be a solitary gift?

MRS. M. *Love,* my dear, is a *chimera,* which has undone your mother!

HARRIOT. Madam!

MRS. M. For your advantage, Harriot, I will sketch some particulars of my life, which I had intended to keep forever from your knowledge.

HARRIOT. If you please, mamma.

MRS. M. When I married your father, although I regarded him as the first of men, yet I felt not for him *what is called, love.*

HARRIOT. [*archly.*] And was you *very happy* with my father, Madam?

MRS. M. I understand you, Harriot. I engaged in a round of dissipation—I continued the most censurable pursuits; and at length *imagined* myself tenderly attached to a person, who was every way the *inferior of* your father.

HARRIOT. Well, Madam.

MRS. M. Your father continued his forbearance, until convinced, by circumstances, that he had a rival in my affections! when, leaving me at our country seat, without a single remonstrance, and taking with him your brother, then only four years old, he departed for this city, leading me to expect he would return with the coming day! [*weeps.*]

HARRIOT. Dear Madam, proceed!

MRS. M. You were then but two months old: The first post brought me a letter, in which he informed me, that, as he was convinced I was unalterably attached to another, he should bid me an eternal adieu!— that he took with him our son, as the only solace of his exile—that he left me the uninterrupted possession of his town and country house, with a sufficient income to support myself and daughter—and he concluded by wishing me, with the man of my heart, all that felicity on which he supposed my fond imagination had calculated.

HARRIOT. For God's sake, Madam, proceed!

MRS. M. I came immediately to town; but he had embarked on board a ship, bound to some part of Europe! From season to season, for a long time, I encouraged hope; but, although nineteen years have since revolved, not a single syllable, either respecting himself or my son, hath ever blest my ears!

HARRIOT. Gracious Heaven! both my father and my brother may be yet alive!

MRS. M. Alas! No—I feel it is impossible! my wounds bleed afresh at this recital! they have long since bid adieu to a world, to which I am chained a miserable captive! [*weeps agonizedly.*]

HARRIOT. Forbear! best of mothers! forbear these tears. Surely, surely, your experience does not decide in favour of an Hymen[1] unblest by love!

MRS. M. Observe me, girl; although I was indiscreet, I was never criminal; and the moment of your father's departure convinced me of my error—*the charm was broke—I detested the author of my sufferings—I never after saw him;* and, to my great satisfaction, I learned that he immediately quitted the continent. I dwelt with unutterable admiration on your father's virtues; and had I possessed worlds, I would have parted with them all to have purchased his return!

HARRIOT. Ah! Madam, your story is indeed instructive: But—

MRS. M. But what, my love?—I am indebted to Major Camden for my life—you have received him with approbation—he is every way

---

1. **Hymen:** in Greek mythology, the god of marriage.

worthy; and, next to yourself, Harriot, he is now the dearest object of my affections!—But alas! my love, you are ill—my woe-fraught narrative has been too oppressive! Heaven guard my child! Let me lead you to your chamber.

Exit Mrs. Montague, supporting Harriot.

END OF THE THIRD ACT.

ACT FOURTH.

SCENE—An Apartment in the Inn.

Enter Patrick.

Ow, if ever I got into such a place before now—by my soul, the Mistress of this same tavern, d'ye see, is the prettiest bit of a *cratur,* as a body may say, that ever a man set eyes on; and, may I never see Killmallock again, if she is not better than a ship load of *peraters,* just landed from the county of Cork—But here comes my master, now.

Enter Mr. Rambleton.

RAMB. Well, Patrick, how wears the day, and what sort of a house have we got into?

PATR. Ow, as to the day, I don't *bodder* myself about that, at all, at all; for, d'ye see, I don't matter time three skips of a grasshopper; but, as for the house, Ow, if I was in my own sweet Killmallock, in the county of Limerick, in dear Ireland *itshelf,* my own born mother could not be better to me; why, they have already given me *three breakfasts,* and as many dinners; and, as to drink, my dear honey, ow, let me alone for that, Master.

RAMB. Why, I believe, indeed, thou hast taken a plentiful portion of the good creature; [*loud knocking without*] but see if thou canst open the door.

Patrick opens the door, Officer enters and gives Rambleton a letter.

RAMB. Hah! where can I have picked up a scribbling acquaintance already? [*Reads.*]
"Mr. Rambleton,
"By virtue of the power delegated to us by the people, we summon you to appear before us, the Select Committee of Public Safety for the City of———. Information has been lodged against you as a spy, employed

by the British government; and we have authorized the bearer of this notification to bring you before us, for the purpose of examination.

ARTHUR VIGILANT, *Secretary of the*
Committee of Public Safety. "

RAMB. [*appears much agitated.*] Can you inform me from what source this officious interference originated?

OFFICER. Sir, my orders are to attend you to the honourable Committee, without answering any questions; but, you may depend on receiving every indulgence, that the nature of the case, and the circumstances of our country will admit.

RAMB. Thank you, Sir. Gracious God! If *Harry Camden* is the *informer,* my hopes of happiness will, indeed, prove the dream of the moment! [*Aside.*]

Walks about, agitated and distressed.

PATR. Ow, then, if it is not a shame now, to be after boddering *a stranger in his own country.* I say, now, little Honey, cannot you be taking your *shelf* off a bit, my dear, and *lave* my poor master *all alone, with his own faithful* Patrick O'Neal, d'ye see?

OFFICER. I do but my duty, friend.

PATR. Your *juty,* do you call it! Ow, by my soul, Mr. Tipstaff, this is the first time I ever heard say it was a *juty* to bodder a man in his *own country after he had got into foreign parts!* Hark'ye, little Honey! will I put a remembrance upon you now?—*suppose you and I should take a bit of a knock for love, my dear?*

RAMB. Patrick, you have nothing to do in this business. Sir, I attend you.

PATR. Arrah, my dear, now, it will never be said that Patrick O'Neal suffered his master to get into the limboes alone, and so I will be after going with you, *that, if we will both be taken prisoners, we may rescue one another.*

RAMB. Patrick, I have nothing to fear—I have valuable articles in this house, and I entrust them to your care.

PATR. Arrah, now, my dear, let them *same articles take care of themselves,* I shall be after going with your worship, d'ye see.

RAMB. Patrick, I command you not to quit the house.

PATR. Arrah, then I shall stay behind; for, he that is *willian* enough not to *plase* a man in distress, ought to have been *assassinated twenty years before he was born—so he had.*

Exeunt Officer and Rambleton.

Ow, if I was but in dear Ireland now, in the borough of Killmallock, in the county of Limerick, may be, I'd soon see the white boys about me—may be I would; and then my shelf would be taking my poor master out of jurance—so I would; but a wet sorrow is better than a dry one, as the saying is, and so I'll be after another little sip of comfort, so I will.

Exit.

SCENE—An Apartment in Mrs. Montague's House.

Enter Obadiah, picking his teeth.

OB. Well, I'll swamp it, now, I have made as good a dinner as if I had eaten baked beans and pudding—Ouns, I could not fare better in Natick.

Enter Mr. Stanhope, senior.

STANH. Is your mistress at home, Obadiah?

OB. At hume, Zir! he, he, he, I cant zay, Zir—*I'll ax her if she chooses to be at hume, Zir.*

Exit Obadiah.

STANH. *May I never take the field,* but this is a fine *musical* custom, which our new form'd States have adopted—we are not always in a disposition to see our best friends, and we have a right to be at home just when we please.

Enter Obadiah.

OB. Yes, Zir, you may zee mistress—walk after me, Zir, walk after me.

Exit Mr. Stanhope, following Obadiah.

SCENE—A Parlour—Mrs. Montague seated.

Enter Obadiah, introducing Mr. Stanhope.
Exit Obadiah.

STANH. Good morrow, fair lady.

MRS. M. Your most obedient Mr. Stanhope, I hope you are in health, Sir?

STANH. Yes, Madam, partly; and yet I am not as young as I was fifty years ago, neither.

MRS. M. Time, Sir, imprints its footsteps upon every thing visible.

STANH. And yet, Madam, *may I never take the field,* if I do not think you look as young as you did twenty years ago.

MRS. M. O dear, Sir!

STANH. Yes you do, yes you do; and if I was twenty years younger, Madam, I do assure you I should feel strongly inclined to strike about myself.

MRS. M. Strike about, Sir!

STANH. Yes, widow, I would make my bow, squeeze your ladyship's hand, whisper soft things in your ear, hint indirectly at marriage, and publish the bans in less time than you could finish your wedding cap.

MRS. M. You are disposed to be pleasant, Sir! but as this is a subject on which I never jest, I beg leave to say, that had you the faculty of renewing your youth, and were to advance with the most serious proposals, I should not hesitate in putting my negative thereon.

STANH. Indeed! Well I profess this is somewhat surprising! but mayhap I am not to your taste; do you not hold matrimony to be a musical[1] thing.

MRS. M. O yes, *musical* enough; but I am principled against *second marriages,* Sir.

STANH. O, is that all? well, then I hope my son may succeed.

MRS. M. Your son, Sir?

STANH. Yes, Madam, my son has taken a violent fancy to a good

---

1. **musical:** *Musical,* a term used in many of the interior parts of the New-England States, to express every thing convenient, excellent or elegant: thus, they say a musical horse, day, garment, &c. &c. [Murray's note].

handsome young woman of whom you have the disposal. I perfectly approve his choice, and have waited on you to endeavour to obtain your consent.

MRS. M. Can my niece have made a conquest of such importance already? [*Aside.*] Why, Sir, the young woman you mention is calculated, both in mind and person, to command affection as well as esteem; had her father lived, her consequence would doubtless have been augmented; but I shall make every effort in my power, which I can suppose will be for her advantage.

STANH. Madam, she cannot stand in need of proper aid, under your care.

MRS. M. Sir, it is my wish to discharge *the duty* of a mother.

STANH. I never heard any thing more musical in my life, Madam; may I inform my son that he has your approbation?

MRS. M. Sir, if your son can render the young lady propitious, he shall have my best wishes.

STANH. Madam, I was made to believe that you were not favourably inclined in this affair, but the best are liable to mistakes; you have done me a very particular kindness, Madam; Alberto will run mad with joy! and I will make all possible dispatch to inform him of his happiness. Sweet lady, I take my leave, and shall ever be your most obedient humble servant.

MRS. M. Sir, your most obedient.

Exit Stanhope.

Quite a whimsical old gentleman, on my word; his way of thinking, too, is rather singular, for Emily's fortune is a mere trifle, and Alberto, accomplished as he is, might form the most aspiring expectations. I will take the earliest opportunity of sounding my niece, and govern myself by her wishes.

SCENE—Another apartment; Harriot and Emily seated on a Sofa.

HARRIOT. Well, Emily, although I have confessed to you that this little heart of mine beats only for Alberto Stanhope, yet you still remain as profound as a pedant who studies obscurity, or as close as Olivia[1] in the Good natured Man. Come, child, you had better make a confession.

EMILY. Dear Harriot, permit me to be a miser of my woes! I would slide through life, performing my little part without observation, and—

HARRIOT. [*Humorously putting her hand on Emily's mouth.*] For heaven's sake, Emily, be not thus humble! Without observation, say you! why I would rather be paragraphed in the newspaper, than not distinguished at all.

EMILY. Paragraphed in the newspaper!

HARRIOT. Yes, my dear, although said paragraph should hold me up in the most ridiculous point of view!

EMILY. I cannot conceive of this!

HARRIOT. Why child, a single scribbler, scratching his malicious noddle, may fabricate his abuse, and the cynic has only to preface his invidious production by the little comprehensive monosyllable *we* think and *we* wish, while he thus hands my name to thousands, who would not otherwise have known *that I had an existence.*

EMILY. Well, but with the knowledge of *your existence,* they would at the same time receive an impression *that would not be to your honour.*

HARRIOT. Yes, Emily; but their *curiosity* would be called into action—it would impel them to *inquire;* I should come out an *innocent sufferer,* be allowed *my full share of merit,* and acquire a *prodigious deal of consequence;* ha! ha! ha! I protest the very idea is enchanting.

EMILY. Mad girl! but however you may divert yourself, I still insist, that were I to be publickly traduced, I should never enjoy peace afterward!

HARRIOT. Then you would be very irrational, my dear, for envy is a powerful stimulus to the misanthropic mind, and *merit is ever the mark at which it aims its most envenomed shafts.* But we have strangely wandered from our subject—I am positive, Emily, that my friend Camden is not indifferent to you.

EMILY. Dear Harriot, spare me.

---

1. **Olivia:** character in *The Good Natur'd Man* (1768), a comedy by Oliver Goldsmith (1730–1774).

Enter Bridget, who presents a billet to Harriot.
Exit Bridget.

HARRIOT. [*reads.*] Raptures—um, um, um! Eternal obligations—um, um, um! Duty—um, um, um! Reverence—O Emily! I am in a delirium of joy! My mamma has sanctioned my wishes! she consents to my union with Alberto Stanhope! Camden shall be your's. Adored parent! but I will go this instant, and on my bended knees I will thank her for her unparalleled goodness.

Exit Harriot, agitated.

EMILY. Well, this is passing strange! my aunt is indeed the noblest of human beings; yet, that she should thus easily relinquish the favourite wish of her soul!—but I will await the issue in my chamber.

SCENE—*The Library*
Mrs. Montague is discovered with a Book in her Hand; Harriot rushes in, and throws herself on her Knees at the Feet of her Mother.

HARRIOT. O my angelic parent! may ten thousand blessings crown your honoured head! You have indeed made me the happiest of human beings!

MRS. M. Gracious Heaven! my poor child has lost her reason!

HARRIOT. No, Madam, reason at this moment imprints on my heart duty, gratitude and love, to the most condescending parent that ever bore that revered name.

MRS. M. Rise then, my daughter, and let me know what has thus discomposed you?

HARRIOT. [*Rising.*] Here, Madam, [*presenting the billet she had received from Stanhope.*] these extatic lines, penned by my Alberto, inform me, that foregoing your former wishes, you now consent to crown our youthful hopes by your maternal approbation.

MRS. M. [*Taking the billet.*] His extacies should have been addressed to Emily Lovegrove.

HARRIOT. To Emily Lovegrove!!! [*Aside.*]

MRS. M. [*After reading the billet.*] You have, child, acted very reprehensibly in concealing your inclinations thus long from your mother.

HARRIOT. I had hoped to have conquered them, Madam, and to have bent me to my duty.

MRS. M. I am disposed to think the best, Harriot. I had thought the father of Alberto solicited me for my niece, and I consented that his son should address Miss Lovegrove. Imagining that you were already regarded as the wife of Camden, I could not expect to receive proposals for you.

HARRIOT. [*Weeping.*] Oh Madam, how cruel is my situation!!!

MRS. M. To say truth, child, I pity you; and I lament my own embarrassments; I cannot break the heart of Harry Camden! he interests me more and more every time I behold him! I have thought, Harriot, that he bears a strong resemblance to your father! But compose yourself, my love; enjoy, with your accustomed vivacity, your evening's entertainment; with the coming day I will converse with Camden, and in the mean time hope every thing from the indulgence of your mother.

Exeunt.

END OF THE FOURTH ACT.

ACT FIFTH.

SCENE—The Inn.

Enter Patrick, tipsy, with a mug in his hand—he hickups and sings:

> Ow! Patrick's *not drunk*, to be sure,
> Although in the liquor *quite drown'd;* [*Drinks.*]
> The wine in his stomach secure,
> His head for pure joy it runs round. [*Drinks.*]
>   Tol de re lol—tol de re lol.   5
>
> I'll stand by my master *all night,*
> And sleep in his hammock *all day;*
> And Patrick, though *dead* in a fright,
> Shall *never be running away.* [*Drinks.*]
>   Tol de re lol—tol de re lol.   10
>
> My *shelf* shall be fighting for him;
> *I'll follow, although I stand still:*
> *Ow! if I am drown'd, I can swim;*
> The world it runs round like a mill. [*Drinks.*]
>   Tol de re lol—tol de re lol.   15

Well, now, if Mistress Van—Van—*juce* take me, if I have not forgot—If she was to see me, she would *be after* taking me off—*Don't they call it taking off?* Well, now, if Master Rambleton should get out of the limboes, *himshelf* would be apt to think I was a little the worse for the good *cratur,* or so; and so I'll e'en turn in; and after taking a nap, may be I would be sober again. Here's good luck to us, Master Rambleton. [*Drinks.*]

    Exit, staggering.
    Enter Mr. Vansittart.

VANS. *Cot a'* mercy! where can *Torothy pe, at this present time?* I have *creat occasions* for *manhoot*—It is a *polt untertaking; ant* I *treamt* all last night of coffins, cross *pones* and the *callows*. O *tear!* I am all over of a *colt* sweat.

Mrs. Vansittart, having forced the trunks, enters, followed by two servants, bearing bags of money—she slips her foot, falls head foremost into the parlour, and, in her fall, overturns a large screen.

VANS. [*Roars out.*] *Cot a'* mercy! *Cot a'* mercy!

MRS. V. [*Rising.*] Why, husband, what ails you? I am sure you are an unmannerly fellow, to leave me sprawling thus.

VANS. [*Trembling excessively.*] *Torothy, Torothy!* vat shall *ve to, Torothy?*

MRS. V. Do! why, put on this here mask and this cloak.

She helps him on with the cloak.

VANS. [*Still trembling and terrified.*] Oh! *Torothy, Torothy!* let me *tie teat,* if I have not *creat* occasions to *tislike* this *pusiness*—it has *creat tangers!*

MRS. V. Well, well—never mind—Come, let's away. [*They all mask.*] We will take the road to New-York, through the woods, and over the mountains.

Exeunt, bearing the treasure—Vansittart still agitated.

*SCENE—A genteel Parlour at Mrs. Montague's.
Mrs. Montague, &c. &c. all in full dress—Alberto and Harriot dancing a minuet—all the rest of the company sitting.—Obadiah enters, and presents a folded parcel to Mrs. Montague, who reads, and, after unfolding another paper, exclaims:*

Gracious God! my own picture! the very miniature, which the man I so deeply injured was accustomed to wear next his heart! Oh! Harriot, Harriot! I am now, indeed, undone! Some villain has murdered your father!

HARRIOT. For Heaven's sake, Madam, explain.

MRS. M. Read that paper, my dear; read it aloud; and advise me, my friends, what step I am to take.

HARRIOT. [*Reads.*]

"Madam,

"Vansittart the inn-keeper, some hours since, parted with the inclosed miniature for a sum of money, by no means adequate to its value. As the picture was set by me, I could not but recognize it. If you think it necessary to take any steps respecting it, you must be speedy; for I shrewdly suspect, Vansittart is on the point of decamping. I have the honour to be, Madam,

> Your most obedient humble servant,
>
> JEREMY TRUEWORTH."

MAJOR C. Madam, Vansittart is my landlord—I will fly instantly, and force him to confess by what means he obtained this picture.

MRS. M. Do, dear Harry: But before you go, it is necessary you should know I am ignorant of the fate of my husband, and that this picture was in his possession when he left me. [*weeps.*]

ALBERTO. Camden, permit me to be the companion of your enterprize.

MAJOR C. With all my heart, Stanhope.

Exeunt Camden and Stanhope.

MRS. M. O my children! my very soul seems to die within me!

HARRIOT. Dear Emily, assist me to bear my mother to her apartment.

Harriot and Emily bear off Mrs. Montague, and the scene closes.

SCENE—*The Inn.*

Enter Patrick, who is supposed to have slept off the effects of his liquor, and who raves and stamps about outrageously.

PATR. Murder! hanging! drowning and quartering! why, every thing which ever happened in this beggarly, rascally world; ow! it was every bit of it no more than the skip of a flea to this—the trunks are all wide open—there is not a soul left in the house; *and nobody that I meet can give me a bit of an answer!*—my poor master clapped up, and Patrick O'Neal in a strange outlandish country! May be the Indian savages shall take my *shelf* prisoner too—may be they shall. Ow! what had I to do, to be after running such a wild-goose chase? But here is some one coming: I'll give *um* a little bit of a taste—so I will. Oh! murder! robbery! bloodshed! fire and thunder!

Enter Major Camden, Alberto Stanhope, Officer and Soldiers.

MAJOR C. Patrick, for Heaven's sake, what is the matter? Where is Mr. Vansittart?

PATR. Ow! Master Camden, Methuselah[1] *himshelf* could not tell that, I believe.

MAJOR C. What do you mean, Patrick? Is he not in the house?

PATR. Ow! I have searched the house from garret to cellar, and the *juce* a bit of a *human soul, except the cat,* is there to be found; and what is more, they have broken open all my master's trunks, and *boddered* him out of a million guineas *more than he had,* my dear.

MAJOR C. Good God! is it possible? Robbed the trunks! Where was you, Patrick?

PATR. Ow! you may say that—shame burn my cheek! My master, d'ye see, had gotten into the limboes; and so, to make my *shelf asy,* I took a drop, or so, and fell fast asleep, and then, before I was awake, the deed was done.

MAJOR C. But what do you mean by your master's being in the limboes, Patrick?

PATR. Why, Master Tipstaff here—Isn't it Tipstaff ye call him?—kidnapped him; that's all, Honey.

OFFICER. Information was given to the Committee of Public Safety against Mr. Rambleton, and I had the honour of attending him before them, Sir.

MAJOR C. Good heavens! I must hasten to his assistance. Mr. Stanhope, I may want your aid. The probability is, that the villainous plunderers have taken the road to New-York; and, by the assistance of these soldiers, Sir, [*speaking to the Officer*] you may surprise and bring them back—their booty will retard their flight. Patrick, you will accompany the officer; you can best designate your master's property.

---

1. **Methuselah:** biblical patriarch who lived for 969 years. See Gen. 5:21-27.

PATR. Ow! that I shall, with the biggest pleasure in life, Sir.

MAJOR C. Mr. Stanhope, we must away to the Committee.

Exeunt severally, in opposite directions.

SCENE—An Apartment in another Public House.
Mr. Rambleton and the Members of the Committee of Safety seated
round the table.

RAMB. Gentlemen, you have detained me many hours—I could clear up all your doubts; but I have private reasons for wishing to remain concealed at present. Yet, however you may be disposed to call my veracity in question, you have so highly obliged me, by assuring me that you received no intelligence respecting me from Major Camden, that I shall not easily take offence.

1ST MEMB. Your attachment to Major Camden would almost induce us to suspect the fidelity of that young soldier.

2D MEMB. Major Camden is a brave, a gallant officer; but so was General Arnold!

3D MEMB. The defection of Arnold has rendered us abundantly more wary; we have every thing at stake, Sir.

RAMB. I commend your caution, Gentlemen. I have already narrated my accidental meeting with Major Camden; but perhaps it might be agreeable to summon the Major; and we will submit to cross examination.

1ST MEMB. This, in my opinion, Gentlemen, is a proper motion.

Enter a Servant.

SERV. Major Camden and Mr. Stanhope crave admittance, Gentlemen.

2D MEMB. Let them enter immediately.

Exit Servant.

3D MEMB. This looks well.

Enter Major Camden and Mr. Stanhope.

MAJOR C. May it please this honourable body, Mr. Stanhope and myself wait on you to offer our joint bonds for the release of Mr. Rambleton; his affairs stand in immediate need of his presence.

RAMB. What mean you, Sir?

MAJOR C. The villain Vansittart, having robbed you of every article of value, hath absconded!

MEMBERS OF THE COMMITTEE. [*all exclaim*] Vansittart! the very man who lodged the information!

RAMB. *The picture of my Louisa, then, is ravished from me!*

MAJOR C. *The picture, Sir!* [*Pauses.*] Yes—*it is possible!*—Vansittart sold the picture to a jeweller; and it is now in the hands of Mrs. Montague, whose soul is harrowed up by agonizing fears for him whose property it was.

RAMB. Oh! give me way; and let me fly, the messenger of peace!

MAJOR C. Explain yourself, Mr. Rambleton.

RAMB. If she can feel so deeply, disguises are no longer necessary. My real name is Montague! the husband of the lady whom you mention.

MAJOR C. Good heavens! what a discovery!

RAMB. Having reason to call in question the tenderness of my wife, I meant this very evening to have learned her sentiments, under a disguise which should have veiled me from her knowledge; and even now, I must insist on being myself the bearer of the tidings of my return: In her emotions I mean to read my fate.

MAJOR C. Upon the truth and firm affection of Mrs. Montague, I'd stake my hopes of happiness.

RAMB. With the good leave of this most honourable Committee, we go to make the experiment.

1ST MEMB. We can no longer doubt.

2D MEMB. Or if we do, these gentlemen will become responsible.

MAJOR C. Most certainly. What say you, Stanhope?

ALBERTO. Ah! to the utmost farthing I can call my own.

Committee rises.
Exeunt severally, in opposite directions.

SCENE—*A Mountain and adjacent Wood.*

Enter Mr. and Mrs. Vansittart, with Servants—Mrs. Vansittart weary.

MRS. V. Oh! I cannot go another step—Was ever woman so completely fatigued? This wood will *clandictedly* conceal us. It would not be doing the thing *jonteelly*, to go any further to-night.

VANS. *Shenteelly!* Why, who ever thought of *shenteelly*, at this present time? Come along, *vife*—come along, *Torothy*, I say.

He pulls her after him.

MRS. V. [*Struggling.*] Dear Mr. Vansittart, you have no *alegunt idears.*

VANS. Elegant *itears! Cot a'* mercy! *Torothy*, you *woult* provoke a saint!

MRS. V. I will not proceed—I insist on sitting down.

They lay down their booty, and seat themselves.

VANS. Vell, if you must *pe opeyt*, you must; *put, vife, vife!* I tell you no *coot vill* come of our *expetition.*

Enter Patrick, Officer, and Soldiers, in different directions—they all rise up, shriek, and endeavour to make their escape; but are severally seized by their pursuers—Mr. Vansittart falls flat on his face, and roars tremendously—Patrick raises him.

VANS. O *tear, plesset* Mr. Patrick! I have *creat occasions* for mercy, *at this present time;* ant so, if you *vill pe* so *coot* as to *parton* me, I *vill* take my *piple* oath, that I *vill* never commit another *roppery*, as long as I *to* live *in this here vorlt.*

PATR. Why, look'ye, my dear, it's none of my affair, d'ye see; but, as you are taken prisoner, or the like of that, my *shelf* shall *be after* making a promise, that if ye cry *pecavia*, Master Rambleton shall never knock your words down your throat—he never *bodders* a poor fellow who can't help *himshelf,* Honey.

MRS. V. What's that you say, husband? I desire you would behave *jonteelly.* I say it is an *alegunt* thing, to take the property of a vile tory, and our country will thank us for it.

VANS. *Holt* your tongue, *Torothy—holt* your *vicket* tongue, I say.

PATR. Ow! *lave* off your palavering, woman; you had better *be after coming along*. Ow! I wish I had the white boys here, for your sake; I would have you fairly trounced—so I would; and *after that you might be carried before the Justice:* But humsomever, d'ye see, these same goods are all Master Rambleton's; and so, Master Tipstaff, you may do your *juty* again, if you *plase*.

Exit, with Officer and Soldiers, bearing the booty, and pushing the delinquents before them.

SCENE—*A Parlour in Mrs. Montague's House.*

Enter Harriot and Emily.

HARRIOT. My mamma, thank Heaven, has reasoned herself into a degree of composure.

Enter Mr. Rambleton, Major Camden, Stanhope senior, and Alberto.

MAJOR C. Miss Montague, this stranger [*Rambleton bows*] has some knowledge of the picture, which he will communicate only to your mother.

HARRIOT. I will inform my mamma immediately, Sir.

Exit Harriot, accompanied by Emily.

RAMB. Exquisite beauty! a perfect transcript of her mother! It was with difficulty I could forbear folding her to my bosom.

ALBERTO. Miss Montague's mind is a fit accompaniment for her exterior. It is strange, Sir, [*speaking to his father*] that you should so immediately recognize Mr. Rambleton.

STANH. Body on me, why he was my old schoolfellow! ah, and a *musical boy* he was too. Why neighbour Montague, my name is not Stanhope if I do not mightily rejoice to see thee.

Enter Mrs. Montague, led by Harriot and Emily.

MRS. M. [*She starts back, draws away her hands, clasps them in an extacy of joy, and exclaims,*] Oh all ye saints and angels! it is my husband! my long lost, highly injured, and dear lamented husband; [*rushing forward, she is on the point of falling, but is saved in the arms of Rambleton.*]

RAMB. O my Louisa, this one luxurious moment is a vast, an ample compensation for every evil which I ever suffered!

MRS. M. [*Kneeling.*] Can you forgive me, Edward? my heart was ne'er in fault; each day, since your departure, has been marked by suffering; and every passing hour hath witnessed my regrets!

RAMB. [*Raising her.*] No more, my love, I have been too severe! But rigid honour demanded much, and I was not apprized how deeply you were wounded!

Mrs. Montague leans on Emily, Harriot comes forward and kneels.

HARRIOT. And is there yet in store for Harriot Montague a father's benediction?

RAMB. [*Clasping her to his bosom.*] Come, my sweet cherub, thy father's heart is open to receive thee, and thou art far dearer to his soul than the life blood which warms him to existence.

MRS. M. Edward, one fond impatient question yet trembles on my tongue—our son—

RAMB. Loved Louisa, he is doubly your's, by virtue and by nature! Camden, come to my bosom! My love, behold our son!

MAJOR C. What say you, Sir?

MRS. M. Harry Camden! Astonishing!!

RAMB. Yes, my soul's treasure—behold the boy whom you so oft have pressed to that maternal bosom! E're I became a voluntary exile, sojourning in Virginia, I left our son with Mr. Camden, a man in whom my soul confided; and 'twas from me, my son, that your *supposed father* received the letters that placed you in the military line.

MAJOR C. I do remember something of mystery about those letters; and with duteous veneration I kneel to such a father. [*Kneels.*]

RAMB. Rise, my brave boy—Cato[1] himself might glory in such a son!

---

1. **Cato:** Roman statesman (234-149 B.C.).

MAJOR C. [*Bowing on the hand of Mrs. Montague.*] Madam, I tender *never ending duty!* my elevation shall be marked by *filial affection!*

MRS. M. Harry, no words can speak the strong sensations which mingle in my bosom!

MAJOR C. Sister, [*to Harriot*] *thou art now* every thing a fond transported *brother* can desire.

HARRIOT. I glory in my *brother,* Sir.

STANH. *A good musical discovery this!* and may I never dance at Alberto's wedding, if I do not think it is best to strike while the iron is hot. [*Aside.*] My son, neighbour, has, I assure you, a very warm heart for Miss Harriot; and I cannot but hope that you will not stand in the way of the young people.

RAMB. It shall be my care to break no tender ties, Sir; if he wins my daughter's love, he shall have my approbation.

ALBERTO. To gain that blissful summit, my most arduous efforts shall not be wanting.

MAJOR C. [*introducing Emily Lovegrove.*] Your beauteous niece, Miss Lovegrove, Sir, to whose superior virtues your son would fain do justice.

RAMB. [*taking the hand of Emily.*] I understand you, Harry; but what says our daughter Emily?

EMILY. That while she blesses Heaven for your return, she marks, with glowing admiration, your brave heroic son.

RAMB. Well said, my good girl! I congratulate you, Harry! a father's approbation shall not be wanting to crown the wishes of his children.

MAJOR C. [*bowing impassioned on the hand of Emily.*] Now I am truly blest!

HARRIOT. [*addressing her mother.*] How is my dear and tender mother?

MRS. M. Ah! my daughter, I shudder at the precipice on which I stood! Had the marriage, I so ardently desired, taken place!—Why, my Edward, our children have been on the point of exchanging the nuptial vow!—a brother and a sister wedded!! How wide the evils, which, but for interposing Heaven, my fatal indiscretion might have originated!

RAMB. Forget them, dear Louisa, and hail thy opening prospects! Now

Rambleton no more—thy Edward Montague—*thy Traveller Returned,* wedded to love and thee.

MRS. M. My enraptured spirit lowly prostrates to Edward, and to Heaven.

HARRIOT. This evening, Sir, we had devoted to a private party—lovers of mirth, who dance away the hours—girls, like thy Harriot, and her chosen friends—e'en now they grace the ball-room, glad at thy return; and, sure convivial joys should mark this happy era!

RAMB. Thank you, sweet cherub! quick bid the dancers enter.

Music plays—Scene draws and discovers the company, which immediately join in the dance, after which the curtain drops.

END OF THE COMEDY.

STORY OF MARGARETTA

The *Story of Margaretta* was published serially in *The Gleaner,* though not in consecutive issues. For the sake of clarity, chapters have been numbered consecutively, and the original *Gleaner* numbers have been indicated in footnotes.

CHAPTER 1

Whether o'er meadows, or through groves I stray.
Industry points her broad directing ray;
With care I glean, e'en in the well trod field.
The scatter'd fragments it perchance may yield.

To the Editors of the Massachusetts Magazine I make my best *congee,*[1]
and without any further prefatory address, I shall, in future, produce
my piece-meal commodities, fresh as I may happen to collect them.

Bless me! cried Margaretta, while, in the hope of meeting something
from the pen of Philenia,[2] she threw her fine eyes in a cursory manner
over the index to the February Magazine. But pray, it may be asked,
who is Margaretta? Curiosity is, without doubt, a useful if not a laudable propensity; and, if it is the parent of many evils, it is but fair to
acknowledge, that it hath also among its numerous sons and daughters
some extremely well favoured children. Curiosity hath given birth to
the most arduous pursuits; its achievements have been of the greatest
utility; and without this stimulus we should have great reason to fear an
universal stagnation in every branch of knowledge. Moreover, this same
curiosity consorts, at this present, very exactly with my feelings; for the
question—Pray, who is Margaretta? involves a subject upon which I
expatiate with infinite satisfaction, and upon which I have never yet lost
an opportunity of being loquaciously communicative.

At the close of the late war, when I was an idle young fellow, fond of
indulging myself in every luxury which the small patrimony that
descended to me from a very worthy father, would permit, I conceived
an invincible desire of becoming a spectator of the felicity which I

Chapter 1. Published in *The Gleaner,* 1:2.

1. **congee:** congée; a ceremonious bow (French).

2. **Philenia:** pen name of Sarah Wentworth Morton (1759–1846), American poet and prose
writer.

imagined the inhabitants of South-Carolina, particularly the suffering metropolis of that State, would experience on their emancipation from a succession of evils, which, for a period of seven years, had continued to occupy their minds, giving them to taste deeply of every calamity consequent upon a war, conducted in that part of our country with almost unparalleled barbarity. I had early connected myself in the bands of wedlock with a young woman of a mild and conceding disposition, who sincerely loved me, and who, accommodating herself even to my caprices, hath made it the study of her life, when she could not convince my judgment, however rational her arguments in her own estimation, to bend to my purposes her most approved wishes.

When I announced my intention of visiting South-Carolina, she could not forbear suggesting some economical ideas; but upon a declaration that I was determined to execute my plan, she submitted with that kind of acquiescence, which our sex is so fond of considering as the proper characteristic of womanhood. For a progress then of many hundred miles, in a one horse chaise, we commenced our journey; we intended to pass on by easy stages; and, moreover, we were accompanied by one of the patriotic exiled citizens of Charleston, with whom, during a struggle which associated the remotest subjects of the union, we had contracted an intimate acquaintance. The kindness of this gentleman, who was well mounted, serving us as a relay, we proceeded expeditiously enough, and I do not remember that I ever in my life passed my time more agreeably. Many scenes novel and interesting, prospects extensive, and views truly picturesque, arrested our attention; and were I not hasting to give a solution to the reader's question, I might perhaps amuse him very tolerably, in the descriptive line, through two or three pages close printing; but in a course of publications, I may possibly again recur to exhibitions which pleased me so highly at the time, when I may be more at leisure to *glean* whatever flower recollection may furnish.

On our arrival in Charleston we found our most sanguine expectations answered; the joy of the liberated citizens was unbounded—it was beyond description; nor can I give a better idea of their satisfaction than by pronouncing it in exact proportion to, and fully commensurate with, their preceding sufferings. Our companion, however, was, by the same unwarrantable measures which had wrecked many a princely fortune, stripped of his whole inheritance; so that being entire strangers in Charleston, we were necessitated to provide ourselves with hired lodgings.

Our landlady was a widow of reputation, whose house was frequented only by people of the utmost circumspection. The second day after our arrival, as the good woman was pouring the tea, which we had chosen for breakfast, a gentle tap at the door drew our attention. My wife, who is in fact the pink of civility, was mechanically rising to open it, when she was prevented by our hostess, who cried, Sit down, Madam, it is nobody but the child. My dear Mary, who is extravagantly fond of children, catching at the sound, eagerly replied, "Then, Madam, you have a young family." "No, Madam," returned the hostess, "it is long since my young folks have been grown up about me; but this little creature belongs to an unfortunate lodger of mine, who is continually weeping over her, and who I am afraid will not long be an inhabitant of this bad world; indeed I suppose her present errand is occasioned by some new distress of her mother's, for the pretty thing is wonderfully sensible for such a mere baby." My poor wife, in whose composition humanity is the paramount ingredient, instantly found her benevolence engaged; all her tender feelings took the alarm; and, precipitately quitting her chair, in a tremulous voice she exclaimed, "Pray, Madam, neglect not the unfortunate sick person for us; I can fill the tea, and I beseech you to admit the little petitioner." The good woman, pronouncing a panegyric upon the tenderness of my wife's disposition, forthwith threw open the door, when a little female, apparently about ten years of age, presented herself; she was beautiful as innocence, and her figure was of that kind, which seems formed to interest every benign principle of the soul; which is calculated to invigorate, even in the bosom of the most phlegmatic, the latent sparks of pity, although nearly smothered there.

"Oh Mrs. Thrifty!" exclaimed the heart affecting pleader, "will you not come to my mamma? will you not give her some more of them blessed drops which yesterday made her so much better? she is—indeed she is"—Here, casting her eyes toward us, whom her concern had before prevented her from seeing, and who were regarding her with a mixture of pity and admiration, a modest blush tinged her cheek, which, even at that early age, had been too often washed by the tear of sorrow; and, bursting into an agony of grief, she remained silent. "Go on, Margaretta, said Mrs. Thrifty; let us know what new complaint you have to make; this gentleman and lady are very good, and will excuse you." Mary took the hand of the weeping cherub, and drawing her to her, imprinted upon her humid cheek one of those balmy kisses which she is always ready to bestow upon the young proficient, thus early enlisted under the banners of misfortune. "Mrs. Thrifty says right, my dear, every body will love and pity you; tell us, how is your mamma?" The child, hanging upon the arm of my wife, expressed by her intelligent eyes a thousand mingling sensations; surprise, love, gratitude, and a corrected kind of joy, seemed to grow at once in her soul; and, bowing upon the hand of Mary in a perturbed manner, she spontaneously expressed the involuntary emotions of her bosom: "Oh my dear lady; will you not see my mamma? certainly you can make her well, and she is indeed very sick; I thought this morning she would speak to me no more—she looked so pale—and was so long before she bid me repeat my morning hymn: Oh if my poor mamma should die—I cannot—indeed I cannot stay here."

Mary, it will not be doubted, bent her utmost efforts to soothe the sweet mourner. But not to dwell longer upon a subject, on which it will perhaps be thought I have already too much enlarged, it shall suffice to say, that, through the good offices of her little friend, Mary soon procured an introduction into the chamber of the sick—that, feelings, which at first originated in compassion for the charming child, meliorated into a sympathetic kind of amity—and that, for the course of one week, she passed a very large proportion of her time in endeavouring to mitigate the calamities of the suffering matron. Her assiduities, however, were not crowned with the salutary effects she wished; the patient, it was but too apparent, was hastening on to the hour of her dissolution; her disorder was a regular decline; the shafts of a deep-rooted and incurable grief, must, of necessity, be unerring; and it was evident, that in the bosom of the fair afflicted, corroding sorrow had infixed its envenomed tooth. My wife often recommended a resignation to, and reliance on, the dispositions of a paternal God; but the dying woman shook her head, and continued her pity moving sighs: And about ten days after our abode at Mrs. Thrifty's, the poor lady recovering from a fainting fit, during which it was supposed she had breathed her last, summoned us into her apartment, and, consigning Margaretta to the care of Mrs. Thrifty, she thus addressed us:—

"You see before you, my friends—for friends, short as is the interval in which I have known you, a number of concurring circumstances evinces you, in the most exalted sense of the term, to be; but you are uniformly, I doubt not, the friends of the unfortunate, and the Searcher of all hearts knows that my claim to your regards in this character is indubitable. You see before you, I say, a very distressed woman; for the sake of the child who is just gone from me, I will briefly recount to you the outlines, if I may so express myself, of my life. She is not, as she supposes, my daughter—I never was a mother—I was the eldest of two sisters, who saw ourselves reduced from affluence to penury; we were orphans, and we were, by the rapacious hand of unexampled fraud, despoiled of our patrimony; our mutual affection, however, survived; and, upon the altar which our misfortunes had erected, we exchanged vows of eternal amity. To a small town in the environs of London we retired, endeavouring to shelter our defenceless heads, and to seek from honest industry, that support, of which, by faithless trustees, we had been robbed.

"My sister was addressed by a young man, whom I conceived altogether unworthy of her; for the pride of my heart was yet unsubdued; she, however, notwithstanding all my remonstrances, persisted in encouraging the pursuit of young Melworth; while, so rooted was my aversion, so impassioned my declarations, and so unyielding the anger which deformed my soul, that I rashly protested, the hour which made them one, should fix between us an everlasting bar, and that I would on no account, after such an event, hold with her the smallest intercourse. Their marriage nevertheless took place, and to my sister's entreaties for a restoration of our former amities, my obdurate heart continued insensible.

"About this time, Captain Arbuthnot made his appearance in our village; a tender friendship grew between us; it meliorated into love, and he, in some sort, supplied to me the place of my lost sister: Hymen[1] sanctified our union, and I esteemed myself the happiest of women.

"Of my sister, I knew but little; common fame indeed informed me, that she was satisfied with her connexion, that her circumstances were easy, that she had given birth to one daughter, and with this intelligence I was well enough contented. It is true, I was, by private whispers, assured that she pined after a reconciliation, and that she had often been heard to say, that a renewal of our once warm and glowing attachment, was the only remaining requisite which was yet wanting to complete her felicity. Still, however, I was unmoved; and I verily believed that every tender sentiment, in regard to my sister, was eradicated from my bosom. It was at this juncture that I accompanied Captain Arbuthnot in a journey of some months; and on my return, being upon a visit, among other occurrences which were retailed to me, I learned that Mr. Melworth, having engaged on board a ship which had foundered at sea, every life had been lost; and that Mrs. Melworth, whose health was before in a declining state, was fast sinking under this calamitous event. The feelings of nature, were now, as by a shock of electricity, instantly roused. Unspeakable was the agony of my soul! with the utmost speed I hasted to her abode; but alas! I was only in time to receive her last sighs! the dart which my unkindness had aimed at her peace, urged by a stroke so fatal, deeply transfixed her spirit, and she was absolutely expiring a martyr to the severity of her fate. Yet, ere she breathed her last, she bequeathed her little Margaretta to my care. The sweet infant, then only two years old, intuitively, as it should seem, threw her arms about my neck; while in the presence of Heaven, and in the hearing of her departing mother, I solemnly swore never to forsake her; and, since that hour, to shelter, to soothe, to restrain, and to direct my lovely charge, hath been the prime object of my life; but, yet a little while, and I shall be here no more. Oh thou sainted shade of my much wronged Margaretta! may my death, so similar to thy own, expiate my injustice to thee, thou first, most indulgent, and mildest of women.

---

1. **Hymen:** in Greek mythology, the god of marriage.

"In one of the regiments stationed in Ireland, and in the year eighty-one ordered to America, Captain Arbuthnot had a command; he was now my only friend, and with my little orphan, who imagined us her real parents, I resolved to follow his fortunes. We had been induced to suppose that ease and affluence awaited us here; that the country was subdued, and that nothing remained for us but to take possession of the forfeited lands; but we have been miserably deceived. Landing in this city, upon the third of June, as early as the seventh of the same month, the troops marched under the command of Lord Rawdon,[1] encountering inconceivable difficulties, in a rapid progress beneath the intense rays of a burning sun, through the whole extent of the State. My unfortunate husband fell a victim to the climate, and to the wounds which he received in the engagement, which took place near Shubrick's plantation. Need the rest be told?—Upon the evacuation of Charleston, I was unable to embark with the troops. For my little Margaretta, my last sigh will be breathed; it is for her, as I said, my humane friends, that I have thus long detained you. By the injuries of which they complain, the benevolent feelings of the inhabitants of this city are blunted—what can I do? strangers as you are, I solicit your advice—was she but provided for, my passage out of time would be easy; for, with regard to myself, I know no prospect so pleasing, as a speedy reunion with my Henry and my much injured sister." Mary cast upon me her intelligent eyes; I understood the reference, and I hastily replied, If, Madam, your confidence in us is sufficient to calm your mind, you may make yourself entirely easy about your girl; for, from this moment, we jointly invest ourselves with the guardianship of the little orphan, and we promise to consider her as the child of our affection. This was enough; the matron yielded up her spirit without a remaining regret; and, after assisting at her obsequies, we returned home, well pleased with our new acquisition.

---

1. **Lord Rawdon:** Lord Francis Rawdon, Marquis of Hastings (1754–1826), general who fought at the Battle of Bunker Hill (1775) and led Rawdon's Volunteers of Ireland at Camden, South Carolina, where the British defeated the Americans in 1781.

CHAPTER 2

Then smoothly spreads the retrospective scene,
When no gigantic errors intervene.

No, I think not—relative to Margaretta, we have no capital errors to deplore; from the hour which consigned to the narrow house the remains of Mrs. Arbuthnot, she hath continued to progress in our affections, endearing herself to us by every act of duty, and having laid her in our bosom, she hath become unto us indeed a daughter. Heaven hath denied us children; but we regret not that circumstance, while this amiable female lives to prop, to soothe, and to slope our passage through the journey of life. Having packed up her little moveables, the most valuable of which was a miniature of her mother, put into her hands by her aunt (whose degree of affinity she hath since understood) just before she expired, we quitted the capital of South-Carolina. I took a place for myself in the stage; and Mary, accommodating herself to the movements of that vehicle, came on with the child. Mary hath the peculiar talent of stealing from the unfortunate their sharpest sorrows; moments of the keenest anguish she can sometimes beguile; and by her address she hath not seldom extracted from the wounded bosom the lacerating shaft. To soothe and to support the little Margaretta, who was at first overwhelmed with grief, she bent her utmost efforts; and as the minds of children, at that early and interesting age, are commonly very susceptible, and easily impressed, she succeeded wonderfully well; while the little creature, assured and comforted, before we had reached the northern extremity of the middle States, with her heart as light as the gossamer, prattled away most delightfully.

When we returned home, we fitted up a little chamber, of which we constituted Margaretta the sole proprietor; my wife informing her that she should establish a post betwixt her apartment and her own, that if they chose, upon any occasion, to separate, they might with the greater convenience open a correspondence by letter. The rudiments of Margaretta's education had been attended to; in her plain work she had made

Chapter 2. Published in *The Gleaner*, 1:7.

considerable proficiency; she could read the seventh, tenth, eleventh and twelfth chapters of Nehemiah, without much difficulty; and when her aunt was taken ill, she was on the point of being put into joining-hand; but Mary very soon sketched out for our charge rather an extensive plan of education; and as I was not entirely convinced of the inutility of her views, the natural indolence of my temper induced me to let the matter pass, without entering my caveat by way of stopping proceedings; and indeed, I think the propriety of circumscribing the education of a female, within such narrow bounds as are frequently assigned, is at least problematical. A celebrated writer, I really forget who, hath penned upon this subject a number of self-evident truths; and it is an incontrovertible fact, that to the matron is entrusted not only the care of her daughter, but also the forming the first and oftentimes the most important movements of that mind, which is to inform the future man; the early dawnings of reason she is appointed to watch, and from her are received the most indelible impressions of his life. Now, was she properly qualified, how enviable and how dignified would be her employment. The probability is, that the family of children, whom she directed, supposing them to possess common capacities, being once initiated into the flowery paths of science, would seldom stop short of the desired goal. Fine writing, arithmetic, geography, astronomy, music, drawing; and attachment to all these might be formed in infancy; the first principles of the fine arts might be so accommodated, as to constitute the pastime of the child; the seeds of knowledge might be implanted in the tender mind, and even budding there, before the avocations of the father permitted him to combine his efforts. Affection for the sweet preceptress, would originate a strong predilection for instructions, that would with interesting tenderness be given, and that would be made to assume the face of entertainment, and thus the young proficient would be, almost imperceptibly, engaged in those walks, in which an advantageous perseverance might rationally be expected. A mother, who possesseth a competent knowledge of the English and French tongues, and who is properly assiduous about her children, I conceive, will find it little more difficult to teach them to lisp in two languages, than in one; and as the powers of the student advanceth, certain portions of the day may be regularly appropriated to the conversing in that language which is not designed for the common intercourses of life. Letters, in either tongue, to the parent, or fictitious characters, may be alternately written, and thus an elegant knowledge of both may be gradually obtained. Learning, certainly, can never with propriety be esteemed a burthen; and when the mind is judiciously balanced, it renders the possessor not only more valuable, but also more amiable, and more generally useful. Literary acquisitions cannot, unless the faculties of the mind are deranged, be lost; and while the goods of fortune may be whelmed beneath the contingencies of revolving time, intellectual property still remains, and the mental funds can never be exhausted. The accomplished, the liberally accomplished female, if she is destined to move in the line of competency, will be regarded as a pleasing and instructive companion; whatever she does will connect an air of persuasive elevation; wherever she may be adventitiously called, genuine dignity will be the accompaniment of her steps; she will always be attended to with pleasure, and she cannot fail of being distinguished; should she, in her career of life, be arrested by adverse fortune, many resources of relief, of pleasure, and of emolument, open themselves before her; and she is not *necessarily* condemned to laborious efforts, or to the drudgery of that unremitted sameness, which the rotine of the needle presents.

But whatever may be the merits of the course which I am thus *apparently* advocating, without stopping to examine the other side of the question, I proceed to say, that the plan of education adopted for Margaretta was, as I have already hinted, sufficiently extensive, and that Mrs. Vigillius (to address my good wife, in her dignified character of governante, with all possible respect) having instructed her pupil in the grand fundamental points of the philanthropic religion of Jesus, was never easy while any branch of improvement, which could by the most remote construction be deemed feminine, remained unessayed; and I must in justice declare, that the consequence, by producing Margaretta at the age of sixteen, a beautiful and accomplished girl, more than answered her most sanguine expectations.

Of needle work, in its varieties, my wife pronounced her a perfect mistress; her knowledge of the English, and French tongues, was fully adequate to her years, and her manner of reading had, for me, peculiar charms; her hand writing was neat and easy; she was a good accomptant, a tolerable geographer and chronologist; she had skimmed the surface of astronomy and natural philosophy; had made good proficiency in her study of history and the poets; could sketch a landscape; could furnish, from her own fancy, patterns for the muslins which she wrought; could bear her part in a minuet and a cotillion, and was allowed to have an excellent hand upon the piano forte. We once entertained a design of debarring her the indulgence of novels; but those books, being in the hands of every one, we conceived the accomplishment of our wishes in this respect, except we had bred her an absolute recluse, almost impracticable; and Mrs. Vigillius, therefore, thought it best to permit the use of every decent work, causing them to be read in her presence, hoping that she might, by her suggestions and observations, present an antidote to the poison, with which the pen of the novelist is too often fraught. The study of history was pursued, if I may so express myself, systematically: To the page of the historian one hour every day was regularly devoted; a second hour, Mary conversed with her adopted daughter upon the subject which a uniform course of reading had furnished; and a third hour Margaretta was directed to employ, in committing to paper such particular facts, remarks and consequences deduced therefrom, as had, during the hours appropriated to reading, and conversing, most strikingly impressed her mind; and by these means the leading features of history were indelibly imprinted thereon. Mrs. Vigillius also composed little geographical, historical, and chronological catechisms, or dialogues, the nature of which will be easily conceived; and she pronounced them of infinite advantage in the prosecution of her plan; she submitted likewise, at least once every week, to little voluntary absences, when my boy Plato, being constituted courier betwixt the apartments of my wife and daughter, an epistolary correspondence was carried on between them, from which more than one important benefit was derived; the penmanship of our charge was improved; the beautiful and elegant art of letter writing was by degrees acquired; and Margaretta was early accustomed to lay open her heart to her maternal friend.

Persons when holding the pen, generally express themselves more freely than when engaged in conversation; and if they have a perfect confidence in those whom they address, the probability is, that, unbosoming themselves, they will not fail to unveil the inmost recesses of their souls—thus was Margaretta properly and happily habituated to disclose, without a blush, each rising thought to her, on whom the care of preparing her for the great career of life had devolved.

No, Mr. Pedant, she was not unfitted for her proper sphere; and your stomach, however critical it may be, never digested finer puddings than those which I, with an uncommon zest, have partook as knowing they were the composition of her fair hand—yes, in the receipts of cookery she is thoroughly versed; she is in every respect the complete housewife; and our linen never received so fine a gloss as when it was ironed and laid in order by Margaretta. Mrs. Vigillius was early taught the science of economy, and she took care to teach it to her daughter; and being more especially economical of time, she so arrangeth matters as never to appear embarrassed, or in a hurry, having always her hours of leisure, which she appropriates to the contingencies of the day. It is true, she does not engage in visits of mere ceremony, seldom making one of any party, without some view either to her own emolument, or that of those about her; and with regard to dress, she spends but little time in assorting an article which is, it must be confessed, too generally a monopolizer of a blessing, that can hardly be too highly estimated. She doth not think it necessary to have her dishabille[1] for the morning, her robe-de-chambre[2] for noon, and her full trimed polanee or trollope,[3] for the evening. The morning generally, except in cases of any particular emergency, presents her dressed for the day; and as she is always elegant, of course she can never be preposterous, extravagant or gaudy. It will be hardly necessary to add, that Miss Melworth was, and is, her exact copiest; and indeed she is so warmly attached to my dear Mary, that I verily believe it would have been in her power to have initiated her into the

---

1. **dishabille:** déshabillé; literally, undressed (French); here, implying bathrobe.

2. **robe-de-chambre:** dressing gown (French).

3. **polanee or trolopee:** polanée, trolopée; loose dresses (French).

devious paths of error; and this is saying a great deal of a mind which possesseth such innate goodness, as doth that which inhabits the gentle bosom of my Margaretta. Upon the subject of dress, I am naturally reminded of the request of my fanciful correspondent Monimia Castalio, relative to the dress of Margaretta, and particularly the height of her head; and I am happy that I can gratify Miss Monimia Castalio, by recollecting a circumstance, which being in point, may serve as a specimen of the general style of Margaretta's dress. I think she was about fifteen, when Mrs. Vigillius conforming as much as her ideas of propriety would admit, to the then fashion of the times, made for her a hat of white satin. I remember there was a prettily fancied ribbon to it; and it had, I thought, rather a jauntee appearance. Margaretta put it on, and sallied forth to pay a visit to an acquaintance, a Miss Preedy; and the next morning, when seated at the breakfast table, with much hesitation she requested her mamma to purchase for her, as an additional ornament to her hat, some beautiful feathers, which she said were to be disposed of at the very next shop. Mrs. Vigillius, with great calmness, replied, "Yes, my dear, without doubt I can obtain for you the feathers; but I have for some time been endeavouring to accumulate a sum, which I had intended to appropriate for the completion of your little library; and a crown laid out in feathers, will take therefrom at least one handsome and instructive volume; it is true, I have some money now by me, designed for another use—Poor Mrs. Lovemore, over whose misfortunes you have shed so many tears, still swells the sigh of sorrow—he, whose presence would turn her little cottage into a palace, yet remains imprisoned! I have long had it in contemplation to dry the tear of anguish from the cheek of that solitary mourner; and I have anticipated the pleasure I should experience while witnessing the mantling joy, and the dimpling smiles, which would, upon an occasion so happy, pervade the faces of the little beings who owe to her their existence—Genius of sensibility! how extatic would be my emotions, could I be made instrumental in restoring to their embraces the husband and the father! The sum for which Mr. Lovemore is held in durance, is small, and his misfortunes could not by human prudence be either foreseen or prevented. From the late expenditures in our family, I have so far economized, as to have at length made up the requisite sum; and I had thought to have taken a walk this fine morning, in order to liberate the poor man—but you want the feathers, and Lovemore must continue in captivity until I can lay by another crown."

Never shall I forget the expression, the animated expression, which lighted up the countenance of Margaretta; tears of mingling pleasure and delicate apprehension, were upon her cheek; with a kind of duteous eagerness, she seized the hand of Mary, and in a most graceful manner bowing thereon, with a tremulous voice she thus questioned—thus entreated—"And will the sorrows of the poor Mrs. Lovemore know an end? O friend, patroness, protectress, preserver, mother—what shall I say?—Already my obligations to you are infinite—but tell me, dear lady, will you still add thereto—shall I accompany you to the abode of Mrs. Lovemore? I know that you will consent—let us go this instant—I will fly for your cloak, and we will not delay a moment."

It is hardly necessary to add that Margaretta obtained her suit, and I subjoin a declaration, that these kind of feathers are the most beautiful, and the highest plumed, of any she hath ever yet worn in her hat or cap.

But while we have been assiduously employed in cultivating the mind of Margaretta, we have been endeavouring to eradicate the seeds of that over-weening self conceit, which, while it would induce an ostentatious exhibition of those talents, natural, or adventitious, which she may possess—like a rampant weed would impede and overshadow the growth of every virtue. Against pride and affectation we have been careful to guard her, by constantly inculcating one grand truth; a truth, to the conviction of which every ingenuous mind must be ever open. Her person, the symmetry of her features, the rose and lily of her complexion, the *tout ensemble* of her exterior, the harmony of her voice, &c. &c.—these are the endowments of nature—while the artificial accomplishments with which she is invested, resulting wholly from accident, and being altogether independent of her own arrangements, confer upon her no real or intrinsic merit.

We are daily assuring her, that every thing in future depends upon her own exertions, and that her character must be designated by that

consistent decency, that elegant propriety, and that dignified condescension, which are indeed truly estimable. We have apprized her, that
in every stage of her journey through life, she will find friends—or a
social intercourse with the circles in which she may be called to move—
constituting one of her principal enjoyments, and that if she is not eager
for admiration, if she avoids making a display of superior abilities, she
will escape those shafts of envy which will otherwise be too surely aimed
at her peace; and secure to herself the complacent feelings of those with
whom she may be conversant.

Margaretta hath a becoming spirit, and dissimulation is a stranger to
her heart; she is rather cheerful than gay; she never diverts herself with
simplicity and ignorance; *double entendres* she detests; she is not an
adept in the present fashionable mode of playing upon words, and she
never descends to what is called jesting; she can deliver herself upon any
subject, on which she ventures to speak, with great ease; but in large or
mixed companies she engages in conversation with manifest reluctance;
and I have heard her declare, that she hath frequently, when encircled
by strangers, felt alarmed at the sound of her own voice; she never comments upon those blunders which are the result of a neglected education, nor will she lend her smiles to those who are thus employed; and
she observes, that such kind of peccadillos have upon her no other
effect, than to excite in her bosom the sensation of gratitude.

With the laws of custom, or fashion, she is thoroughly acquainted,
and she consents to follow them as far as they square with the dictates of
rectitude; but she never sacrifices to their documents either her humanity, or her convenience; she regards, as extremely venial, an ignorance of
their despotic institutions; (indeed the multifarious requirements of
mere ceremony, strike her in so trifling a point of view, that she conceives it rather a matter of course that they should sometimes be omitted) and she prefers plain manners to all the glitter of a studied or
laboured address.

But it is against the unaccountable freaks of the capricious, that all
the artillery of that humour, of which she possesses a natural fund, is
levelled; frank and ingenuous herself, she laughs at the vagaries of the

whimsical, and her heart is ever upon her lips; she reflects much, and her judgment is fashioned by reason; she cannot be seen without pleasure, nor heard without instruction.

But I am rather describing what Margaretta *is*, than what she *was*, at the period of her history to which we are arrived. Three or four years have matured her talents, presenting the daily improving and promising girl, a truly lovely and accomplished woman, abundantly answering the fondest expectations which were formed of her.

When our beloved charge had completed her sixteenth year, we conceived it full time to introduce her an interesting and beautiful object to a world, of whose deceptions we had been careful to warn her, and for whose intercourse, we flattered ourselves, she was as well qualified as girls at her age generally are.

It was at this period that Mrs. Vigillius, in compliance with the pressing entreaties of a friend in whom she entirely confided, reluctantly consented that Miss Melworth should pass a few weeks in the city of New-Haven.

But it may be proper to refer the opening of a new, and important scene, to a separate essay; and we shall proceed to bring forward the appropriate number, with all possible dispatch.

CHAPTER 3

Important period, when the opening germe
Bursts into life—to each impression warm.

It was a first parting—and it cost a shower of tears on both sides, but avoiding as much as possible scenes which may be better *imagined* than *described*, I proceed in my narration. Margaretta had been absent but two weeks, when the following letter, giving the alarm to our most anxious feelings, was read by Mary and myself, with uncommon perturbation.

Chapter 3. Published in *The Gleaner*, 1:8.

New-Haven, May 10th, 1789.

Ever honoured, and ever dear Friend,

The tear is still wet upon my cheek! yes indeed, and well it may; for I never think upon the morning on which I took my departure from—, but the pearly drops, as my good papa would call them, chase each other down my cheek; the truth is, that since the hour which closed the eyes of my poor aunt, I have never known affliction so severe. Well, but my mamma hath taught me not to dwell upon the dark side of events; and finding an adherence to her precepts my surest path, I wave every thing of a melancholy nature, and proceed to say—that Mrs. Worthington received me with much affection; that she treats me in all respects with the same tender attention which she bestows upon her own daughter, Miss Amelia; and that I do not believe, if I except my own dear mamma, that there is in the whole world a better woman. Col. Worthington, as we were told, is at present absent from home; so that, excepting the domestics, who are decent and obliging people, our family consists only of Mrs. Worthington, Miss Amelia, and myself. I am delighted with New-Haven, with its beautiful plains, its high surrounding mountains, its neat built houses, its ample streets, and the tall trees by which on either hand they are shaded. Yale College, an episcopalian church, and three dissenting meeting houses, are situated contiguous to each other. You know, my mamma, you directed me to write as if you were a stranger to every particular. As I walked over the green, the neighbourhood of these buildings seemed to consecrate the spot, rendering it, as it were, hallowed ground. Yale College is not near so spacious as the description which we received from Edward Hamilton of the seminary in which he was educated; indeed, ever since the evening upon which Edward entertained us so agreeably with an account of Harvard College, I have had a very strong inclination to behold those venerable domes. Many students, however, prosecute their studies here; and I cannot but esteem every young creature happy who hath the disposition, and is presented with the opportunity, of acquiring knowledge. As I have been introduced by Mrs. Worthington as the adopted daughter of Mr. and Mrs. Vigillius, and as the characters of my dear parental friends are so properly revered here, I have received the most marked attentions. If I might be allowed to give an opinion, I would say that the gentlemen of New-Haven appear to me to be friendly, and hospitable, and that the ladies are truly polite. Perhaps I may be permitted to pronounce, that those whom I have seen, answer very exactly to the idea of genuine urbanity, which you, Madam, have taught me to form. Among the many who have most obligingly distinguished me, the limits of a letter will only allow me to mention Mrs. Edwards. Mr. Edwards, you will recollect, Madam, is an eminent barrister; and the person who is permitted to mingle in their social circles, cannot but enjoy a satisfaction of a superior kind.

The ladies of New-Haven are remarkably fond of cultivating flowers; and a disquisition upon the beauties of the parterre[1] makes a part in almost every conversation. Mrs. Edwards counted in her garden at one time, no less than eight hundred tulips all in full blow, among which the various streaks and shades were innumerable. Doubtless I could be very happy in New-Haven, if it was the residence of my papa and mamma, but were it the paradise of the globe, I should sigh for the village of their abode; and the elegant saloon which my mamma devotes to sentimental friendship; the social breakfasting parlour, the ample dining room, the chamber, of which with such unexampled goodness I was constituted sole proprietor, the sweet little flower garden, the smooth gravel walk terminated by the woodbine alcove, &c. &c. these would all live in my idea as the haunts of perfect happiness. Mrs. Worthington insists on my tarrying here until the expiration of the Commencement holidays; but in truth, I am well pleased that my leave of absence extendeth not near so far; and I am glad that my mamma hath fixed precisely the time of my return; for I always feel assured and tranquil when I am entirely under her direction. You will please to assure all my young acquaintance, particularly Serafina and Edward Hamilton, that they are often present to my imagination; that in my dreams I still mix in their little parties; and that it is impossible I should cease to remember them, or to love them very sincerely.

---

1. **parterre:** flower bed (French).

Well, I have written more than two pages, and yet have not executed the purpose I formed when I sat me down to this employ: You have accustomed me, dearest lady, to unbosom myself to you, and though this is my first separation from you, yet the epistolary correspondence, with which I have for such a length of time, though continued under your roof, been indulged, hath given me the habit of expressing myself to you in this way, with the utmost freedom; and as a proof that I will never wear disguises, when addressing her whose care hath rendered life to me a valuable gift, I will confess that I make the following communication with more reluctance than I ever yet, upon any occasion, experienced; but truth shall be my motto, and to my loved patroness I will have no reserves. I had been but one hour in the family of Mrs. Worthington, when a young gentleman, Mr. Sinisterus Courtland, made his appearance in that lady's drawing room; he entered with the air of an established acquaintance, and indeed he stands high in the esteem of Mrs. Worthington; a large party was collected, all of whom he addressed in a manner truly engaging, and upon my being introduced, payed me a compliment in a style so new, so elevated, and so strikingly pleasing, that my heart instantaneously acknowledged an involuntary prepossession in his favour; sensations with which I was till that moment unacquainted, pervaded my bosom; I felt my face in a glow, and a pleasing kind of perturbation took possession of my faculties. My opportunities of seeing Mr. Courtland have been since frequent. Three days afterwards he declared himself my lover; his assiduities are unwearied; he professes to live but in my presence, and he protests that my rejection of him will make him the most miserable of men. Mrs. Worthington assures me, that Mr. Courtland is a gentleman whose addresses no lady need blush to receive; and I will own to you, Madam, that if a few years more had passed over my head, as you have taught me to conceive a union with a man of worth may rationally be the ultimatum of a woman's wishes; I should think I stood a greater chance for happiness with this gentleman, than with any other individual of his sex.

Mr. Courtland is a native of V—— in the State of —— he says he had formerly the honour of an acquaintance with my papa. He is tall and well made, his address is easy, and commanding; the contour of his face is strikingly agreeable; indeed, his whole exteriour is a combination of elegance and dignity, and his manners are confessedly descriptive of the finished gentleman. I am told that he adds to these superficial accomplishments a substantial and cultivated understanding; that he is a man of erudition, and possesseth also, with a general knowledge of books, an extensive acquaintance with the world. On my return, he will present himself before my parental friends. Perhaps they may not approve a connexion so disproportioned in regard to years, Mr. Courtland having numbered full thirty, and I but little better than sixteen. I confess that I feel a degree of culpability while detecting my heart, thus audaciously leaning toward an election, until my honoured benefactors, pointing the finger, had unitedly pronounced, "There, Margaretta, there is your congenial soul; behold the person whom we direct you to regard, as him who is destined the associate of your future life;" but my fault is altogether involuntary, and I pray you, my dear lady, to present to my papa my respectful regards; and to assure him that from his honoured lips, and those of my mamma, must proceed the award which will decide the fate of their ever duteous, ever grateful, ever affectionate

MARGARETTA MELWORTH.

This letter, I say, inflicted upon my bosom the most pungent anxiety. Full well I knew Sinisterus Courtland. I knew him much better (for my personal interviews with him had been but few) than he was apprized of; I knew him to be base, designing, and however incongruous these qualities may seem, improvident also; his father had bred him a gentleman, leaving him only a slender patrimony to support his pretensions, while he was wholly destitute of the means, disposition, or talents, to add thereto; nay, even his small inheritance, without spending a single thought on the future, he had deeply involved, until pressed upon by his creditors, he was finally induced to an effort to extricate himself, by the very *honourable method* of deluding some woman whose expectations were tolerable, into an affair of the heart, the matrimonial termination of which, he considered as an axiom, which was too irrefragable to admit of doubt; he had spent the morning of his life in fluttering from town to town, paying his devoirs[1] to every inconsiderate girl, who, allured by his flattery, and charmed by an exteriour which is indeed unexceptionable, and deceived also by the ease, brilliancy, and eclat[2] of his appearance into a good opinion of his finances, became the dupe of her own vanity, finding her inclinations betrayed, in favour of an impostor, who on his part, possessed not depth of understanding sufficient to render him capable of a serious or lasting impression.

It is scarcely necessary to add a finishing to the character that now presented a formidable candidate for the heart of my girl; and, in addition to the unfavourable light in which I beheld Mr. Courtland, I had long entertained other views for Margaretta, adjusting my plans in such a manner, as I conceived well nigh precluded a disappointment: I was sensible, that as I had no near relation of my own, it was generally supposed Miss Melworth would be my heir, and I shuddered at the idea of the little fortune which, with much industry, application and economy, I had accumulated, being squandered by a spendthrift, while my daughter, and her descendants, were left pennyless! For a moment, regarding myself as a shipwrecked voyager, bereaved of every hope, I was ready, yielding the point, to stretch myself upon the barren heaths of despair; but after deliberating the matter, I conceived, that though my fabric tottered, it was not absolutely whelmed; and though I was aware that, manured by the prejudices prepared in the hot-bed of novel reading, the impressions made upon young minds, with the passions implanted in the tender soil, were not easily erased, or up-rooted; yet I conceived that the task, however arduous, was not altogether impracticable; and while apprized that the business in which I was about to engage required in the management thereof the utmost delicacy, I concluded, nevertheless, that an object so desirable, was at least worth any attempt to obtain it. Thus having made up my mind, Mary, who was

---

1. **devoirs:** respect (colloquial French).
2. **eclat:** éclat; brightness, splendor (French).

hand in glove with me, began our operations, by responding to the letter of Margaretta, in the subjoined manner.

Village of ——, County of ——, May 16, 1789.
I persuade myself, my dear Margaretta, that it would at this time be wholly superfluous to express to you the very high satisfaction which both your father and myself mutually experience, at that unfeigned complacency in your situation, which you take every opportunity so gratefully to avow. Once for all, my dear girl, you may assure yourself that your affectionate regards are abundantly reciprocated; that we have no idea of a warmer attachment than we have conceived for you; and, that if the hearts of natural parents beat with ardours stronger than those which expand our bosoms, they must border so nearly upon anguish, that we are not ambitious of being able, experimentally to ascertain the difference; neither shall I, at this time, expatiate upon the merit of your letter—my opinion of your epistolary talents, you already know, though perhaps I should not so easily deny myself a repetition of those fond expressions of admiration, to which I am accustomed, and which, possibly, in some degree originate in the predilection which my maternal feelings hath induced—were it not that the important communication you have forwarded to us, absorbs in my soul every consideration of less weight.

I hardly know where to begin, or how to express to you the anxiety to which you have given birth in our bosoms. Is it possible, that my Margaretta can *love* where she cannot *entirely esteem!* and can she have so far forgot the lessons of her youth, as *entirely to esteem* Mr. Courtland! What is the conduct of a man of honour in so delicate a conjuncture as you delineate? doth he wait till he hath, as he supposes, irrevocably fixed himself in the heart of a young woman, before he deigns to apprize those whose nights and days have been spent in watching for her welfare? Certainly not—but immediately after his proposals have been made to her, who I grant is the person principally concerned, if he can discern the smallest appearance of success, (and men are eagle eyed upon these occasions) he will solicit the sanction of her guardian friends, that he may either avail himself of them as auxiliaries in his pursuit; or, if necessary, set about conquering a passion which cannot be consecrated by duty—reverse the picture, and the man of duplicity stands confest; he will steal into the confidence of the unsuspecting virgin, obtaining what he conceives an unalterable and undivided ascendancy over her mind, and then, *merely as a compliment*, the parents are made acquainted with the business, who, if they presume to enter their caveat, however improper the connexion may in fact be, are accused of tyranny, barbarity, and what not.

Thus Mr. Courtland—the post passes by our door, but he hath not condescended to pen for us a single line, which might inform us of his enterprize. Doubtless his intention is to assail your passions during the whole period of your purposed visit, when deeming the matter irremediable, he will make us a genteel bow, and *insult* us by requesting our advice! But from you, my dear child, we expect a decision more upright—you have deviated, it is true, but you have as yet taken but one step, and we doubt not that you will very speedily recover the path of discretion. You see that our objection to Mr. Courtland is not altogether on account of his years, though this of itself is in our opinion insuperable; at present, sixteen and thirty may move in the same sphere; but pass a few years, and we may almost trace their orbits in opposite hemispheres; *seventy is the age of man*—while fifty-six may enjoy the utmost vigour of mental and corporeal powers—indeed, if *similarity of dispositions, sentiments and attachments are requisite to constitute matrimonial felicity, surely an equality, or nearly an equality of years, ought to be deemed of some importance in the calculation.* I know that to almost every general rule there are exceptions; but yet, nevertheless, I would not give my voice in favour of a gentleman's having more than two or three years at farthest, the advantage over her whom he selected as the partner of his life.

Ask yourself, my dear, what opportunity have you had of becoming acquainted with the views, habits, or temper of Mr. Courtland; and yet, although, when your letter was written, only *ten days* from the moment of your introduction to him had elapsed, you *seriously pronounced him*

the individual, who of all his sex was the most capable of making you happy!
Such is the natural good sense of my Margaretta, that I assure myself I
need not comment upon this declaration.

I am rather surprised at the part which my friend Mrs. Worthington
hath taken in this affair; surely, in this instance, she hath been misled by
the goodness of her own heart. Mr. Courtland is only a visitor in New-
Haven; the place of his nativity and usual residence is at a great distance; and she can only know in general that he is a man of family and
education. But in truth, I myself have been wrong; I ought not to have
parted with my Margaretta. Yet, while I palliate my fault, by a declaration that I conceived her extreme youth would have protected her from
overtures so important; I trust, that the tears which I have shed upon
this occasion, will expiate it.

Yes, my love, your father knows Mr. Courtland—*he knows him well;*
and without further investigating the character of that gentleman, he
bids me tell you, that he hath long entertained views of establishing you
in our own neighbourhood. Edward Hamilton—start not, my dear, at a
name, which in the innocence of your heart you have a thousand times
declared you loved—hath now completed his nineteenth year; he bids
fair to be every thing which a fond father could wish for the man, to
whom he yielded the beloved daughter of his affections; his character is
bottomed upon integrity; he is every way accomplished; his prospects
are good; his knowledge of the profession of his election, indeed his
extensive acquaintance with mercantile affairs, is, for his years, prodigious; with regard to his exteriour and address, if we allow for the charm
of novelty, he might rival even a Courtland; and I declare I know not
the youth who can equal him for gentility of mein, and beauty of person. But these are attractions, simply considered, to which the heart of
my Margaretta, when she suffers herself calmly to reflect, will, I am persuaded, ever remain inpregnable. Before the death of your reverend
friend, old Mr. Hamilton, the plan of uniting our children, supposing
their hearts were not reluctant, was adjusted. The good gentleman
regarded his son as almost an affianced lover; otherwise I imagine he
would not have left his ward, the beautiful and accomplished Serafina,
situated as she is in regard to Edward; who, however unblemished his

character may be, is nevertheless, as a young man, a very ill-judged guardian for a young and unconnected woman. Hitherto, being desirous of leaving you wholly unrestrained, we have kept our secret close locked in our own bosoms; and until the receipt of your letter, we have beheld with pleasure the gradual advancement of our wishes. For Edward, he is wholly devoted to you, and while hardly conscious of the motives by which he is actuated, he is assiduous in every thing which relates to you; even trifles are invested with importance, if they are inscribed with your name—if you are unexpectedly mentioned, his whole frame is visibly agitated, his complexion assumes a more animated glow, his voice is mellowed into an unusual softness, and his tongue is never tired in rehearsing your praises; but, fear not my girl—if we cannot convince your judgment, and woo your best affections, you shall never be the wife of Hamilton.

Your interest and happiness is the sole motive of our actions; it is the pole star[1] by which all our movements are directed, and if we can but see you pleasingly established, and in possession of tranquillity, we shall lay us down in perfect peace. We regard the unfolding our plan to you at this time, as premature, and we *feelingly* regret that our measures are thus unfortunately precipitated. We have not yet disclosed ourselves to Edward; we are not in favour of early marriages; and though the laws of Heaven and of good citizenship, have ordained the sexes for each other, yet we think that years are requisite to ripen the judgment, and to ascertain the choice, which a young person may have every reason to suppose immutably fixed. We have conceived, that a female who takes a step so important, at the age of twenty-three, or upwards, hath lost no time; and it was only in compliance with the dying request of Mr. Hamilton, that we consented, supposing our young people should be propitious, that you should, at the period when you shall have completed your nineteenth year, exchange your vows with his deserving son.

But, waving these matters for the present, I have to say, that your father, after presenting you his paternal regards and blessing, directs me to inform you, that business will soon call him to New-Haven, and

---

1. **pole star:** directing principle.

that, if curtailing your visit, you can find it agreeable to return home with him, you will confer on him a very high obligation; in this request, my dear, I, for my part, most sincerely join; and, if your wishes meet mine, you will please to express to Mrs. Worthington, my thanks for her indulgence to you—to offer her my respects, and to acquaint her, that, sickening for the dear child of my love, I can no longer deny myself the gratification of her society. Present my compliments to Miss Amelia, who, I trust, we shall soon see at our village; and think of me at all times as your truly affectionate and tender mother.

Mary Vigillius.

CHAPTER 4

Low should they bend at sovereign Wisdom's throne,
Who are ambitious of that fair renown,
Which wreathes with honour the parental brow,
And wings with fervour every tender vow.

It will not be doubted but the urgency of my affairs, very soon made my New-Haven expedition a matter of necessity; nor will it, I presume, be regarded as problematical, that Miss Melworth, with duteous acquiescence, became the companion of my return. But alas! that cheerfulness, which had so long presided in her bosom, had taken its flight; and though joy gladdened in her countenance at the entrance of our village, and at the appearance of our habitation; though she seemed, while clasped in the arms of Mary, to be lost in extacy—yet, upon her lovely countenance the cloud again gathered; her eye beamed a melancholy languor; the rose upon her cheek visibly gave place to the lily of her complexion, and we were well nigh distracted by the gloomy forebodings which her altered figure originated in our souls. We had concerted our plan, the ultimatum of which was her felicity; and we were determined, if we could not bend her to our wishes, to follow her through all the vicissitudes her unfortunate preference might involve, with every alleviation which we could furnish. We contemplated the yielding her to the youth we loved, with her full and deliberate choice. Nothing short of this would satisfy our affection, or restore to us the entire possession of that peace, which the late event had invaded; yet we abhorred constraint, and we regarded persuasion, considering the tender and conceding mildness of that heart which was almost in our hands, as no better than a specious kind of tyranny. But being infidels in regard to the doctrine which extends the empire of *genuine love, in any virtuous bosom, beyond the existence or agency of esteem*, we doubted not, if we could erase from the breast of our orphan, those high ideas she had conceived of the merit of her lover, the *belle passion* would very speedily evaporate. Our business then being to convince the judgment, while we assured ourselves, if this was possible, the consequences we wished would inevitably follow, against a confidence which we conceived so highly misplaced, the whole force of our artillery was, of course, levelled. Having, however, so great a stake, it became us to deliberate much, to be very cautious in our movements; a precipitate step might ruin our measures, and it was our aim to be guarded at all points. Courtland very soon made his appearance in our village, we extended to him the rights of hospitality; and, as an admirer of Miss Melworth's, we gave him every decent opportunity of advocating his cause. To this mode of procedure we were impelled by the following considerations: Should we refuse, to this pretender, that uniform civility, with which we have distinguished every stranger, the wound thereby given to the feelings of Margaretta, might very possibly add to the strength of her attachment; and the idea of his suffering upon her account, interesting her gratitude, would still more have endeared him to her; while, in the inmost recesses of her soul, accusing us of injustice, she would syllogistically have concluded, that error in one particular involved a possibility of mistake in another. And it would, in truth, have been in a very high degree absurd, to have denied his claim to common attentions, merely because he had eyes for the charms of a person, whom our partiality induced us to think, had merit sufficient to captivate every beholder. In this arrangement we also made ourselves witnesses of every movement, precluding all necessity for, and possibility of, clandestine views; and we conceived, besides, that as Miss Melworth possessed a penetration far beyond her years, frequent interviews with *Sinisterus Courtland* would infallibly develope to her understanding his true character, effectually destroying that mask under which he had continued to betray the unwary; and we well knew, that could *she herself* make the discovery we wished, such an event would operate more propitiously than any information, however important, which might be handed her from any other quarter. Perhaps it may be matter of surprise, that being myself in possession of such material documents, I did not come to an immediate explanation, thus adjusting the business agreeably to my own designation. But though, as I apprehend, the preceding remark anticipates this observation, I have yet to say, I was aware of the subterfuges to which bad men often have recourse: Had I declared my knowledge of what I termed Courtland's enormities, it would have been easy for him to have availed himself of the plea of youth and inexperience, of a change of system, reformation, present regularity, &c. &c. and, for his poverty, it was an objection which the ardour of young affection would not only find a *laudable generosity* in palliating, but it would, with glowing zeal, assay to enlist against so *mercenary* and *unworthy* a consideration, the most virtuous propensities of the soul. I knew that to erase impressions, made upon the youthful bosom, violent efforts must generally be inadequate; that they would much more frequently lacerate, than obliterate; and I was not willing to leave in the bosom of Margaretta the smallest scar. I had not forgotten the integrity and the ingenuity which characterizes the morning of life; and I remembered also, that the enthusiasm of an early love, is fruitful in its vindications of the object of its preference; and that it is ready to accuse every objector as prejudiced and unjust. Taking the matter up in this view, we thought best to await some fortunate crisis, holding the *unquestionable facts* of which we were possessed, relative to Courtland, as our *dernier resource*.

Mean time, we descended not to disguises: Upon the application of that gentleman, we informed him of our prior engagement to young Hamilton's father; of our wishes for the success of the projected union; of our determination to take every proper step, which we should deem likely to propitiate the mind of Margaretta, respecting an event which we regarded in so eligible a view; and we grounded our objections to him on the disparity of years, the short date of his acquaintance with Miss Melworth, and the distance of his residence; nevertheless, we added, that if we had the power, even of natural parents, over the final decision of that young lady, we should not hold ourselves authorized to direct her any further than reason pointed; and that we left him at full liberty to prosecute his suit with what advantage he might, only promising, that we should not consent to dispose of Miss Melworth, even to Hamilton himself, until she had completely rounded her nineteenth year. Courtland, upon this assurance, reddened excessively; he had hoped *his happiness might have been much sooner accelerated, and some very pressing circumstances, relative to him, demanded a very early establishment.* Our determination upon this head continued, however, unalterable; while our espousing, as we apparently did, the interests of Hamilton, occasioned in the bosom of our daughter such a struggle between inclination and duty, as still looked with a very serious and unfriendly aspect upon her health. Upon our grand subject, both Mary and myself held with her many conversations, which, I am vain enough to imagine, might be useful to young persons thus circumstanced, and which, did not the limits prescribed to a writer for the Magazine, set bounds to my encroachments, should most certainly be recounted; but should they be demanded, as they were immediately committed to paper, future Gleaners shall certainly record them. One sentiment, however, which dropped from the mouth of Mary, which I accidentally overheard, and which was perfectly new to me, I cannot excuse myself from giving. She was, one fine afternoon, while seated with Margaretta in the arbour to which they were both so much attached, endeavouring, in a manner peculiar to herself, to sooth the feelings of her daughter; thus encouraging her to lay open her whole soul, that she might, from such confidence, the better judge of the nature of the remedy she was to apply; when Miss Melworth, sensibly regretting that she was so unfortunately situated, as to feel a disposition to act contrary to the wishes of her best friends; by turns lamenting and accusing the treachery of a heart which had thus betrayed her, concluded a very tender harangue, by a declaration, that though Hamilton was every thing amiable, yet she was certain she could never feel for him that preference which she did for Courtland; she could never regard him in any other view than that of a brother. "Will you, my sweet girl," replied Mary, "*re-consider* this affirmation? you are fond of reasoning, you know; and trust me, my dear, when I assure you, that an attachment which embraceth not reason as its auxiliary, is not worth cherishing. You own that Hamilton is every thing amiable; but you can only love him as a brother! you pretend not to point out a single virtue, a single accomplishment, a single grace, in which Courtland can claim a superiority over Hamilton; yet you can only love Hamilton as a brother, while you love Courtland as— as what, my dear? Will you, Margaretta, please to point out the distinction between those attachments which you feel for the one and the other? You blush, my love; let me kiss off that conscious tear—Say, my charming reasoner, would these over nice distinctions, for which you cannot find a name, ever have found entrance into the bosom of a virtuous girl, were it not for that false taste which is formed by novel reading? What is this something which you feel for Courtland, and which you cannot feel for Hamilton? Certainly it is, at best, but the fever of the imagination, the delirium of fancy; and every experienced votary of this *ignis fatuus,*[1] if under the direction of truth, will tell you, that the duration of the paroxism is extremely short, that the sober and healthy age of reason awaits, when love and friendship wear the same face, when only solid advantages can please; and, they will add, that no well informed person would sacrifice to the illusion of a moment, the happiness of a life. Did you never, my dear, reflect upon the connexions which must have been formed by the immediate descendants of the pair who were created in Paradise? brothers then interchanged the nuptial vow with sisters; they were unacquainted with the refinements of modern times; the virtues which endeared the brother, rendered the husband amiable; and we have no authority for supposing, that their matrimonial felicity was more circumscribed than that of their posterity. It is true, that the multiplication of our species have rendered other regulations, relative to the marriage contract, or the parties contracting,

---

1. **ignis fatuus:** literally, foolish fire (Latin); a deceptive goal or desire.

both necessary and proper; and it is undoubtedly true, that an observation of these regulations, is religiously obligatory; but yet, in my opinion, the absurdity of holding a character in great estimation, and highly
accomplished, as a brother, which we should at the same time regard
with reluctance as a conjugal companion, is still palpable; and I must
repeat, that the prevalency of such romantic ideas can originate only in
the regions of fancy." Thus far my honest woman. But Margaretta, in a
letter to Miss Worthington, which lately came under my observation,
hath best described her own sensations; I subjoin it therefore, *verbatim*,
as it flowed from as susceptible and upright a heart, as ever beat in the
bosom of humanity.

Miss MELWORTH to Miss WORTHINGTON.

Village of ——, June 30th, 1789.
I am, my dear Miss Worthington, highly pleased, that my account of
my reception in—I had almost said, my native village—hath been productive to you, of even a momentary satisfaction; and I do assure you
that I am not a little elated, when I am told, your honoured mother
pronounces my description replete with some of the most beautiful
traits of nature: I know, that to her partiality and candour, I ought to
impute much; but, by the commendation of so respectable a judge, I
am nevertheless exhilarated, and I am almost induced to think it allow-
able, to plume myself upon an award so honorary. You will please to
offer to the dear lady my acknowledgments, accompanied by my most
respectful regards.

You ask me if I have recovered my tranquillity; alas, no! and I fear,
my Amelia, that peace hath fled forever from my bosom. Mr. Courtland, as you suppose, is here; would I had never seen him—I might
then have been happy. Edward Hamilton—the bloom hath forsaken his
cheeks—the lustre of his fine eyes is no more—I never saw so total a
change in a youth, who but lately might have figured as the personifica-
tion of health, enlivened and informed by the most endearing vivacity:
Would I had never seen Courtland—I might then have been happy.
When Edward Hamilton suffers, I feel that I cannot stand by regardless; I follow him with the affection of a sister; but of late, he studiously

shuns my advances: It was but yesterday, that with trembling eagerness, he grasped my hand; something he was about to say; but, as if recollecting himself, instantly, like the spectre of a dream, he fled away. Am I not justified in saying, that if I had never seen Courtland, I might then have been happy? Serafina too, is often drowned in tears. Serafina is the sister of my heart. Why will she not exchange her vows with Edward? how rich should I then be, with such a brother—such a sister. You ask if Mr. Courtland is an approved lover—alas, no!—alas, yes!—You will be at no loss to explain this seeming paradox. I sometimes suspect that my guardian friends must be in possession of some secret, relative to Mr. Courtland, which they have not yet unfolded; for surely they could not be so strongly opposed, on account of inequality of years. The engagement entered into with old Mr. Hamilton was conditional; and you know, my dear, that though I am—though I *was,* I should say, cheerful, it never could be said that I was gay; and I think I could accommodate myself to the gravest humour: But my parents, you will say, are the best judges; and you, Miss Worthington, are a good girl, while I, methinks, am become a faulty, a very faulty creature. My mother—but my mother is an angel—I do assure you, my dear, that I not seldom feel a degree of awe, while contemplating the character of so divine a woman, which absolutely deters me from arrogating to myself the title, with which her condescending indulgence hath invested me. This superior woman, you will recollect, assured me that I should never be the wife of Hamilton, except both my judgment, and my best affections were consenting; exactly with this declaration, doth every arrangement correspond; and, while neither she nor my father produce a single argument in favour of the man of their election, which reason doth not fully authorize, they unitedly and repeatedly engage, that however I may ultimately determine, they will never cease to be my parental friends. Tell me, my dear, what returns doth such matchless generosity merit? And help me to discharge as I ought, with becoming decency, a daughter's part. Unexampled indeed is their consideration for me; and still the more to enhance their goodness, and ally it to perfection, they assay to wear a tranquillity which is foreign from their hearts; for alas! do I not hourly observe the anxious solicitude but too visibly pourtrayed in the manly features of my father—often have I wiped the tear from the swoln eye of my mother—often have I witnessed the chagrin which they have mutually and involuntarily manifested at any discovery which I have unwarily made of my attachment to Courtland; and I have but too well marked the joy of their brightened countenances, at the smallest instance of my tenderness for Edward. What right do I possess thus to stab the bosoms which have so long fostered me? Better I had been whelmed beneath those waves which gave death to him from whom I derived my existence, than thus to become the source of corroding anxiety, to characters so exalted. Every pensive look of theirs pierces me to the soul; and I seem to move an evil genius, doomed to chace peace from their revered bosoms. Amelia, I could not be other than miserable, even possessed of the man of my heart, if I thus implanted in the pillow of my guardian friends, the rankling thorn of disappointment.

Forgive, my dear, this incoherent letter; it is expressive of my feelings; the pressure upon my spirits is extreme; my situation is truly melancholy; it is precisely that which I would wish to avoid. Could I unite my hopes and wishes with the expectations of those who have a right to my utmost obedience, how enviable would be my lot? You demand a long, a very long letter; but what can I write which will not be calculated to cast a cloud over the charming vivacity of my lively friend. Yet you would acquaint yourself with every movement of my soul! well then, as you have expressed a predilection for my little poetical attempts, I will transcribe for you some lines which I last night hastily penned, after I had retired from my parents, enriched with their affectionate and joint benediction; they delineate my wishes; they delineate my feelings, and they are the fervid breathings of a much agitated, and deeply wounded spirit.

Invocation to Duty.

Low, sacred duty, at thy shrine,
  Behold thy suppliant bend,
All conscious of thy right divine,
  To thee my vows ascend.

With pity bland regard a maid,   5
    To soft obedience form'd;
Who, though by tenderness betray'd,
    Is still by virtue warm'd.

Goddess all radiant, enshield
    This fond, this treacherous heart;   10
The arms of bright discretion wield,
    And all thy powers impart.

These wayward passions—oh reclaim—
    Each dear illusion hide;
Give me a faultless virgin's fame,   15
    Blest prudence for my guide.

By thy just influence arrest
    Each wandering wish of mine;
Bind all thy dictates to my breast,
    And every hope entwine.   20

Of Lethe's[1] waters let me drink,
    Forgetful of the past;
My errors in oblivion sink,
    The veil of candor cast.

Give inclination to recede,   25
    Each rising thought chastize;
Let naught my righteous steps impede,
    The tranquil joys I prize.

Give acquiescence to my grasp,
    A mild conceding mind;   30

---

1. **Lethe's:** in Greek mythology, the river that flows throughout the underworld; drinking its water causes forgetfulness.

Give me bright fortitude to clasp,
  To all my fate resign'd.

Give me no more their breasts to wound,
  My orphan life who guard;
Let me not be that ingrate found,   35
  Who angels thus reward.

My God! those tears in that mild eye—
  My dear maternal friend;
That anxious brow—paternal sigh!—
  Where will my sorrows end?   40

For still I struggle—still complain,
  But, sovereign Duty, hear,
My righteous purposes sustain,
  And make my steps thy care.

Adieu, my dear Amelia—that you may still be happy, is, and will continue to be, the very sincere wish of your

MARGARETTA MELWORTH.

CHAPTER 5

Yet pressing onward, with the goal in view,
More ardent still our hopes and wishes grew.

Thus, for a considerable time, matters remained stationary as it were, in my family. Courtland continued his pursuit. In the bosom of Margaretta, the conflict between duty and inclination was unyieldingly severe; and Hamilton, with a noble consistency, persevered in declining a competition, which he deemed unworthy that rational, disinterested and

---

Chapter 5. Published in *The Gleaner*, 1:10.

fervent attachment, which every faculty of his soul had long acknowledged for Miss Melworth.

Courtland, evidently exulting in his success, felicitated himself upon
his opening prospects; and calculating upon the tenderness of Margaretta, he became confident it would be in his power to obtain a much
earlier day, than the very distant era which we had so peremptorily
named.

We were thus circumstanced, when the following little poem that
made its appearance in the Gazette, however inconsiderable it may in
fact be, from the important consequences by which it was attended,
merits a place in my narration.

> As on the shorn bank I delightedly stray'd,
> Admiring the meadows, the woods, and the glade,
> A nymph whose attendance enlivened the scene,
> In airy meanders tript over the green;
> And thus, as she rambled, she carelessly said—   5
> Come, depict, if you can, your favourite maid.
>
> My favourite maid, all enraptur'd I cry'd,
> My favourite maid, of her sex is the pride;
> The standard of elegance, formed to please,
> Her movements the portrait of dignifi'd ease;   10
> While each brightening charm which floats on her mien,
> Announces her bosom as virtue serene.
>
> Her tresses *not borrow'd,* so neatly entwin'd,
> Proclaim the good taste which so well hath design'd;
> And her dark auburn locks as so glossy they flow,   15
> Contrast as they wave the smooth forehead of snow;
> While her soft, mildly beaming, sky tinctur'd eye,
> Evinceth bland pity, and sweet sympathy.
>
> The rose and the lily are blended in vain,
> Her sway to extend, or her triumphs maintain,   20

For though on her face as they dazzlingly glow,
The polish of beauty's own hand they bestow;
Yet rivall'd by graces which dwell in her mind,
To mental inthralment my heart is resign'd.

She knows to distinguish—she knows to reflect,   25
What measures are proper, and how to direct;
Her manners correct, by fair decency form'd,
To complacency sweet, by tenderness warm'd,
Inmingles true dignity, chaste and refin'd,
With soft condescension, for soothing design'd.   30

And thus gem'd by loveliness—thus gem'd by worth,
The virgin of innocence, beauty and truth;
That swain will be happy, to whose faithful heart,
The gods shall a gift of such value impart;
For amity lives in a bosom so fair,   35
And love will ameliorate when planted there.

From floods of old ocean the nymph was receiv'd,
From white clifted Albion[1] the angel deriv'd.

Hold, hold, 'tis enough, my fair prompter exclaim'd;
This hint is superfluous; each trait you have nam'd   40
Belongs to your Melworth—your Melworth alone,
No maiden so perfect our circles have known;
E'en as you delineate, the object expands,
And sweet Margaretta conspicuous stands.

These lines, by accelerating our movements, soon put our affairs in a
train, giving us at least a perspective glance of the completion of our
plans. The lighted match is soon in a flame, and the smallest spark will

---

1. **Albion:** According to ancient British legend, Albion, the son of Poseidon and Amphitrite, brought astrology and shipbuilding to England; his name became synonymous with England.

enkindle it; but I will lead to the catastrophe in course. The lines, as I said, made their appearance in the Gazette; they had no signature, and who the writer was, we could not even conjecture. Hamilton, upon pretence of business, had absented himself from our village for more than two weeks; and besides, though we knew that when a boy he had indulged an itch for scribbling in rhyme, yet we conceived that his ripening years had induced him to relinquish every intrigue with damsels y'cleped the muses, whose favours are so hardly earned, and who so seldom invest their votaries with that portion of success, which is in any sort adequate, as a compensation for the unwearied diligence requisite in the pursuit.

We, however, were not greatly concerned about it; and Margaretta was too much accustomed to praise to be highly elated by, or interested in the matter. But the amiable qualities of my girl, (the extensive charity of whose wishes encircled even those sufferers whom her powers of alleviation could not reach) her well known benevolence, her condescending affability to her inferiors, her complacently dignified deportment to her equals, and her veneration for all those whom years had rendered her superiors—had so well established her in the hearts of our connexions, as to render her an object generally beloved; and, indeed, the propriety and equality of her conduct had been such, as to produce a solecism to the adage, which creates envy as the shadow of merit; nor did we know that the passion of malevolence was in exercise toward her. It was soon noised abroad that Margaretta had been eulogized in the news-paper, and it furnished a topic for those circles in which she moved; her partial favourers found beauties in the piece, which perhaps a critic would have been far from allowing it. They made it their business to find out the Author; they applied themselves with much avidity to the pursuit; and they determined, if they should be so fortunate as to succeed, to hail him as the prince of poets.

We had, among the number of our visitors, an old lady by the name of Clacket, who was also much attached to Miss Melworth, and whose curiosity was upon this occasion raised to the highest pitch. She roundly taxed Courtland with being the author of the poem; and the embarrassment which he discovered, abundantly justified her suspicions.

The piece had, as I hinted, its admirers; and Courtland either saw, or thought he saw, an advantage in adopting this fugitive relation of the Parnassian[1] lasses: He managed the matter with some adroitness; his servant was authorized to whisper, as a profound secret to lady Clacket's maid, that his master had in truth composed the favourite lines, which had originated so much speculation; and she reporting it in confidence to her lady, it was in a few days entrusted to the taciturnity of the whole neighbourhood. Courtland was repeatedly complimented upon his poetical abilities, and he hesitated not to wear the bays.

It happened about this time that Courtland made one of a large circle which were collected round our social board, when the before mentioned lady introduced the subject of the poem, and proceeded with all the loquacity of talkative volubility, to pronounce a panegyric upon our gentleman, as the author. The poet bowed, blushed, and looked silly. Margaretta was evidently pleased; while I, regarding the whole affair, as another *much ado about nothing*,[2] should have passed it without further observation, had I not accidentally glanced the face of Serafina, who was also of our party, and whose countenance, in the course of a few moments, expressed the most lively sensations. Her heightened complexion during the conversation, now changing to the clearest white, and now assuming the deepest colouring with which the most impassioned feelings could tinge it. I marked Serafina, but I marked her in silence; for, from these suspicious appearances, I was induced to fear that the specious manners of our gallant, had made also upon the youthful mind of this young lady, an impression which would be with difficulty eradicated! But I was not suffered to remain long under this deception; our company soon separated, and only Courtland, Margaretta, Serafina, Mary and myself, remained. The chagrin upon the face of Serafina was still visible, when, standing up with much dignity in her manner, she instantly accounted for the appearance, by which I had been misled.

Addressing Mr. Courtland, she thus expressed herself: "I am, Sir, the

---

1. **Parnassian:** referring to Parnassus, a Greek mountain considered sacred to the muses.

2. **much…nothing:** title of a Shakespearean comedy.

friend of Edward Hamilton; we have been educated together, almost
from the first moment of our existence, and every secret of his soul is
reposed in my bosom. I am not sure that he would approve of what I
am about to say; nay, feeling my mind at this present in a great measure
governed by indignation, I am not myself positive, that I am quite right;
however, like all angry folks I am hurried on by an impetuosity which I
find altogether irresistable. Is it not enough, Sir, that you have sup-
planted that unhappy young man in his dearest hopes? Is it not enough
that you have stepped between him and that hoard of felicity which he
fondly fancied was treasured up for him? but must you also *poorly steal*
that pittance of fame, which justice reserved for him? You know, Sir,
that you never wrote the piece for which you have been contented to
receive the praises of so many admirers. I have at this moment the original lines upon Miss Melworth, which were written by Edward, in my
pocketbook; they were penned upon yonder verdant bank, during Miss
Melworth's continuance at New-Haven, while I was prattling by his
side. It is true he imagines they are destroyed; he requested that I would
destroy them; but I have imprudently and unkindly given a copy of
them to Miss Predy, and thus they have found their way to the press."

What would I have then given for the pencil of a Hogarth,[1] that I
might have sketched the group which my parlour at that instant exhibited. Need I tell thee, reader, that I am not even a descendant of Hogarth's? I trow not; but I add, by way of information, that having a
mortal aversion to daubing, it is therefore that I pass hastily over every
expressive feature, which was then replete with the deepest meaning,
and only observe, that Courtland, almost immediately recovering himself, suddenly seized the outstretched hand of Miss Clifford, and pressing it with much address to his lips, burst into an immoderate fit of
laughter, affecting great surprise, that she took the matter so seriously,
and declaring that he meant nothing more than a jest, and merely to
amuse himself with the simplicity and credulity of lady Clacket.

For my own part, my astonishment at the impudence of the fellow,
absolutely struck me dumb; and I suffered him to give his adventure
what turn he pleased, without even the capability of interrupting him! I

---

1. **Hogarth:** William Hogarth (1697–1764), English painter.

saw, however, by the altered looks of Margaretta; by a degree of disgust which pervaded her fine countenance, and the pointed reprehension which she darted from her charmingly expressive eyes; from all these auspicious indications, I gathered, that the full time for executing my scheme, was at length arrived, and that the mine being thus accidentally and advantageously sprung, it became me to continue my operations with all possible expedition.

Courtland, therefore, had no sooner taken his leave for the evening, than without taking the least notice of the rhymes, or their effect, I observed to my daughter—that having long noted with much concern her wasting frame, and impaired constitution, I was at last come to the resolution of bending myself entirely to her wishes; that upon the next morning's visit which we should receive from her lover, I would lead him immediately to my library—that possibly I might have mistaken his character, but that I would then enter into a conversation with him, of a nature so serious, as fully to ascertain our man—that I would request her, accompanied by her mother, to seat herself in the adjoining apartment, where they might be ear witnesses of our discourse—and that if, after the investigation to which I should oblige Mr. Courtland to submit, he should still continue the object of a choice, which would then be so deliberate, I would myself lead her to the altar, at any hour which she should judge most proper; and, furthermore, that I promised on behalf of Mary, as well as in my own name, that we would continue through life, in every event, to partake her felicity, and to gild for her, to the utmost of our ability, every misfortune which might await her.

Margaretta trembled excessively; her complexion now reddened to the deepest dye, and now changed to the most deadly pale! we were fearful that she would faint. Mary addressed her in the most soothing language; this had the desired effect; and, bursting into tears, she raised her clasped hands, while a kind of agonized expression was depictured upon her countenance, and, ere we were aware, with a sudden and tremulous emotion, quitting her seat, she sunk down upon her knees before us. "Oh Sir, oh Madam!" in a broken voice she exclaimed, "spare your child, spare me this trial; your condescension is sufficiently manifested; never more do I wish to behold the man who hath this evening passed your doors; I am convinced that he is poorly mean, that he is capable of the most deliberate baseness; and never shall my soul bind itself in alliance with an unworthy pretender, who can thus pitifully stoop to purloin the fame, with which undoubted merit had invested his superior."

"Nay, my love," rejoined Mary, "you are now again too precipitate; would you discard the man of your heart, merely because he is ambitious of adorning himself with the poet's laurel? besides, these tears, these looks of anguish, these broken accents, and heart-affecting sighs; these all betray a mind not sufficiently at ease, to make up a determination so important; should you thus hastily proceed, you may possibly repent at leisure. Come to my arms, my daughter—let me press this throbbing heart to the bosom of friendship; let us take time, my love; your father, whose wisdom not seldom leads him through the labyrinth of the human heart, shall prosecute his plan, while we, summoning the aid of mild resignation, abide, with patient acquiescence, the event."

Thus, then, we adjusted our measures; and the returning sun, according to custom, presenting Mr. Courtland, ushered in an hour which I regarded among the most important of my life. My unalterable intention was to constitute Miss Melworth sole heiress of every shilling which I possessed; yet, regarding our spark, in pecuniary matters, as another *Zeluco,*[1] I conceived myself justified in practising a little address, in order to the unmasking an impostor, who, by methods so unwarrantable, had obtained such hold of the affections of my daughter.

Behold me then, gentle reader, with these impressions, seated in my library, and Courtland, with *unblushing effrontery,* lolling upon a sofa before me; listen, also, while with a solemn, but composed countenance, and in a resolute and peremptory tone of voice, I thus deliver myself.

"I have requested this interview, Sir, in order to obtain your ear upon a very important subject. I observe that your pretensions to Miss Melworth, notwithstanding your knowledge of our predilection for Mr. Hamilton, are still continued; and I repeat, that no parental friends,

---

1. **Zeluco:** 1786 novel by John Moore (1729–1802).

ought *unduly* to influence in an affair, which cannot so deeply interest them, as the individuals who are principally concerned; we consent, therefore, supposing Miss Melworth's preference should remain, to yield you her hand, and we assure you that her matrimonial choice shall, in no sort, influence her fortunes." Here Courtland bowed exultingly, and I proceeded to say—"But, Sir, it is just, that upon this occasion, I add, that, as Miss Melworth is not in fact, our daughter, she is not by nature entitled to our inheritance. My heart, Sir, my paternal heart, acknowledges for that young lady the strongest affection; but family claims are respectable, and the pride of relationship is seldom wholly eradicated from the bosom. There is now living in a certain metropolis upon this continent, a distant relation of mine, who bears my name; it is true he is rich, but his family is large, and as I am fond, I confess, of establishing my name, the world, in general, will not condemn me, should I devise the greater part of my real estate to this my kinsman; while prudence directs me to secure to Margaretta and her posterity, whatever part of my possessions I shall judge proper to endow her with; and I am positive that Miss Melworth will not accuse me of want of affection for her, whatever arrangements I may be induced to make."

I assay not to describe the agitated alterations, which the countenance of Courtland underwent, during the latter part of my harangue; anger, disappointment, and the deepest chagrin, were marked there; when, starting from his seat, with an indignation but ill concealed, he expressed himself to the following effect: "I was informed, Sir, that you had no relation in existence; I was informed that Miss Melworth would undoubtedly succeed to your estates; and I was moreover informed, that you had destined a very handsome sum, as a nuptial present, for the husband of that young lady, upon the day of marriage; if I am deceived, Sir, though I *adore* Miss Melworth, yet neither my fortune nor my family will admit of my union with a young lady, who, (excuse me, Sir) doth not seem to have *any* well grounded expectations, and who cannot claim a single person in the world, as her natural relation."

It was with difficulty that I stifled my resentment; but, assuming an air of calmness, I returned—"I am ignorant, Sir, who was your informant; but I am confident I have never before explained myself upon this subject, to any one, and I am not answerable for the erroneous conjectures of the busy multitude: But, Sir, you, in your turn, must excuse me, when I say, that I should imagine a person upon the eve of bankruptcy, if he really loved the woman whom he was seeking to affiance to penury, would be happy to find her invested with a share of property, which, being independent of his failure, would set her above absolute want."

This was enough; it worked him up to a degree of frenzy; and, clenching his fist, with a menacing air, he approached my seat.

"What, Sir, can you mean? What do you mean Mr. Vigillius? I demand an explanation."

"Compose yourself, Sir," I rejoined, "I am not to be intimidated by those big looks, or that air of haughty defiance. Had you, Mr. Courtland, when you presented yourself in my family, as a candidate for the affection of my daughter, ingenuously favoured me with a *real* statement of your affairs, I would have used my interest to have adjusted them amicably with your creditors; and had the attachment of Margaretta been permanent, while I regarded you as a worthy, though an unfortunate man, I should, notwithstanding my conditional engagement with Mr. Hamilton, have viewed the matter with tolerable complacency; but, when you pass yourself upon us as a man in affluent circumstances, when you act, in every instance, the deliberate deceiver, I should greatly grieve, did I not know that my daughter's eyes were already opened: She, even at this moment, regains her former tranquillity. You are no stranger to me, Sir; your *amours,* your *improvidence,* the *ruined state of your finances,* &c. &c. I have this moment letters in my pocket, from your principal creditors, and I could long ere this have apprized Miss Melworth, had I not judged it expedient that she should make the discovery for herself—she hath made it, and I am again a happy man."

Courtland's cowardly soul now shrunk from my gaze; but assuming, with his wonted finesse, the air of an injured man, as he darted from the library, and from the house, he said, "It is well, Sir, it is well that your connexion with Miss Melworth is your protection; otherwise I should not fail to call you to a very severe account, for falsehoods and absurdities, which the bosom of malevolence hath doubtless originated."

From the library, I immediately passed to the adjoining apartment. Margaretta hid her blushing face in the bosom of her mother; and while I pressed those beautiful females to my heart, I protested, by the tenderness which I bore them, that I was, at that instant, the happiest of human beings.

Margaretta proposed a thousand questions in a breath; and, while she blessed the hour of her emancipation, she begged to learn the residence of the dear family I had mentioned, who, from their affinity to me, she gratefully said, were already imaged in her heart, and to whom she wished speedily to devote the page of tender acknowledgment, for the share they undesignedly had, in liberating a mind which had been so unworthily enslaved. Tapping her cheek, I expressed my wonder that she too had been deceived; for, my dear, I added, though there is actually, in the city of ——, a gentleman of my name, circumstanced exactly as I have stated, yet I am not personally acquainted with him; nor do I know that there is the remotest consanguinity between us, in any other line, than as we are alike descended from the honest couple who had their residence in Paradise.

In fact, not having, in my conversation with Courtland, absolutely avowed an intention of alienating from Margaretta any part of my estate; only simply suggesting the rationality and equity of such a procedure, and having fully accomplished my design, I was not anxious to guard my secret.

Courtland, who still continued in our neighbourhood, was soon apprized of the stratagem which I had so successfully employed; and such was the egregious vanity of the coxcomb, that he entertained no doubt of being able to reinstate himself in the bosom of Margaretta; to which end, he addressed her by many expostulatory letters; imputing the part he had acted in the library, entirely to surprise, and disavowing every tittle of what had been alleged against him; declaring, that those calumnies had undoubtedly been fabricated by some friends of Hamilton's, on purpose to ruin him in his love; and, that however she might determine, his inviolable attachment to her would never permit him to be other than the humblest of her *adorers*. It was in vain Miss Melworth assured him, that his real situation, his wishes, or his pursuits, could affect her in no other way, than as she was a general well-wisher to her species; and that, having outlived the esteem she once avowed for him, she must beg leave to decline all correspondence with him in future. No sooner were his letters returned unopened, than he persisted in besieging every door which she entered; and, having once crossed the threshold, his clamorous protestations bore a stronger resemblance to those of a madman, than to a rationally attached lover. Miss Melworth, however, acquitted herself upon every of these occasions, with that cool and determined consistency, which was necessary to the establishment of her character, which confirmed the general sentiment in her favour, and placed the whole affair in its true light.

But many days elapsed, before my girl regained her wonted *self-complacency.* She often lamented the weakness which thus, subjecting her to so humiliating an attachment, had involved us also in the utmost anxiety; and not being able to forgive herself, for a time she continued to deplore. But the good sense she so eminently possessed, leading her at length to impute her error to inexperience, finally banished every remaining regret, and enabled her to pen a letter to Miss Worthington, which I produce as a contrast to that which appeared in my last Gleaner.

Miss MELWORTH to Miss WORTHINGTON.

Village of ——, July 31st, 1789.
News, joyful news! my beloved girl. Your Margaretta is restored to her senses, and she is now the cheerfullest, the most contented, and the happiest being in the universe. Yes, thanks to the unworthiness of Courtland, my liberated heart is at this moment lighter than a feather; and I can now behold this once formidable man without the smallest perturbation, save what is excited by the recollection of that imbecility, which so poorly subjected me to an indiscretion which must, as often as it is recurred to, suffuse my cheek with the blush of conscious error! The story of my emancipation is too long to relate in the little moment allowed me, for the post is on the wing, and as my dear Amelia has

given me reason to flatter myself I shall soon see her at ———, a bare sketch of this happy event shall suffice, while I voluntarily engage to fill up the outlines during some *tete a tete*,[1] which we will sweetly enjoy, in the woodbine alcove, you have so often heard me mention.

For some time, being left by my matchless parents wholly to the exercise of my own reason, I had begun to discover that Courtland was not the faultless being which my imagination had almost deified. He let slip no opportunity of piqueing Hamilton; he seemed ungenerously to aim at pointing the shaft which so apparently wounded the bosom of my early friend; and his triumphant exultation partook a degree of meanness, at which I felt my bosom involuntarily reluct. Once or twice, too, I looked in upon some poor neighbours of ours, who were struggling with disease and penury, in order, in my little way, to afford them what relief my angel benefactor had commissioned me to yield; methought his soul was not formed for pity or for sympathy; no tear started in his eye; and while his complaisance induced him to accompany me in my walk, his features gathered a severe and rigid kind of austerity; that gentle and engaging demeanor, for which we have together admired him, was no more; his air was haughty and forbidding, and he deigned not to pour even the oil of soothing words, into the lacerated bosom of sorrow! Upon these occasions disgust grew in my soul, and I was conscious that my attachment was gradually diminishing. A little poem, written by Edward Hamilton, he had the weakness to claim; this also, exhibiting him in a new and disagreeable light, made large inroads upon that esteem, which, while with you, (not considering, that I thereby violated the duty I owed my revered friends) I had so fondly cherished; but the finishing stroke was reserved for the investigating wisdom of my father. By the dictates of equity Courtland was tried, and he came out—I will not say what he came out. In short, my Amelia, no longer enslaved by that dangerous man, it is not my business to pursue him by invectives; he mingles, in regard to me, with the rest of his species: I owe him no ill-will, and I am only solicitous that no unhappy young body, not

---

1. **tete a tete:** tête à tête; literally, head to head (French); a private interview.

patronized and directed, as I have been, may fall a victim to the wiles which an enemy so fascinating may prepare for her.

For myself, my utmost wishes are gratified; joy once more illumines the revered countenances of my parental friends: I am conscious that I have banished anxiety from their bosoms, and this consciousness seems to dignify and render my existence of importance; it is of itself a sufficient compensation for years of suffering; from a mighty pressure my soul is relieved; every thing wears its accustomed face; I skip about the house as usual, and this dwelling is the same blessed mansion which it heretofore was. Serafina, too, embraces me with returning rapture; and though Edward Hamilton, who hath long been absent from our village, may probably reject a heart which hath been capable of so improper an attachment, yet he will allow of my sisterly regards; in his fraternal bosom, I shall find an abode of sincerity; and I shall still be in possession of the approbation of my next to divine benefactors, and of the unalterable affection of my much loved Serafina. Possibly also—but whither am I wandering? I forget that the post will be gone; but having at length recollected myself, I hasten to offer my respects to your mamma, and to assure you that I am, with very sincere affection, your ever faithful

MARGARETTA MELWORTH.

CHAPTER 6

When crimes despotic in the bosom reign,
The tears of weeping beauty flow in vain.

Scarce an hour had elapsed, after Margaretta had forwarded her letter to Miss Worthington, when the following interesting account from that young lady, which had been written some days before, was put into her hand.

Chapter 6. Published in *The Gleaner,* 1:11.

Miss WORTHINGTON to Miss MELWORTH.

NEW-HAVEN, July 25th, 1789.

Gracious Heaven, what are my sensations! Never did I expect to address my dear Miss Melworth under a consciousness of having contributed (as the event may prove) to her ruin: But in deed, and in truth, we have not intentionally erred; and surely the tale which I have to unfold, will banish from a mind, where integrity and every other virtue have taken up their abode, a wretch, who ought never to have profaned a temple so sacred.

My poor mother weeps incessantly; she says she shall never know peace again, if you are not enabled to assure her, that tranquillity is restored to a bosom, where she hath been accessary in planting so sharp a thorn. Listen, my beloved Margaretta, to the recital I have to make; and let the virtues of Hamilton obtain their due estimation.

About six years since, a gentleman by the name of Wellwood, was one of the most respectable dwellers in this city; his family consisted only of his lady and daughter, with their domestics; his daughter had been educated with the exactest care, and she was, at eighteen, a beautiful and accomplished young woman. Just at this important period, Mr. Wellwood paid the great debt of nature; and so deep an impression did this melancholy and calamitous event make upon the mind of Mrs. Wellwood, who was one of the first of women, that after languishing a few weeks, under all the pressure of a rapid decline, she also obtained her passport, resigning her life, a confessed and lamented martyr to grief.

Thus, in a very short interval, the unfortunate Frances Wellwood saw herself precipitated from a situation the most eligible, with which the dispositions of paternal Providence can possibly endow a young creature, to that of an unprotected orphan; no guardian father, no indulgent mother remained, to direct her steps, or to approbate her movements! She had been accustomed to regard her parents as the source of wisdom; no design had she ever executed, unsanctioned by the parental voice, unpropitiated by the maternal smile; and the authors of her existence had, in every sense, continued the prop and the confidence of the being they had reared. Neither Mr. nor Mrs. Wellwood were natives of this city; none of their kindred resided among us: So that the beauteous orphan viewed herself as alone in the universe; and when she cast her distracted gaze upon the clay cold tenements of a father and a mother; upon those eyes, now for ever closed, which, while the least vestige of life remained, had still darted upon her the most benign and unequivocal testimonies of affectionate tenderness; upon those lips never again to be unsealed, which had opened but to enrich her with advice, admonitions, directions, or benedictions; when, with folded arms, she contemplated those trophies of relentless death, the unutterable anguish of her spirit, depriving her for a time of reason, suspended the operation of the silent sorrow, which afterward reduced her to the very verge of the grave! Not a benevolent heart in this city, but deeply felt for the lovely mourner; never did I see a more pathetically interesting object. But time, that sovereign physician, and the soothing of those friends, to whom her virtues and her misfortunes had inexpressibly endeared her, at length effectuated in her bosom precisely that state of tender melancholy, which, in a delicate and sentimental mind, is described as finding a luxury in tears; and her youth and an excellent constitution, surmounting the ravages which had been made in her health, she was gradually restored to a pensive kind of serenity.

The effects, of which Mr. Wellwood had died possessed, exclusive of his household moveables, which were very genteel, consisting altogether of navigation and articles of merchandize, he had directed in his will that they should be immediately converted into ready money; and the gentleman whom he had appointed his executor, with that integrity and dispatch, which are such conspicuous traits in his character, speedily disbursing every arrearage, and adjusting every affair relative to his trust, delivered into the hands of Miss Wellwood the sum of two thousand pounds in cash; this being the whole amount, after such settlement, of what remained of her deceased father's estate; and of this her patrimony, she was, agreeably to his direction, the sole and uncontrolled possessor. Behold her then, before she had completed her nineteenth year, absolute mistress of herself and fortune: Her apartments were elegantly furnished; she was in possession of a handsome library, and two thousand pounds in ready specie; but her discretion was unquestionable, and no one presumed to dictate to Miss Wellwood.

Just at this crisis, Courtland made his first appearance at New-Haven. His exteriour and deportment, we have mutually agreed, are pleasingly fascinating, and our unguarded sex are but too easily captivated. His arts of seduction must be prodigious. When I see you, I will recount the gradual advances, by which he undermined a virtue, that would have been proof against a common assailant. Hoodwinking her reason, and misleading her judgment by arguments the most sophistical, *he induced her to view, as the result of human regulations, the marriage vow;* it was not to be found in the law of God, and it (or rather, the calling a priest to witness it) was calculated only for the meridian of common souls: True, the institution answered political purposes, and it might be necessary to preserve a character; but for him—his nuptial hour—should it take place previous to the death of a capriciously obstinate old uncle, who was a bachelor, and who had made his succeeding to his estate to depend upon his continuing single, would mark him the most imprudent of men. Mean time, his love for Miss Wellwood was unbounded; he could not possibly exist without her; he could not bear the idea of seeing her hourly exposed to the solicitations of those numerous pretenders, who thronged about her, while he was conscious that he possessed no superior claim to her attention; and surely, as they had the sole disposal of themselves, they might, in the sight of Heaven, exchange their vows; while that Heaven, which would record the deed, would also sanction and crown with success, a union so pure, so disinterested, and formed so wholly under its own sacred auspices; this transaction would in fact constitute their real nuptials, and upon the demise of the old gentleman, they would immediately submit to authorise their union by modern rites.

Miss Wellwood loved the villain—Horrid wretch!—he succeeded but too well, and she was involved in the deepest ruin! My tears blot the paper—would to God that they could cancel her faults, and serve as a *lethe* for her sufferings. Not a soul was apprized of their intercourse; and so well were their measures taken, that when, six months after, the young lady disappeared, amid the various conjectures which were formed, not even the shadow of suspicion glanced upon Courtland; every one expressed, in their own way, his or her wonder, grief, and apprehension; the whole town took an interest in her unexpected removal, and Courtland was with the foremost to express his astonishment; but as Miss Wellwood was entirely independent, no one was authorised to commence an active inquiry or pursuit.

The attention excited by any extraordinary event, after having its run, at length subsides; and Miss Wellwood ceased by degrees to be the subject of conversation; nor hath her strange flight been in any sort accounted for, until two days since, when Bridget introduced into our breakfasting parlour this forlorn female, who, immediately upon fixing her eyes on my mother, sunk down almost breathless at her feet! It is hardly necessary to add, that we instantly raised the hapless orphan, and that after recognizing, with some difficulty, the well-known features of Miss Wellwood, we received from her lips the foregoing particulars.

Upon her quitting New-Haven, she repaired directly to apartments, which had been taken for her by Courtland, in a distant village; her patrimony, you will not doubt, was relinquished to her betrayer. After sacrificing her honour, every thing else became a trifle. At first, he vouchsafed to support her; but for these two last years, either wanting ability or inclination, she has not been able to obtain from him the smallest sum! Of her furniture, of her valuable library, of every thing she is stripped; and for some months past she hath been reduced to the necessity of parting with her clothes, and of availing herself of her skill in needle work, for the subsistence of herself and three sons, whom she hath borne to Courtland; and the little wretches, with their injured mother, have long been in want of the common necessaries of life! Yet, through all this, she hath been supported, being buoyed up by the hope of an ultimate residence with the father of her children: By the laws of Heaven, she regards herself as already his wife, while she hath repeatedly, with floods of tears, besought the abandoned man to confer upon her, by the rites of the church, a title so honourable; and, though still repulsed, and often with severity, she hath never despaired, until the tidings that Courtland was on the point of marriage with a young lady, who had abode for some time with us, reached her ears; this heart-rending intelligence produced her, upon the before mentioned morning, in our parlour; this hath also procured you the sorrow, which so melancholy a recital will doubtless occasion.

The once beautiful form of Miss Wellwood is now surprisingly emaciated; the few past weeks hath made dreadful havoc in her constitution; we assay to pour into her lacerated bosom what consolation is in our power; we have made her acquainted with your character, with its marked integrity and uniform consistency; and we have encouraged her to hope every thing from a goodness so perfect. The desolated sufferer will herself address you. Alas, alas! what further can I say! it is with difficulty that I have written thus far; but this information we have judged absolutely necessary. May God preserve my dear Miss Melworth from so black a villain—every thing is to be feared. For myself, I stand, in my own apprehension, as a culprit before you. Forgive, I entreat you, my sorrowing mother; and with your wonted kindness, forgive—O forgive—your truly affectionate, and greatly afflicted

AMELIA WORTHINGTON.

Miss WELLWOOD to Miss MELWORTH.
[*Inclosed in the preceding.*]

NEW-HAVEN, July 25th, 1789.
Will the most faultless of her sex deign to receive a line from one, who, but for the infatuation of a fatal and illusive passion, meeting her upon equal ground, might have drawn from so bright an example, a model by which she might have shaped her course, through an *event-judging* and *unfeeling* world. I am told that your virtues partake the mildest qualities, and that pity, bland and healing, is empress in your breast; if so, sweet mercy must administer there; and you will then not only tolerate the address of an unhappy stranger, but you will be impelled to lend to the prayer of my petition, a propitious ear. Miss Worthington hath condescended to become my introducer, and she informs me that she hath unfolded to you the story of my woes!

For myself, I write not, most respected young lady, either to exonerate myself, or to criminate an unfortunate man, who hath had the presumption to aspire to such daring heights! Registered in the uncontrovertible records of heaven, the wife of Courtland, in walks so reprehensible, it would ill become me to be found. No, Madam, I write to supplicate, and on my bended knees I am prostrated before you—I write to supplicate you to use your interest in the heart of Courtland, in my favour. Help me, O thou unblemished votary of virtue! help me to reclaim a husband, who, not naturally bad, hath too long wandered in the dangerous paths of dissipation; who hath drank too deeply of the empoisoned cup of error; and who, if he is not soon roused from his visionary career, may suddenly be precipitated into the gulph of perdition!

I said that Mr. Courtland was not naturally bad; and believe me, good young lady, I have, in a thousand instances, observed the rectitude of his heart. Early indulgence, and a mistaken mode of education, hath been his ruin; but the amiable qualities which are natal in his bosom, have, nevertheless, through the weeds by which they have been well nigh choaked, occasionally discovered themselves. Yet, whatever are his faults, they can never obliterate my errors; *doubtless he observed in me some blameable weakness,* or he would never have taken those unwarrantable steps, which were the consequence of our acquaintance; and now, circumstanced as we are, a failure of duty in him, can never apologize for the want of every proper exertion on my side. He is the father of my children; I have a presentiment that he may be recovered to the bosom of equity; and, if he will permit me, I will watch over him as my dearest treasure. Let him but acknowledge the honourable and endearing ties, father and husband; let him but sanction them in the face of the world, and I will soothe his aching head; I will smooth his thorny pillow; and, in every circumstance, in sickness and in health, I will continue that faithful Fanny, whom he hath so often sworn never to forsake, and whom, in the fulness of his heart, he hath called Heaven to witness, he would ever prefer to all created beings.

Perhaps he can no more command the sums which I have yielded into his hands—be it so, they were mine, I made them his, and he had a right to dispose of them—Nay, I think I had rather find him destitute; for such a situation will acquit him of that cruelty, with which he is otherwise chargeable on account of his late neglects. What are pecuniary emoluments, compared to that real felicity, which is to be derived from a mutual, a faithful, and an unbroken attachment? I have made the experiment, and I can confidently pronounce it in truth a fact—*that we want but little here below*. Let him know, Madam, that I will draw the impenetrable veil of silence over the past; that we will commence anew the voyage of life; and that if he will at length be just, his returning kindness, by invigorating once more this poor, this enervated frame, will restore alacrity to my efforts; and that I am, in that case, positive, our combined exertions will procure for ourselves, and our little ones, the *necessaries of life*.

What can I say? It is for my children I am thus importunate; were it not for their dear sakes, the story of my sufferings should never interrupt the felicity of Miss Melworth. No, believe me, no—but I would seek some turfed pillow, whereon to rest my weary head; and, closing forever these humid lids, I would haste to repose me in that vault, which entombs the remains of my revered parents, and where only, I can rationally expect to meet the tranquillity for which I sigh. Innocent little sufferers!—observe them, dearest lady; to you their hands are uplifted—Courtland's features are imaged in their faces, and they plead the cause of equity.

Nor will we, my children, despair—we cannot sue in vain: Miss Melworth being our auxiliary, doubtless we shall again be reinstated in the bosom of your father.

Forgive, inestimable young lady, forgive this incoherent rambling—distraction not seldom pervades my mind. But grant, I beseech you, the prayer of my petition, and entitle yourself to the eternal gratitude of the now wretched

FRANCES WELLWOOD.

It was well that my girl had discarded Courtland from her heart, and that she had almost entirely recovered her tranquillity, previous to the receipt of these letters; otherwise, the sudden revolution they would have occasioned, must, in a young and impassioned mind, have uprooted her reason.

Old Mr. Wellwood had been one of the first of my friends; and from his countenance and advice, on my setting out in life, I had derived material advantages. The disappearance of his daughter had much perplexed me. I was fearful she was ill advised, but from the idea I had entertained of her discretion, I had not the least suspicion of the truth. Yet she never rushed upon my memory, without giving birth in my bosom to sensations truly painful; and I had been constantly solicitous to discover the place of her retreat.

Thus, under the influence of equity and gratitude, I hope my readers will do me the justice to believe, that in Miss Wellwood's affairs, I found myself naturally impelled to take a very active part. Margaretta speedily responded to both the ladies; but as her letter to Miss Worthington is not absolutely essential to my narration, I shall omit it: The following is a copy of her reply to Miss Wellwood.

Miss MELWORTH to Miss WELLWOOD.

Village of ——, August 1st, 1789.

I have, my dear Madam, received your pathetically plaintive epistle; and, over the melancholy recital of your woes, I have shed many tears. I lament your sorrows, and I honour the propriety of your present feelings and wishes; but a letter which I yesterday wrote to Miss Worthington, and which she will soon receive, will, I persuade myself, convince you of the indelicacy and inutility of my interference relative to Mr. Courtland. Before the name of Miss Wellwood had been announced to me, I had been convinced of my error, in entertaining the most distant views of a serious connexion with that gentleman; and the preference my inexperienced heart had avowed for him, was eradicated from my bosom.

Doubtless, if the ever honoured guardians of my unwary steps, had not still been continued to me, *ensnared as I too certainly was,* Miss Wellwood's *wrongs would not have exhibited a solitary trait in the history of the unfeeling despoiler!* You must excuse me, Madam, if I do not adopt *your mildness of expression,* when speaking of a *betrayer,* whose atrocious conduct hath blasted in their early blow, the opening prospects of a young lady, whose fair mind seems eminently formed for all those social and tender intercourses, which constitute and brighten the pleasing round of domestic life. Surely, Miss Wellwood—yet, sensible that painful retrospection will avail us nothing, I stop short.

But, my amiable panegyrist,[1] though I, myself, am ineligible as a mediatress, between parties whose interests *ought indeed to be considered as one,* I am authorized to offer you the extricating hands, and protecting arms of those matchless benefactors, who, with unexampled condescension, have dignified the *orphan* Margaretta, by investing her with the title of *their daughter;* nor is this an empty title; their parental wisdom, their parental indulgence—*but come and see.* I am commanded to solicit you immediately to repair to an asylum, and to hearts, which will ever be open for your reception. My father, Madam, confesses essential and various obligations to your deceased parent; and he hath long been anxiously desirous to render the arrears, which were due to Mr. Wellwood, into the hands of his ever lovely representative. The bearer of this letter is commissioned to pay you the sum of fifty pounds, which you are requested to receive, as a *part of the interest,* which hath been, for such a length of time, your due; it may answer your present exigencies, and the *principal* is still in reserve. It is with much pleasure, I avail myself of the orders which are given me, to repeat my solicitations, that you would, without hesitation, hasten to this mansion. An elderly man and woman, who are to return to our village in the next stage, and who have long been our very respectable neighbours, will call upon you at Colonel Worthington's, to take your commands; and if you will be so obliging as to put yourself under their care, they will see you conveyed in safety to one, who, in addition to the general and unquestionable humanity of his character, feels his heart operated upon, in regard to Miss Wellwood, by the ancient and inviolable claims of gratitude.

Mr. Courtland, though not at present our visitor, is still a resident in this neighbourhood; and my father bids me assure you, that every rational step shall be taken, which can be supposed to have the remotest tendency toward the restoration of your peace. He himself will undertake your cause; and as his plans are always the result of wisdom and penetration, he is not seldom gratified by the accomplishment of his wishes. He will seek Mr. Courtland; he will assail him by those invincible arguments, with which equity, reason and nature will furnish him; and

---

1. **panegyrist**: creator of eulogies or elaborate praise.

should he still remain obdurate, my dear and commiserating father will, nevertheless, aid you by his counsel, and continue unto you his protection; he will assist you in educating your young people, and in disposing of them in a manner, which will render them *useful members of society:* In short, no efforts which benevolence can command, will be wanting, to alleviate your misfortunes. Cheer up then, lovely mourner; the orphan's friend is ours: I predict that the smile of tranquillity will again illumine your grief-worn countenance; and should I yet have to raise to you the voice of felicitation, *good, in that event, will be educed from evil,* and I shall then cease to regret a circumstance, which at present, as often as it is remembered, tinges my cheek with the blush of confusion. Were it necessary, I would add, that no means shall be left unassayed, which may be within the reach of, dear Madam, your truly commiserating, and sincere well-wisher,

MARGARETTA MELWORTH.

Taking it for granted, that the candid reader will allow for the partiality of a young creature, *whose high sense of common benefits,* and whose gratitude had rendered her almost an enthusiast,—I intrude no comment thereon. Margaretta's letter soon produced Miss Wellwood in our family; and upon the morning after her arrival, I sat off in pursuit of Mr. Courtland. My most direct course brought me to rap at the door of his lodgings, and as I was rather early, I made myself sure of finding him within. My astonishment, however, was not equal to my regret, when I was informed by his landlady, that a writ of attachment, being the evening before served upon him, at the suit of Mr. ——, and he not being able to procure sureties, he was then lodged in the county jail. I hesitated not in regard to the measures which were best to be taken; a few moments produced me in that abode of the miserable; and I found little difficulty in obtaining an interview with the prisoner.

Courtland—never shall I forget his appearance—all those airs of importance, which had marked his innate consciousness of superiority, were whelmed in the storm of adversity, that had at length burst upon him. His haggard looks proclaimed, that sleep, in her accustomed manner, had forsaken his dreary abode; his dress was neglected; his hair in disordered ringlets hung upon his shoulders: In short, scarce a vestige of

the finished gentleman remained; and his folded arms and vacant countenance, as I beheld him unobserved, were almost descriptive of insan-
ity: But the jailer announcing my name, his agonized and unaffected
discomposure commanded my utmost commiseration; an expression
indicative of mingling confusion, surprise and apprehension, instantly
suffused his cheek; and, with extreme perturbation, he exclaimed,
"Good God! Mr. Vigillius—this is too much—but, forgive me, Sir, *the
uniformity of your character* will not permit a continuance of the idea,
that you are come hither either to reproach or insult me."

"To insult you, Mr. Courtland! God forbid. I come hither rather the
petitioner of your favour; and it is a truth, that I at this moment feel, in
regard to you, all the father predominating in my bosom; but, having
matter for your private ear, I must beg the indulgence of this gentleman
for a few moments."

The humane keeper withdrew with much civility; and the consternation of our delinquent was unutterable, while I proceeded to inform
him of the early knowledge I had obtained of the commencement and
progress of his career; of my information in regard to the ruined state of
his affairs; and of my actual correspondence with his principal creditors.
"I have opened my business, Sir," I added, "by this exordium, on purpose to let you know how well qualified I am to serve you; and however
you may have smarted, while I have thus taken it upon me to probe
your wounds, I flatter myself you may be induced to bless the hand,
which is furnished also with a specific. In short, Sir, I am this morning
authorized to act in your affairs—*a fair plaintiff hath constituted me her
attorney, and I come to offer you terms of accommodation*—Miss Wellwood, Sir——" At the sound of this name he changed colour, bit his
lips, groaned deeply, and vehemently articulated—*"Jesus God, have
mercy on me!"* and, as if that injured female herself had been present, he
thus continued: *"Miss* Wellwood—*lovely, but too credulous fair one—
wretched woman!—I have undone thee; but, Madam, my death shall soon
present you the only compensation in my power."*

"I came not, Sir," interrupted I, *"to point to the defenceless bosom the
shaft of despair:* If you please, I will read a letter, which was written by
Miss Wellwood to my daughter." I read; and, as I folded the paper, I

beheld with astonishment, the tear of contrition bedewing his pallid cheek! *"Welcome stranger!"* he exclaimed—*"lovely woman—injured saint—forgiving martyr!—Yes, Heaven is my witness, that the tenderest affection of which this obdurate heart hath ever been capable, hath still been the undivided, unalienated possession of* Fanny Wellwood—but, Sir, she knows not the depth of my misery—God of heaven! my crimes have already precipitated me into the gulph of perdition, and there remains no remedy."

But not to fatigue my readers by further circumlocution, I found that our gentleman had become as wax in my hand; and I proposed to him, that if I could procure his enlargement, he should retire immediately to my dwelling, where he would meet Miss Wellwood; and that the nuptial ceremony being *legally* performed, my house should become his castle; that I myself would undertake his affairs, thoroughly investigate every point, and endeavour to adjust matters with his creditors.

My proposal was accepted, *with the most extravagant and rapturous demonstrations of joy;* and my interest, combined with that of a substantial neighbour's, soon liberating the captive, produced him a *happy and a grateful bridegroom.* The rites of the church were performed; not a single ceremony was omitted—while Margaretta and Serafina, blooming as Hebe,[1] and cheerful as the morning, officiated as bride-maids.

Agreeably to my promise, I very soon opened my negociation with the different claimants upon Mr. Courtland. New-Haven furnished me with many auxiliaries; it was sufficient to produce the daughter of Mr. Wellwood, to command, in her favour, the most energetic efforts: We speedily obtained a very advantageous compromise: our debtor was, by the joint assistance of many respectable characters, set up in business; and the deficiencies of nature and education, which we have noted in him, were abundantly supplied, *by the abilities, application, and economical arrangements of* Mrs. Courtland. Every year, a regular dividend of the profits of their business is remitted to their creditors; a large part of the old arrears is discharged; and they bid fair, in the run of a few revolving seasons, to possess themselves of a very handsome *competency.*

---

1. **Hebe:** in Greek mythology, the goddess of eternal youth.

CHAPTER 7

And now the ripening harvest clustering round,
With fruits mature our well form'd hopes were crown'd.

I am sometimes wonderfully amused by the various comments upon these my lucubrations, which in the course of my peregrinations are frequently poured into my ear. It must be confessed, that as I journey from place to place, I am sufficiently solicitous to collect the sentiments of my readers; and that although I am often subjected to extreme mortification in this my anxious pursuit, yet I have, upon some occasions, inhaled, from the voice of the genuine critic, the fine effluvia of well-judged praise.

But during a late tour, which I made to a distant metropolis, I was not so fortunate as to observe that my laurel crown was much indebted to the brightening hand of fame; for although I then breathed the natal air of the Massachusetts Magazine, yet I found that upon the ear of *the many,* even the name of the Gleaner had never vibrated; and that a considerable majority of those whose attention he had engaged, seemed more occupied in detecting the *real author,* than in essaying to investigate the merit of his productions! An old lady, (taking off her spectacles, and laying down her knitting-work) informed me she had been credibly assured, that the Gleaner had in fact never been married; that he was a young man, a dweller in Worcester, and that he never having had a *bit of a wife,* it was impossible to tell what to believe.

A *facetious divine,* sitting by, gravely replied, "Well, if the scoundrel has imposed upon the public by a fictitious tale, he ought surely to be tossed in a blanket; and I, for my part, am willing to lend any assistance in my power, to deliver a delinquent, so atrocious, to condign punishment."

A sober young woman next joined in the conversation, proceeding with great solemnity to give in her evidence: She said she had but just returned from New-Haven; that she happened to be there when the

---

Chapter 7. Published in *The Gleaner,* 1:12.

story of Miss Wellwood came out; and that she was, by unquestionable authority, positively assured they had never heard the name of Margaretta Melworth, until they saw it in the Magazine; that the Wellwoods, the Courtlands, and even the Worthingtons, (as described by the Gleaner) were wholly unknown in that city.

"Pshaw, pshaw, young woman," said a pedant, who had eyed the fair speaker with an air of supercilious contempt, "you know nothing of the matter; but ignorance is always forth putting. I tell you that I had the honour of receiving my education at Yale College; I was there at the very period, on which the Gleaner represents his Margaretta as having passed some time in the city of New-Haven, and I more than once saw that young lady at church, and in several private families; it is true that being then but a youth, (for it was my first year in the seminary) I was not very intimate with Miss Melworth, otherwise, I doubt not, I should have been made acquainted with every particular which he records." A testimony so decisive, could not be controverted; the old lady resumed her knitting, and an air of general complacency took place.

I cannot help regarding this *hunting after names,* as descriptive of the frivolity of the human mind: No sooner does an anonymous piece make its appearance, than curiosity invests itself in the stole of sagacity, conjecture is upon the rack—Who is he? Where does he live? What is his *real name,* and occupation? And to the importance of these questions, considerations of real weight give place; as if the being able to ascertain a name was replete with information of the most salutary kind. Whereas, if the writing is in no sort personal, and cannot be construed into a libel, a knowledge of the author can be of no moment, neither can a name designate a character. *Facts, real events,* have often been communicated to the world *under feigned names;* and instruction not seldom arrays itself in the decent and alluring veil of allegory.

The business of the reader is to scan the *intrinsic value* and *general tendency* of the composition; if that is considerable, if that is laudable, he ought to leave the author to announce himself under what auspices he shall judge proper.

Passing from these *name-hunters,* I joined a select tea party, when I had an opportunity of hearing the work itself very freely descanted upon; and while I was humbled by the uncandid and satirical disquisition which I underwent, I was proportionably elated at observing that my daughter was as much a favourite in the world at large, as in the village in which she hath been educated. In Margaretta every one appeared interested; and, however questionable the merit of the Gleaner was deemed, Miss Melworth obtained her full share of applause. A damsel, verging upon thirty, the height of whose feathers was enormous, pronounced the poetry of the Gleaner *pitiful;* declared his essays in general much *below a mediocrity;* and she added, that in her opinion they depreciated as rapidly as the paper currency of insolvent memory; that his last numbers were *monstrously* unnatural; that the library scene in particular was quite *outree,* [1] since it was impossible to conceive of a man so *truly polite,* thus passionate; that her friend Mrs. G—— condemned those writings altogether, and that Mrs. G—— having *travelled, and seen the world, must undoubtedly be acknowledged a competent judge.* Yet she allowed Margaretta to be a decent young person; and she doubted not if she had been left entirely to herself, she would have generously chosen the *man of her heart,* whatever might have been the embarrassments in which his *juvenile errors* might have involved him.

"*Juvenile errors!*" repeated a female who sat next her. "Is it possible, Madam, that you can bestow an epithet so gentle upon crimes of so deep a die? O! that our sex were conscious of their true dignity; *that they were just to themselves;* then should we no longer behold the unprincipled betrayer obtaining the confidence of virtue; then would the despoiler, banished from society, be necessitated to press forward to the path of rectitude, and a uniform pursuit of goodness becoming the price of his restoration to the privileges and immunities of a social being, he would be compelled to array himself in the garments of consistent equity. For my own part," continued the fair rationalist, "I am free to own, however singular it may be deemed, that unblemished virtue is, in my estimation, as essential in a man, as in a woman; and that as *man is commonly the primary aggressor,* I regard a *male prostitute* with even greater detestation than I do an abandoned female. I profess myself

---

1. **outree:** outrée; exaggerated (French).

an admirer of the Gleaner. I conceive him to be a moral writer; and I must own that far from thinking the library scene *unnatural,* I have conceived it inimitably drawn. *Courtland* is represented from the beginning as a man extremely superficial; that shallow waters are not seldom noisy, is a common observation; and it is as true that in silent majesty the great profound may stand collected. Mr. Vigillius, with infinite address, had wrought up to the highest pitch, the sanguine expectations of his man; he is in fancy placed upon an eminence at which he had long aimed; and having, as he supposed, at length obtained the enviable summit of his wishes, he is suddenly dashed therefrom.

"Is it then surprising to find him off his guard, especially when it is remembered, that his reasons for keeping measures with the Gleaner were no longer in force? Viewing the matter in this light, I confess, it appears to me rather extraordinary, that his passions discovered *no greater excess.* But, be this as it may, I declare to you, that Margaretta captivates my very soul; that the virtues attributed to Hamilton strike me most pleasingly: I am charmed with the open integrity, and the manly consistency of the character of that youth; and I cannot but hope that the ensuing Gleaner, recounting his union with Miss Melworth, will give us an opportunity of contemplating the most faultless pair who have ever lighted the torch of Hymen, since the lord of paradise received our general mother from the hand of her Creator."

"What in the name of ingenuity," interrupted the lady who was filling tea, *"has he done with Hamilton?* I protest I am enchanted by that divine fellow; his disdaining to enter the lists with Courtland, and his absenting himself during the pursuit of that unworthy pretender, was a deportment at once dignified, proper and manly. I confess that it hath been no small disappointment to me, to find him in the several last Gleaners but barely mentioned; and I am absolutely impatient to hear of his return from exile, and of the restoration of his hopes."

The lovely sentimentalists here adverted to, will recollect a conversation so recent; and, from the throng which upon that occasion crowded the levee of Mrs. ———, they may possibly recognize the Gleaner; but even in this case, I feel pleasingly assured, that in the bosom of candour, discretion and good-nature, *my secret is perfectly safe,* while I am confident, that by *the many I shall remain untraced.* My amiable panegyrists were unconscious that they delivered their sentiments in the presence of an *interested man, who hung upon their lips, engraving their words in characters indelible upon the tablets of his breast;* yet, as I am happy in an opportunity of rendering to superior merit the tribute of esteem; so I hasten with alacrity, to pen the acknowledgments of gratitude; and while, in a manner as succinct as possible, I proceed to bring down my narration to the present period, it is with substantial satisfaction I confess that my hopes are invigorated, and my efforts stimulated, by a knowledge that persons so worthy await, with some impatience, the recital of a catastrophe which hath long since gratified my utmost wishes.

It happened that Mr. Hamilton returned home upon the very evening which witnessed the nuptials of Mr. Courtland and Miss Wellwood. Being ignorant of his route, it had not been in our power to follow him by letter; and he was consequently unacquainted with every thing that had passed in our village, during his absence. This plan he had purposely concerted, with an expectation of banishing from his bosom those tender sentiments of Margaretta, which were inconsistent with his peace; and fondly imagining that he had effectuated his wishes, he alighted at the lodgings of Serafina, whither he first repaired, in tolerable tranquillity; but, on inquiring for Miss Clifford, being rather abruptly informed by her maid, that her young lady passed that evening in the family of Mr. Vigillius, in order to assist at the marriage of Mr. Courtland, he discovered, in a single moment, the cruel fallacy of those hopes he had so confidently cherished. He was unacquainted with the existence and even the name of Miss Wellwood: It was Courtland's wedding night; he could think of no one but Margaretta; a thousand varying ideas rushed instantaneously upon his mind; all his purposes were broken; and he saw that, so far from accomplishing the laudable end which he had proposed, by tearing himself from the beloved object, he had too probably accelerated his own ruin.

In speechless agony he clasped his hands, and raising his fine eyes to Heaven, he hastily withdrew to the retirement of his own chamber, where, summoning reason, fortitude and religion to his aid, he endeavoured to rally his scattered forces, to recollect those resources which, in prospect, had appeared so pregnant with consolation; and, upon this occasion, pressing into his service every *balancing* auxiliary, in a manner becoming the mind conscious of its divine origin, of its transitory abode in tabernacles of clay, and of its beatified and immortal destination—in a manner honorary to philosophy, and honorary to manhood, he sought to make head against those passions which were ravaging all before them, and which were seeking to precipitate him into the abyss of despair! What progress he would have made in this conflict, and on which side victory would have declared, I pretend not to determine; for after the combat had continued, with various success, from twilight grey, until the sober hour of twelve, the whole phalanx of discretion was thrown into disorder, by the following little harmless scrip of paper, received from the hand of Serafina; true, it bore on its milk-white surface certain *caballistic*[1] inscriptions, which seemed endowed with magic influence; and Hamilton read with no less ardour than it was penned, the language of friendship.

"A delicious moment is at hand—I myself will be the narrator—*come to me, my friend, this instant.* I would rather lose whole years of my existence, than the luxury of an hour, which Fortune (I thank her *goddess-ship*) hath reserved for her, *upon this occasion, devout admirer,*

SERAFINA CLIFFORD."

CHAPTER 8

> To the blest haunts of amity he flew,
> Hope lent him wings—and wild predictions drew:
> But sovereign truth explanatory rose,
> And sweet oblivion whelm'd his tender woes.

It is scarcely necessary to add, that Edward immediately obeyed this flattering summons: He was at a loss what to conceive, and he was ready to hope for impossibilities; but a short interval presenting him before

---

1. **caballistic:** mysteriously artistic.

Chapter 8. Published in *The Gleaner,* 1:13.

the companion of his youth, he had little time for conjecture; and the propitious explanation was no sooner given, than, absorbed in a delirium of joy, he lost sight of every ill, and pronounced himself wholly invulnerable, altogether superior to the shafts of future sorrow.

The ensuing morning produced him, the image of rationally complacent happiness, in our bridal circle. He attended Miss Clifford; Mary and myself were addressed by him with pleasing respect; and while he bowed upon the hand of Margaretta, his eye beamed unutterable tenderness; a refined and animated kind of affection, and a glow of ineffable satisfaction, swelled every expressive feature, mantled upon his cheek, and seemed to invest him with supernatural graces: In short, the fine manly open countenance evidently assumed a celestial contour, and the charming youth was never before so completely captivating.

In the beautiful face of Margaretta, mingling surprise and pleasure were agreeably blended; a blush of sensibility pervaded her cheek; and an attachment, which I dare believe will be lasting as her life, gradually enlisted every faculty of her soul; an attachment, raised upon the superstructure of esteem, entwining a full growth of amity, and finally attaining the honorary wreath of rationally approved love. Such an attachment was alone worthy the bosom of Miss Melworth; and I had the happiness to observe, that her meliorated passions, rectified and confirmed, at length pointed to the centre of true and chastised felicity.

No sooner was she assured of the continued, and even augmented tenderness, and of the confiding friendship of her Edward, than she yielded up her whole heart, without hesitation, to the sweetly fascinating impression. Sanctioned by duty, authorized by reason, and borne forward upon the feathery sails of white-bosomed hope, she did not see that she ought to blush at avowing those sentiments of preference, which her youthful heart acknowledged; and they were, in truth, as pure as those which are impressed upon seraphic bosoms, amid the paradise of their God.

During the period which preceded her marriage, she gave and received many visits to and from Miss Worthington. She made many little tours round the country; and, possessing a strikingly commanding exterior, with manners so truly pleasing, she was, of course, followed by a train of admirers. Courtlands, Bellamours and Plodders, of every description, crowded about her; and, assailed on every side by the perniciously enervating and empoisoned airs of adulation, the uniformity of her character was put to the severest test.

Miss Melworth, however, was fully equal to the ordeal which was thus prepared for her; and she continued to receive her admirers of every description, in a manner which was truly worthy of approbation. The impassioned feelings of the devoted heart, never contributed, in the smallest degree, to her amusement: She had not to charge herself with inflicting a single moment's unnecessary pain; and no sooner did the serious pretender advance his claim, than his professions of love, though received with grateful respect, were decisively rejected. Obligations for every honorary testimony, she was free to acknowledge; but she was not ambitious to enlist a train of danglers. Her heart, tremblingly alive to the merits of Hamilton, although the nature of their connexion was not publickly known, was ready, almost indignantly, to resent the officious competition of those, whom her delicacy induced her to consider as intruders. But reason, true to its office, corrected the fervid ebullitions of passion, and always brought her back to that tranquillity of mind, so necessary to the full exercise of her fine talents. Observation, experience, reason and judgment, these all combined to confirm her in the election she had made; and, on the bosom of serenity, her hours rolled on.

Both the mental and exterior accomplishments of our children were still improving; their mutual attachment seemed daily to augment, and the prospect still brightened upon us. We often addressed them upon the importance of the vows they were destined to exchange, representing, with all the energy which language could command, the necessity of a permanent and unabating affection, to render silken the bands of wedlock.

Expect not, we exclaimed, a continuance of those vernal zephyrs,[1] which will fan the genial flame of your early loves: It is true you may embark upon a summer's sea, but the unavoidable evils, the vicissitudes,

---

1. **vernal zephyrs:** gentle spring breezes.

and too probably the storms of life, will arise—rocks and quicksands await the voyager, and eagle-eyed discretion ought to set at helm, if you would pass safely between extremes, which may be regarded as equally dangerous! Mutual esteem, mutual friendship, mutual confidence, *begirt about by mutual forbearance*—these are the necessary requisites of the matrimonial career; and there is not a virtuous endowment that can fall to the share of mortality, which may not be called into action.

We conjure you to consult each other's humours, dispositions, sentiments, and pursuits—an interval is given you for this purpose: Congenial tastes, congenial spirits, you ought to possess, *or at least a similarity of views is absolutely indispensable, if you mean to secure the social enjoyment of your lives.* Be not afraid, dear children of our fondest hopes, be not afraid to come to the test. Submit with cheerfulness to the most scrutinizing ordeal; the present is your era of experiments. Look well to your *individual faults;* forbear to *emblazon your virtues;* and, if you find you cannot wholly eradicate any little peculiarities, which the imbecility of human nature may perhaps have interwoven with your constitution, examine if you can *tolerate them;* and seek not, at the risk of your future quiet, during these peace crowned days, to shut your eyes upon each other's errors! If you entertain the shadow of a preference for any other object; if your long cherished attachment experiences abatement— shrink not from the voice of public censure—*you are still at liberty*— other pursuits yet open themselves before you—your most direct step is an open declaration of what passes in the inmost recesses of your bosoms, to parents, who will not fail to patronize and uphold you in every action, which is, strictly speaking, the result of undeviating rectitude.

Reason authorises us at this time thus to address you; but when once the hallowed hour, that shall witness your plighted faith, is past, the transaction of that hour will be indissoluble! Death only can set you free; and we shall then, in one particular, dictate for our children a reverse of conduct. A familiar figure will elucidate our meaning. You are to behold *each other's virtues with a microscopic gaze,* while we shall hardly permit you to glance at a *blemish,* even through the *telescope of affection.* It was to this effect we occasionally, frequently, and solemnly addressed our children, while we were peculiarly happy in remarking, that even to the searching eye of anxious solicitude, not a single moment of apathy, hesitation or regret was at any time apparent.

Thus rolled on the weeks, months, and years, until revolving time produced the promised era: It took place in the last vernal season, when the humid steps of April were on the point of resigning their tear gemmed empire to the bland and flowery feet of the wreath crowned and odour breathing month of May. Margaretta had then just rounded her nineteenth year; and, much sooner than would have been our *uninfluenced wish,* we resigned our lovely charge into the hands of him, who had long been the deliberate choice of her heart.

Arrayed in majesty serene, the morning broke. The orb of day assumed to our grateful view an uncommon cheerfulness—all nature looked gay—the flowers seemed just expanding with emblematic sweetness—and the birds carolled most divinely.

We were not solicitous to collect a throng about us upon that auspicious day. With happiness innate in our bosoms, the *pomp* and *parade* of *joy* we were contented to spare; and our circle consisted only of those, whose faces we should have contemplated with pleasure upon every rising morn and setting sun.

But though only a select party were summoned to partake our felicity, and to gild, by their presence, our bridal day, yet we were ambitious of diffusing the face of gladness over our village; and we therefore appropriated the sums which we might have expended in the flowing goblet, and at the festal board, to the preparing nuptial presents for those who mourned beneath the iron sway of penury, and who, by this well-timed relief, felt their hearts once more attuned to the genial voice of pleasure; who hasted to entwine for us the wreath of gratitude, the perfume of which was as the sweetest incense to our souls; and who, bending at the footstool of paternal Deity, supplicated Heaven to confer upon us the choicest blessings.

The bride appeared among us arrayed in spotless white; her robe was a delicate muslin, drawn in many a flower, from the rich variety of her elegant fancy, and neatly wrought by her own fair hands. She beheld the approach of her wedding day, unconscious of those terrors attributed to her sex. Upon the evening preceding the appointed morning, she enter-

tained us, at our first request, with many of our favourite airs, upon her
piano forte. I did not perceive her heart flying through her bodice! and
her tremors being of the governable kind, she was all her own agreeable
self. What passed between her and her mother, with whom she retired
for a few hours, I am yet to learn; but this I know, that the day itself was
not ushered in either by fits, or any violently agonized emotions. Virgin
delicacy only served to animate, to heighten, and to new point the
exquisite beauties which adorn the finest face I have ever seen; and she
accompanied us to the altar, where the ceremony was performed, with a
sober and chastised expression of complacency, which seemed to say—*I
have taken sufficient time to deliberate—I am under the direction of my
best friends*—every sentiment, every passion of my soul approves the
man who is this day to become my husband. Undoubtedly he is every
way worthy; I possess his tender and entire affection—his entire confidence. I am assured; I am satisfied; I am happy.

For Hamilton, the unbounded rapture which took possession of his
bosom, was blended, however, with a dignified and manly manifesta-
tion of tenderness, which served to tranquillize his deportment, and to
present him in a state of mind becoming the sacred rites which were to
be performed: Yet, when he received the hand of Margaretta, the big
emotions of his bosom refused to be wholly suppressed—"Condescending excellence!" he exclaimed "may He, who thus enriches me,
render me worthy of so much goodness." The ceremony, excepting this
interruption, passed agreeably to its sacred arrangement; and, after the
good Urbanius had pronounced the benediction, we adjourned to our
own mansion; and, since, what halcyon days, weeks and months have
revolved! Not a cloud has yet obscured our horizon.

Last week, Margaretta presented Edward with her first born—it is a
male infant. Let me see—eleven months of uninterrupted felicity!! Can
this last? The present is a checkered state.

Reader, though we bid adieu to Margaretta for the present, I would
not have thee lament it too seriously. I know thou art tenderly attached
to her; and I therefore give thee my word, that if thy acquaintance with
me continuest, we will occasionally peep in upon her, and thus learn,
from time to time, how matters go on.

CHAPTER 9

Then are the shafts of disappointment barb'd,
When of her well form'd hopes the soul is robb'd.

"All is not right at Margaretta's"—said my poor Mary, some nights since, as she laid her head upon her pillow. It was an involuntary expression, and from the fullness of her heart it escaped her: She would gladly have recalled it, or at least have palliated its effects, but it was too late, for the impression was indelibly made—*all is not right at Margaretta's!* Her words reverberated through the inmost recesses of my soul; they seemed to possess a deadly power, which, at a single blow, annihilated the serenity of my bosom. A thousand painful ideas rushed in a moment upon my mind, and they originated the most alarming and affecting conjectures.

I had observed, that a kind of pensive melancholy had for some time clouded the fine open countenance of my wife; that her wonted equanimity was interrupted; that her slumbers were disturbed and broken; and that the admirable regularity of her movements were evidently discomposed. As I possessed a perfect confidence in her prudence, I had forborne to press her upon so distressing a change, well knowing, that whenever it was advantageous or proper, discretion would not fail of prompting her to pour into my ear the sorrows of her heart.

Maternal affection had armed her with an anxious and vigilant attention to her daughter; she had for some months marked a visible alteration in her child; the dimpling smile of complacency no more spontaneously welcomed her approach; thick glooms encircled her brow; and while she visibly struggled to preserve appearances, the tenor of her soul was apparently lost! Whenever Mary occasionally looked in upon her Margaretta, if her visit was unexpected, she was sure to find her bathed in tears; and the apologies which she seemed to study, but ill concealed the discomposure of an agonized bosom.

Mary, with all her penetration, could not divine the cause of an

---

Chapter 9. Published in *The Gleaner,* 1:20.

event, which she so greatly deplored; she imagined that her daughter was in possession of every thing which could conduce to the most pleasing kind of tranquillity; and she conceived that the grateful affections of her heart ought to be in constant exercise. Competency beamed its regular, mild, and equal blessings upon her; her infant was not only lovely and promising, but he seemed almost exempted from those disorders, which are usually attendant upon his imbecile age; her own health was uniformly good; and though Edward Hamilton partook, of course, the morbid contagion of her grief, yet he was still the pensively pleasing and entertaining companion.

Mary concluded, that nothing remained, but for Margaretta to re-assume the accustomed equability of her temper, in order to the perfect restoration of that sunshine, which had for a season illumed her hours; and tenderly interested, while her heart was torn by anxiety, she could not forbear to interrogate—but the only replies she could obtain were sighs and tears, interrupted by broken assurances, that indeed she was —she was very happy; and that she supplicated her dear Mamma to put upon every appearance the most candid construction. Her mother, however, made wise by the observations she had collected from books, from the study of her fellow mortals, and from a large share of natural discernment, could not be thus easily deceived.

Curiosity was, upon this occasion, her smallest inducement; and she trembled at the impervious darkness of a cloud, which she rationally apprehended involved the dearest hopes of her Margaretta! Baffled in repeated attempts to fathom a mystery, which had yielded her bosom a prey to the keenest anguish, she changed the mode of her attack; and, addressing her daughter by letter, in the language of discretion, in the language of tenderness, she penned the feelings of her soul.

To Mrs. HAMILTON.

Is it possible for Margaretta Hamilton to conceive her mother a calm spectator of that corroding inquietude, which is gradually and too surely undermining the peace of a child, who is, she had almost said, dearer to her than any other human being? As I have not been stimulated by an idle wish to obtain your secret, I am hurt that my inquiries have proved so ineffectual. Can Margaretta wish to veil herself from the eye of the guardian friend of her early years? Believe me, I seek only to probe the wound, that I may the more assuredly arrest the progress of the envenomed poison, and be enabled to judge what prescription may operate as a specific.

But, for the tender age of innocence, the advice of the physician is the superstructure of conjecture; and in this instance I am necessitated to follow the example of the benevolent practitioner, at all hazards assaying to throw in something, which may possibly preserve the opening life of those budding joys, the growth of which I had fondly hoped to have watched, until I had gratulated their confirmed maturity.

When we gave our Margaretta to Edward Hamilton, *we conceived that we had yielded her to the man of her heart;* and, believing him to be every way worthy, we congratulated ourselves upon the establishment of the felicity of our child. What, my love, can have produced a change so affectingly agonizing? Whenever you *appear* tolerably composed, it is *evident* that you are *acting* a part.

I tremble lest your father should penetrate the thin disguises which you assume; and, sanguine as his expectations in regard to you have been, it is difficult to say, what serious consequences his disappointment might produce.

Oh, my child, my soul is torn by the most fearful conjectures! will you not endeavour to assuage the sorrows of my heart? will you not at least relieve me from the pangs of suspense? Can it be, that Mrs. Hamilton is so far subjected to sexual weakness, as to have delivered herself up to the most alarming chagrin, merely because, perhaps, she receives not from the husband such *adulatory devoirs* as distinguished the lover? Surely I ought to regard this idea as inadmissible; and yet, the strongest minds may have their moments of imbecility; and, my Margaretta, all accomplished, all lovely as she is, must nevertheless still be considered as a young and inexperienced woman.

If this is indeed the source of your perturbed anxiety, I persuade myself that some such reflections as the following, will ere long awaken you to reason.

It is impossible to change the order of nature. Delighted admiration of pleasing novelties, is the spontaneous growth of every bosom; a sec-

ond view finds us more calm; a third, a fourth, may possibly rouse us to
pleasure; but a constant repetition will create that indifference, which
will constitute a perfect contrast to the keen edge of our new-born feelings. The impassioned ardours of the soul must of necessity subside; *they
are but created to expire:* But I pity the mind which prefers not the calm
rational affections that succeed, to all the hurricane of the passions.

Love, as it is commonly described, is undoubtedly a short-lived
being; it is a luxurious glutton, that invariably gormandizeth to its
destruction; but from its perfumed ashes ariseth a star-gemmed soother,
that the wedded pair may either crush in the birth, or agree to cherish,
as the security of their mutual happiness. Esteem may sometimes be
traced as the *parent,* but I think it will be found that it is oftener the *offspring* of love. Young esteem, entwined by smiling confidence,
enwreathed with sweet complacency, how fragrant is its rosy breath,
how necessary to the hymeneal career, and how much is it in the power
of the affianced friends to render its existence permanent!

Behold your Edward in a large circle of ladies; doubtless, he is all
attention; his features are animated; and if they are young, beautiful
and sentimental, he is all soul; he seems to tread on air, and he hath no
eyes or ears, but for them; he will address to them the most refined gal-
lantries, and he will appear lost amid a constellation so splendid. But
think you, my love, that he would experience sensations thus highly
wrought, were he to mingle every hour in their society? and would you
wish to exchange for such *mental gewgaws,* if I may so express myself,
the solid pleasures of endearing familiarity; the advantages resulting
from unbroken confidence, from a social intercourse, uninterrupted by
the fopperies of language, and from all the matchless and serene enjoyments which wedded friends may know?

Are you not apprehensive that the continued clouds which gloom
your lovely face, may prematurely destroy your bloom, and, by imperceptible degrees, alienate the affections of your husband? If once you
relinquish your place in his bosom, it will require a series of the most
arduous efforts to restore you to the possession you will have thus
imprudently abdicated!

I am not an advocate for undue gentleness, or submissive acquiescence; such conduct may border upon meanness; a woman should be

just too, she should reverence herself. I am far from conceiving that the female world, considered in the aggregate, is inferior to the male; but custom hath established a certain order in society, and custom is a despot, whose chains, I am fearful, it will be in vain that an individual will assay to burst.

I know too, that it is for the interest of every person who singly considers either him or herself, to cultivate an *equal* and *serene* temper of mind. If you array yourself in the garments of tranquillity, if you seek to clothe yourself with innate cheerfulness, *habit* will at length render you in *reality complacent,* and it will not be you who will derive the smallest share of advantage therefrom.

In short, my dear girl, you have every inducement to call forth your most unremitted exertions. Parents tenderly anxious for your welfare— Parents, whose felicity is inseparably entwined with your own; a husband acknowledged as highly deserving, and a beauteous infant, whose little eyes are raised to you for protection, for instruction, and for peace: Oh! cloud not his budding life by a grief so strange and unaccountable; his lovely cheek should not thus early be washed by the tear of sorrow. Oh, pierce not thus the bosom of her who hath reared you to womanhood, whose prime hopes of temporal enjoyment rest with you, and who, in consequence of that authority, which by high Heaven is vested in her, demands of you an account of that latent woe, which, *gaining strength by concealment,* is thus preying upon all your promised joys. Speak, I conjure you, speak; and let your communications mitigate the pangs, which cease not to lacerate the bosom of your afflicted and commiserating mother.

The evening of the day, which had presented the foregoing address, returned Mary the subjoined reply.

To my dear and honoured MOTHER.

Pitying angels—and must I then speak? assuredly I must—every consideration unquestionably points out an explanation.

I have sunk, mortifyingly sunk, in the estimation of her whose *appro-*

bation I would die to preserve; and I have inflicted upon her the severest anguish; yet, probably, her tender bosom may be disburthened, by a knowledge that her Margaretta is not altogether so culpable as she hath apprehended: And duty seems to impel an unreserved confidence; for the honoured woman, to whom I am primarily indebted for every thing that can render life valuable, hath commanded me to be explicit.

But stop!—can duties clash? Ought the discreet female to accuse him to whom she hath voluntarily yielded her most sacred and solemn vows? Can Margaretta criminate her Edward!!!!

Yet, possibly, what I have to urge in my own defence, may not exhibit my Hamilton in a censurable point of view; from a mutable being we are not to expect immutability; and if my conjectures have their foundation in truth, though I may be wretched, I will not be unjust. It is necessary that I justify myself to my mother; but I will not dare to cast a shade upon the character of a man, whom I regard as the first of created beings.

Hardly three months after our marriage had elapsed, when Edward exhibited marks of a growing and deep-felt inquietude! an impenetrable gloom overshadowed every feature! Had you witnessed, as I have done, and still do, the lasting and serious sorrows of his bosom, your maternal remonstrance would have been addressed to him, rather than to your unfortunate child. Often hath he regarded me with a fixed and melancholy attention; and when, alarmed and terrified, I have sought the cause of his mysterious deportment, as if unable to command his grief, he hath fled with precipitation from my importunities. To induce him to disclose the fatal secret of his heart, no means within my power have been left unassayed; and although failing in my well intended efforts, I have still endeavoured to soothe and woo his steps to the sweet and flowery paths of peace.

With the severe eye of unrelenting rigour, I have examined my own conduct: Probably I am under the dominion of *self-partiality;* for, in regard to him, I cannot view myself as reprehensible either in thought, word, or deed.

When, by your direction, I announced to him my expectation of presenting him with a little being, who would bring into the world with it,

its claims to his fondest affections,—Oh, Madam! instead of the effect
which we naturally imagined, the sorrows of his heart became ungovernable; with convulsed and agonized emotions, he clasped his hands—
Never shall I forget his exclamation; it sounded like a death-warrant to
my ear—*"Gracious God! wretch, wretch that I am!"*—What he would
have added, I know not; for, overpowered by my grief and my surprise,
I sunk lifeless at his feet; and when, by his endeavours, and those of the
attendants whom he summoned to my relief, I was recalled to sense and
to recollection, I found him kneeling by my bed side, assiduously and
tenderly employed in my restoration, and his transports at beholding
me, as he expressed himself, once more open my eyes to love and to
him, at seeing the bloom again revisit my cheeks, were, he declared, the
most exquisite he had ever experienced!

You will not doubt, that I seized this tender moment, to expostulate
with him relative to his heart-affecting and soul-piercing expressions of
grief, and continued melancholy; but, although he beheld me, as I then
supposed, with unabating affection, although he soothed my spirit by
the most delicate and unequivocal assurances, he nevertheless turned a
deaf ear to the voice of my supplication! Edward Hamilton hath a
strong and determined mind; fortitude is innate in his bosom; he can
wear to the public eye, and even to the circle of his friends, a face of
tranquillity, while his breast is a prey to the most perturbed sensations.

Fearful of disgusting him by my persecutions, I banished from my
lips every expression of my anxiety; and, as far as was in my power, I dis-
missed from my features the inquietude of my bosom. I studied, by my
every movement, his pleasure; and I flattered myself, that the birth of
my child, by giving a new turn to his ideas, would restore my felicity. It
is true that I had nothing to complain of, except the corroding grief,
with which he evidently struggled, and which, notwithstanding his
efforts to conceal it, was generally the companion of his private hours:
For the rest, I judged myself in possession of his heart, and his deportment was descriptive of the most refined and faithful attachment.

Thus passed the days, until the arrival of my pangful hour. You, dear
Madam, were a witness to the distressing agitation of his soul, during
that perilous and tremendous period; you heard and repeated his fervid

vows for my safety; they were music in my ears; doubtless they were sincere, for the heart of Edward Hamilton is as tender as it is manly. You also witnessed the rapt sensation of his grateful spirit, when he received his son; you heard and marked the paternal blessings, which he poured upon his youngling head; and, it is true, that the little creature is as dear to him, as the vital spark which warms him to existence—*but alas! this is the sum total of my enjoyments!* The anguish of heart, which is destroying the *father of my child,* seems daily to augment! The tears, of which he is apparently unconscious, often bedew the face of my infant! Frequently, as if by mutual consent, we gaze in silent sorrow upon the dear innocent, and when Hamilton supposes himself unobserved, his eyes and hands are raised toward heaven; and in all the majesty of innate woe, he pathetically makes his appeal to the Searcher of all hearts, while rectitude, it should seem, is the motto of his life.

Yet, I will not withhold some circumstances, that have produced inferences, which my full soul hath recoiled at admitting. Alas, my mother! will you not esteem me wretched, when I confess to you, that I have but too much reason to suppose *myself the origin of his misfortune.*

Some weeks after the birth of my little William, I was alarmed by the frequent absence of Hamilton; and as I *forbore any remarks thereon, being unwilling to embitter, by my expostulations, the few moments which he allowed me,* I continued ignorant of the manner in which he appropriated his time. *Accident,* at length, informed me that all those hours of which he had robbed me, were devoted to Serafina! and from her he always returned a prey to the deepest and most fearful chagrin.

The shock which my tenderness and my sensibility received, in a moment so replete with anguish, I assay not to describe; but reason, I bless God, darted athwart the region of my soul her beamy[1] influence. Serafina was the sister of my heart; she was a lovely and an amiable woman. Edward and Serafina had been educated together from early life; their habits of intimacy were confirmed; and I considered, that if her society possessed more charms than mine, Edward was unfortunate, but not culpable.

---

1. **beamy:** radiant.

I immediately formed the resolution of soliciting her to become an inmate in our house; and when I made my proposal to Hamilton, *he received it with more satisfaction than my feelings could well tolerate;* he kissed my hand with rapture; a gleam of joy vermilioned his cheek, and he flew to acquaint Miss Clifford with the wishes which I had expressed.

Serafina too demonstrated the highest complacency; a residence with her Margaretta, she was pleased to say, would complete her felicity; and she could not hesitate, when a situation every way eligible was tendered to her acceptance.

Our plan was no sooner concerted than put into execution: Miss Clifford was established in this mansion, and Hamilton no longer wandered abroad! When I am present, Hamilton hath never, for a single moment, abated his marked attentions to me; and he regards Serafina in his accustomed manner; but if I unexpectedly join them, although they have apparently been engaged in the most affectingly interesting conversation, they are immediately silent, embarrassed and uneasy!

The fine eyes of Serafina are often drowned in tears, and the grief of Hamilton seems to know no bounds! Two weeks since, upon the morning of the day on which you surprised me yielding up my whole soul to sorrow, supposing Hamilton in his closet, I took my needle-work, with a design, while sitting beside him, to make one more effort to allure him into the sweet and flowery walks of tranquillity. He was not there—but an open piece of paper lying upon his scrutoire,[1] written by the hand of Serafina, in which I saw my name in large characters inscribed, caught my attention. I read it—its contents are indelibly engraven upon the tablets of my heart; and, with a trembling hand, I transcribe them for your perusal.

"That I love not my own soul better than I do my Edward Hamilton, I trust he will always believe. I have received his *expostulatory letter,* and by that *love which we mutually avow,* I conjure him to consider, weigh, ponder, and reflect. *Can Edward consign Margaretta to ruin? Can he be forgetful of the interest and well-being of his infant son?* If Hamilton will

---

1. **scrutoire:** a small desk.

give to these claims their *due weight,* I persuade myself that he will then listen to the voice of prudence—of that prudence which is *in this instance,* regent in the bosom of

Serafina Clifford."

I read, I say—and the agony of my spirit was inexpressible—with a wild air I turned toward the window; and, as if fate had determined to make me completely wretched, I beheld Edward and Serafina, arm under arm, walking down the gravel-walk of our little flower garden: This, at such a moment, was too much. With precipitate and unequal steps, impassioned almost to frenzy, I hasted from the closet, flying, as for refuge, to my own. It was at this distressing juncture, that you, Madam, looked in upon me; you saw, and your eye condemned the irregular expressions of a sorrow to which you was a stranger; but I flatter myself that you will, in future, rather pity than censure your Margaretta.

Real illness, through that fatal day, served me as an apology for not making my appearance at dinner, or at evening tea time; and, in the course of the night, reason taught me sufficient self-command, to *appear* tolerably composed at breakfast the next morning. As I left the writing precisely as I found it, there cannot be an idea entertained of the suspicions which wound my bosom; and if it is mine to suffer, I am determined to suffer in silence.—Thus, dear and honoured Madam, you will see that I have no common cause of sorrow—that I am not so very faulty as you conceived. Thus have I entitled myself to your advice; and thus you will be induced to pity your

Margaretta Hamilton.

Mary hesitated not to dispatch the following approbating reply.

To Mrs. Hamilton.

No, my poor sufferer, you do not stand in need of advice—persevere as you have begun—Mr. Hamilton is a man of sense and feeling; he will rouse to a recollection of your virtues, and your *reward* will be great.

Believe me, I glory in my child.—My tears flow so fast, I cannot add; and I can only say, that I am indeed your commiserating and tender mother.

CHAPTER 10

Worth, sterling worth, amid the ordeal shines,
Conviction gems it—truth the polish gives;
Asbestos like, it whitens in the flames,
And in eternal records brightening lives.

Sitting, last evening, in the little apartment which I have devoted to pleasures, properly termed sentimental, I was endeavouring, while Mary was seated by my side, to amuse the hours which she employed at her needle, by a re-perusal of Gibbon's[1] Roman History. We had passed our afternoon, in a vain attempt to investigate the cause of the infelicity of our daughter; we went over and over the ground, we traced and re-traced, we exhausted the powers of retrospection, until wearied amid the wilds of conjecture, we attained the precise point from which we at first sat off.

I had forborne to question either Mr. or Mrs. Hamilton, imagining that the discretion of Margaretta must inevitably become finally triumphant; and I conceived, besides, that any interference, considering the exquisite sensibility and delicate circumstances of the parties, must unavoidably increase the evil we lamented.

But to delineate the agonized perplexity which tempested the bosom of Mary, is impossible! the perturbed sigh, humid cheek, and swoln eye, proclaimed the anguish of her spirit; while she in vain endeavoured to reassume the wonted fortitude and equability of her disposition.

Last evening, however, wiping from her face the tear of maternal woe, and calling into action all those efforts which it is the privilege of

---

Chapter 10. Published in *The Gleaner,* 1:21.

1. **Gibbon:** Edward Gibbon (1737–1794), English historian; author of *The History of the Decline and Fall of the Roman Empire* (1776–88).

tender esteem to embody, I so far succeeded in my attempts to soothe her mind, as to procure a temporary calm; and pressing, as an auxiliary, my admired historian, my purpose was to draw her off, at least for the moment, from the contemplation of the melancholy consequences of her daughter's marriage.

We had but just invested our pensive *tete-a-tete*, with a degree of apparent serenity, when Mrs. Hamilton, without being announced, rushed hastily into the apartment. Our astonishment at so unexpected a visit, was in no sort abated by the wild extravagance of which her air and manner were descriptive; it was, however, the mania of joy; and, without giving us time for reflection or interrogation, throwing herself suddenly at my feet, with clasped hands, and all the delirium of rapture, she exclaimed—"O Sir! O my father! bless, bless, your happy child!—delay not to bestow your benediction upon this, the most blissful period of her life; thus giving the paternal voice, to sanction and complete that measure of felicity, which perhaps her wayward and desponding heart hath but ill deserved."

Alarmed and apprehensive, I would have folded her to my breast, at no moment hesitating to pronounce a blessing, which was ever the spontaneous dictate of my heart; but ere I could utter a word, springing up and hasting forward, she threw her snowy arms around the neck of Mary. "O my mother, my more than mother! embrace your now not sorrowing, but perfectly assured and extaticaly enraptured Margaretta!"

Mary, alternately clasping her to her bosom, and regarding her with looks of agonized terror, struggled in vain for utterance; the impassioned feelings of her soul disdained language, and the perturbed emotions which agitated her spirit, were expressed only by an affecting and descriptive silence.

For myself, I am free to own, that the scene had almost unmanned me; and, that trembling equally for my wife and daughter, I could not have supported it a moment longer. It was interrupted by the entrance of Edward Hamilton and Serafina. "Ah, my love!" cried Hamilton, "why do you thus cruelly deprive me of your presence; at a moment too, when you have, as it were, renovated my existence; when you have relieved me from a burthen that, by its mighty pressure, had well near crushed my every hope of happiness this side the eternal world; when you have new pointed every felicity, and taught me still more highly to appreciate the inestimable worth of yourself, and of your ennobling affection! Were it possible I could call my Margaretta unkind, her absence at such a time, would be the only plea that could justify my accusation. *But who talks of accusation?* Margaretta, like the Being from whom she originates, and who hath formed her a near resemblance of his blessed self, *unreservedly forgives;* and, influenced also by an example so fair, while urged by their own lenient benevolence, our revered benefactors, parents, friends, will likewise condescend to sign my acquittal; and thus their once almost despairing culprit, restored to peace and to them, will new plume his hopes, and, re-embarking upon the voyage of life, he will trust that prosperous gales may attend his once shipwrecked prospects."

Margaretta, encircled in the arms of her husband, bent her sweet face upon his bosom, while Serafina, enthusiastically pressing her hands to her lips, murmured in broken sentences—"Lovely and forgiving *sister!* a sister indeed! angelic Margaretta! May God in heaven greatly reward and forever bless my indulgent Margaretta."

But not to fatigue the reader, by the incoherently agitated manner, in which we finally obtained an explanation of these mysterious appearances, I will piece together materials which, through many breaks and pauses, I received, and present a succinct narrative of circumstances, that have produced an ecclaircisement,[1] which hath rendered Margaretta, in her own estimation, the happiest of women.

The opening dawn of yesterday presented a serene autumnal morning, and the advancing day confirmed the pleasing indications of its rosy harbinger.

The ripened fruits of autumn gathered in, the industrious swain once more hailed the interval which, crowning his hopes, permitted him to indulge a suspension of his labours; the very air, gently moving the motley foliage of the grove, impregnated with the seeds of bland and social

---

1. **ecclaircisement:** éclaircissement; enlightenment; explanation of a mystery (French).

peace, and disburthened of the undulating and busy clang, seemed to breathe the true spirit of grateful and unmolested contemplation; while all varying nature apparently wore the semblance of tranquillity.

Margaretta made the comparison—she could no longer support the dreadful contrast which her bosom exhibited; and, asserting herself, she determined to be peremptory in her demand of an explanation. For many hours she revolved her important purpose; her spirit laboured with its interesting design; her breast was the seat of inquietude, and her soul was heavily oppressed. How to present herself; how to introduce her subject; in what language to clothe those sorrows which she had hitherto so assiduously sought to veil from the eye of Hamilton—these were questions which strongly agitated every faculty of her mind; but all her attempts to concert a plan of operation were ineffectual, until at length, tortured by reflection, hesitating, trembling and irresolute, she bent her steps toward that saloon, which Edward had consecrated the scene of his most retired moments; thither, at certain hours of the day, she knew that he repaired; upon this solitude she had never before ventured to intrude; yet, by slow and solemn movements, urged by despair, she now approached: She drew toward the recess, the door was but half closed; Edward and Serafina, for the purpose of obtaining an uninterrupted conference, had previously retired there. Serafina was seated on a sofa, her face bathed in tears; Edward, evidently overpowered by grief, reclined by her side; he pressed the left hand of Serafina to his lips, while her right was thrown affectionately over his shoulder!

"O Edward!" with a voice almost choked by sorrow, exclaimed Miss Clifford, "why are you thus unkindly persevering? False sentiments betray you. My attachment to you is closely interwoven with my existence. I stand upon the brink of a precipice, down which your unyielding obduracy will not fail to plunge me! Again I assure you, that my happiness or misery is involved in yours! If you become an exile from your country, doubtless I shall be the companion of your flight; but whither shall we go? in what recess can we hide ourselves? Is it possible that we can voluntarily consign to irremediable ruin, the *lovely and affectionate Margaretta?* Is it possible that *you, that a father,* can deliberately resolve to blast the just budding prospects of him, who now, unconscious of the threatened danger, lulled in the cradle of innocence, smiles with celestial sweetness?"

Margaretta had entered unobserved; she had beheld the attitude of two persons whom she had accustomed herself not only tenderly to love, but reveringly to esteem. The most envenomed pangs of despair at that moment pervaded her bosom—a feverish kind of anguish seemed to drink up the purple stream of life—her voice was lost, and her sight well near absorbed. Unable to proceed, she sunk upon the ready settee, which the second step presented—she distinctly heard the exclamation of Serafina!!—and the powers of animation suspending their operations, she sunk motionless upon the settee—a sigh burst spontaneously from her bosom—a sigh, that might well be imagined the immediate harbinger of death; it first drew the attention of Serafina—Hamilton started from his seat, and with mingling surprise, anguish and terror, they mutually flew to the supposed expiring sufferer. Their applications were in part successful; the active principle of life resumed its functions, and a gradual resuscitation pervaded the system. Reason, nevertheless, as if indignant at the outrages which she had sustained, stood aloof; and it was but too evident, that Margaretta possessed not that fine arrangement which had hitherto regulated the feelings of her dignified and gentle mind.

Her wanderings, however, imbibed the hue, and partook the prevailing bent of her natural disposition; and amid her incoherent ramblings, the true situation of her soul was expressed.

In pathetic language she lamented her own hard fate; and, addressing Serafina, whom she believed to be Mary, she questioned her in regard to the propriety and eligibility of a separation from Edward. She said that her attachment to her husband could never know abatement; but (lowering her voice, as if fearful of being overheard) as he was devoted to another, she thought it was becoming her character to relinquish her claims; she wished, indeed, that Edward and Miss Clifford had sooner understood the nature of their mutual attachment—But perhaps they might have much to plead in their own defence; and that, for her part, though she was at a loss to trace the origin of the calamity which had overtaken her, and could not justly accuse herself of intentional error, yet she wished every body well. That they need not be reduced to the necessity of abandoning the country; for if she could but obtain one of those moss-grown caverns, which she had heard were so numerous in the dominion of Old Ocean's God, in those watery abodes she would seek her deceased father; possibly too, her supplications might draw down the sainted spirit of her injured mother; and if she might be permitted to take with her the darling boy, for whom her last sigh would arise, they would be a family of love—she would soothe the woe-fraught bosoms of her parents—she would prepare for her infant son an oozy bed, the sea-green turf should pillow his little head, and, by the murmuring waters of some coral grove, he should be lulled to rest.

Hamilton, agonized beyond expression, in the frenzy of the moment, would have put a period to his existence; but by Serafina, who is ever present to herself, he was wooed, and awed to some degree of composure.

Serafina, by the assistance of a faithful female, conducted Margaretta to her chamber; and, while she offered up to Heaven her silent and fervid vows for the perfect restoration of her friend, she availed herself of the idea she entertained that she was her mother; and, assuming the mildly commanding air, she had so frequently observed Mary to wear, she gently remonstrated, pressed and soothed, until she had placed Mrs. Hamilton upon her pillow, when, seizing the exact crisis, in the softest key, she proceeded to chaunt[1] the most plaintive, harmonizing and dulcet strains, within the compass of her musical voice, until she beheld the disordered mourner embraced by those slumbers, from which she doubted not she would awake, in the full possession of her charming intellects. Having thus effectuated this salutary purpose, leaving Margaretta to an attendant, her next care was to rejoin Hamilton.

It was impossible not to understand the nature of the suspicions, which, it was apparent, had so deeply impressed the soul of Margaretta; and a retrospection convinced them, that even in the bosom of apathy, reason, from a variety of circumstances, would have originated

---

1. **chaunt:** chant.

conjectures. Edward acknowledged, that a desperate disease demanded a decisive remedy; he trembled for the consequences; but his dearest hopes now pointed out the most unreserved confidence. Alas! had he known the heart of my daughter, how many pangs he might have spared her. But the limited pages of this publication forbid remarks.

Serafina, obtaining full power to act agreeably to her own discretion, returned to the chamber of Margaretta, fraught with a sovereign specific for her wounded spirit; when, dismissing the girl, and seating herself beside her, she impatiently waited her release from that salutary repose, to which she had been so solicitous to consign her.

Margaretta at length opened her grief-swoln eyes; the traces of deep-felt melancholy were visible in her countenance; but reason, it was evident, had resumed her operations, and the expression of every feature was descriptive of a mild and affecting kind of resignation.

"How are you, my sweet friend?" soothingly questioned Serafina.

"Not well, Serafina;" returned Margaretta; and, after a moment's pause, letting fall some tears, in an affecting tone of voice, she added; "I am, Miss Clifford, the daughter of misfortune; my parentage was early announced; and though the interposition of my blessed friends and benefactors, would, by adopting me into their family, have snatched from me the bitter cup of adversity, yet, to struggle against the unalterable decrees of an all-wise Providence, it is in vain we assay!"

Serafina, inexpressibly affected, delayed not her remedy, but immediately taking her hand, which she bedewed with her tears, she delivered herself to the following effect:—

"You are undoubtedly an angelic woman; hardly any lot could be considered as fully adequate to your uncommon merit; yet, if my admeasurement of the mind of Margaretta is just, the secret which I have to communicate, will banish from her bosom its most corroding sorrows.

"I shall make my recital in as few words as possible; and, although I may criminate the everlastingly absent, yet I will not be so unjust to myself, as to suppose that the fact which I have to state, will lessen me in your esteem. The bosom of my Margaretta is the natal habitation of candour; and, while I inform her that Edward Hamilton and myself, owe our being to the same father, the sensation that is most prevalent in my breast, is a pleasing kind of conscious pride.

"While Mr. Hamilton, the elder, transacted business in Europe, he saw and distinguished my unfortunate mother. A circumstantial narrative of the tender, though unwarrantable connexion, which was the consequence, you will find in these sheets, *which are the hand-writing of my father: the characters are familiar to your eye,* and I yield them cheerfully to the perusal of some serene hour.

"It appears, that the only fault of which my ill-fated mother could be accused, was her unjustifiable and fatal attachment to my father: the struggles of her soul were great; her sufferings were accumulated; a number of *extenuating facts* the narrative faithfully records; and the filial feelings of a daughter's heart, naturally suggest a persuasion, that when, at the moment of my birth, she yielded up her life, the sacrifice may be regarded as an expiation for her indiscretion.

"My father called me by her name; and, returning to America, presented me, then only six months old, to his lady, as an orphan, whose person and fortune were entrusted to his care by her expiring parents, and to whom he was determined to discharge the part of a tender and faithful guardian.

"The soul of Mrs. Hamilton was the seat of *unsuspecting virtue,* and she received me to the bosom of commiserating affection; but I had not passed my third year, when this excellent lady was summoned to the mansion prepared for her; and my father exchanged no second vows. The attention which he paid to my education, hath often been remarked to you; and though, until I had completed my twelfth year, I viewed him only as my guardian friend, yet upon the tablets of my heart the sincerest veneration for his character was inscribed. Edward, born during the absence of his father, had only one year the advantage of me, and it was on the twelfth return of my natal day, that, leading us to his library, and putting into my hands those papers, which I have now committed to yours, he thus expressed himself: 'Receive—Serafina Clifford'—and the big tear rolled down his venerable cheek— 'receive the recital of your mother's woes. I have marked, with a perturbed and anxious kind of pleasure, the uncommon attachment by which my children distinguish themselves; yours is the age of innocence, and your affections bud on the stem of virtue; but a little onward, and the passions of youth too often assume a baleful and fatal hue—these, alas! may perhaps precipitate you into a gulph of ruin—I judge it proper to commit to you a *secret*—that I command you never, but in an hour of *unavoidable necessity,* to divulge—*Know, Edward Hamilton, that Serafina Clifford is your sister; she is the daughter of your father—Know, Serafina Clifford, that Edward Hamilton is your brother; he is the son of your father; and upon the heads of my children may the blessings of Heaven descend!* Here the emotions of his soul became too big for utterance; he was unwilling to submit them even to the eye of duteous affection, and he hastily withdrew.

"For us, our bosoms were awake only to the mingling sensations of surprise and joy. I, for my part, never experienced a rapture so sincere; and, no longer restrained by the presence of our father, we flew into each other's arms, eager to exchange those vows of eternal amity, which we have ever since inviolably observed.

"With one half of his ample fortune, my father, by gifts, investitures and last testament, scrupulously endowed me; and, as I enjoy no maternal inheritance, my every pecuniary emolument is derived from him: Yet, he so well concerted his measures, as to lead every one concerned to imagine, that he was only relinquishing a trust that had been reposed in him.

"The remainder of my account I shall pass rapidly over. When Mr. Courtland's pretensions were apparently approbated by you, my brother, struggling in vain to rise superior to an attachment, which he then deemed unfortunate, sought a remedy in absence; and, flying for refuge to the southern States, melancholy, and almost despairing, he assayed the various rounds of dissipation; gaming became his favourite amusement; and, in a few weeks, it is scarcely credible what immense sums of money were squandered! Mortifying embarrassments were the consequence; and had it not been for the extraordinary interposition of a friend of uncommon merit, his immediate ruin would have succeeded.

"Viewing himself, however, as young, and unconnected, he was prepared to meet the frowns of fortune; and supposing he had obtained the cure of a passion, that had gained strength with almost every added year of his life, he returned home, well pleased with his expedition. The event proved what an erroneous calculation he had made; and when he received your hand at the altar, he trusted that future successes, economy and application, would retrieve his affairs. What shall I say?— every month he hath accumulated misfortunes; and the rapid decline of his finances hath operated as a severe check upon his dearest pleasures. When you communicated to him your expectation of augmenting his felicity, by presenting him an invaluable pledge of love, he was then struggling under the pressure of a recent disappointment; he reflected upon himself as a prodigal, who had wasted the patrimony of the unborn. You must recollect his unguarded and impassioned expressions, with the alarming effects which they produced upon you. He accuses himself as a wretch who hath deceived you; and he is miserable. The generous forbearance of his southern friend, hath hitherto upheld him; but that benevolent creditor hath himself become a bankrupt, and the state of my brother's affairs can no longer be concealed. My lovely sister must soon have known, that her husband is some thousands in arrears, which he hath not a shilling to discharge. My fortune would completely reinstate him; often have I tendered it—Interrupt me not, my love;"— for Margaretta was eager to express her feelings; "I have written, I have repeatedly remonstrated: To effectuate this favourite purpose of my soul, I have revolved a variety of plans; my nights have been spent in tears, and my days in attempts to conceal from you my chagrin.

"Edward is withheld, by false principles of delicacy, from availing himself of what the laws of his country, but for the regulations of his father, would undoubtedly have invested him with: Gladly would I commit myself wholly into the hands of my brother. The good or evil which awaits him, I would wish to share; I would have but one interest between us, and I would be regarded only as the sister of his heart.

"But for him, he styles himself a wretch who hath deceived and betrayed you, and, under this appellation, he shuns your presence; he cannot bear to appear before your parents, the victim of extravagance; he meditates absconding from America, and if he cannot be induced to

relinquish his design, his sister will bear him company in exile: But if
matters can be adjusted, Edward may receive my interest, at least as a
loan. If Margaretta can forgive, and will become my auxiliary, she may
yet possess tranquillity; and she will ensure to herself the eternal gratitude of two persons, who will, upon all occasions, devote themselves to
the promotion of her felicity."

As Miss Clifford proceeded in her narrative, Margaretta had quitted
her couch; she had continued highly agitated, traversing up and down
her apartment. Now her clasped hands, raised eyes, and accelerated
movements, expressed the big emotions which struggled in her bosom;
now she threw abroad her hands in admiration, and now raised them to
Heaven, in a delirium of joy: Vehemently seizing the first pause, she
repeated— "*Tranquillity!*—Gracious God!—Can Serafina Clifford
Hamilton—my divine sister—my angel friend—my peace-speaking,
hope-inspiring genius—can *she give so cold a term to the extatic rapture of
this blissful moment?* Creator, and Almighty Preserver of my life, how
have I deserved this fullness of felicity, which, like a mighty torrent,
now bursts upon me? O Edward! my *faultless, my injured husband!* but
instantly, on my knees, I will supplicate the benign tenderness of that
manly bosom, to intercede in my favour."

Margaretta glided through the passage—Hamilton met her in an
adjoining chamber; where, with a perturbed and anxious spirit, he had
waited the result of what he termed the crisis of his fate. It was not in his
power to prevent the humble posture of his charming wife; Margaretta
bent before him; and, with streaming eyes and supplicating hands,
besought his pardon for the error, into which a hasty, inexperienced and
suspicious spirit had precipitated her. Edward in vain assayed to raise
her; by the events of the day her reason was still in a degree disordered,
and she insisted upon receiving her forgiveness in form.

"My God!" cried Edward, flinging himself beside her, "this is too
much; receive once more your offending Hamilton; endeavour to erase
from thy lovely bosom every painful remembrance of his past irregular-
ities, and you may then number him among the happiest of human
beings. Dearer to my soul than the light of heaven, my Margaretta hath
ever been: All amiably consistent, and mildly good as she is, she hath
not, she never could be found in a reprehensible walk; and conse-

quently, her husband must have marked her progress with an approbating eye; consequently, he can have nothing to condemn, nothing to forgive."

The appearance of Miss Clifford suspended their tender contention; and Margaretta embraced the opportunity of hasting to impart to us, the astonishing change which had taken place in her favour.

The subsequent scene, in my reading parlour, naturally resulted; and, I only add, that if there are, who do not greatly admire, and highly applaud the unequivocal demonstrations of joy, with which my daughter received the knowledge, that she must relinquish the independence of affluence, and descend to the humble grade, which *scanty and precarious circumstances enrolls,*—I pity the frigidity of their bosoms.

CHAPTER 11

Rich are the splendors of that golden day,
    Which breaks triumphant on a night of storms;
The fleecy clouds pursue their azure way,
    And every heart with grateful transport warms:
So oft when wrapt about in shades of woe,   5
    When the lorn bosom swells the length'ning sigh,
In copious streams when tears of anguish flow,
    And mem'ry can no beamy ray supply,
Some blest event bursts radiant on the sight,
And every sense proclaims the new-born light.   10

With sensations of ineffable complacency and high glee; with feelings, the felicity of which it would be difficult if not impossible to delineate, I set me down, upon this 27th day of May, 1794, to recount unto the *good-natured reader* an event, which, if I have not been extremely erroneous in my calculations, will render him, in no inconsiderable degree, a partaker of my joy.

I say, good-natured reader; for, without incurring the charge of

Chapter 11. Published in *The Gleaner,* 1:28.

credulity, I conceive I may fairly presume, that persons of this description have, from time to time, been constrained to take an interest in the fate of Margaretta Melworth Hamilton. I say, *good-natured reader,* because *the Gleaner* hath never yet had the arrogance to conceive his powers sufficiently energetic to arrest the attention of the phlegmatic, the saturnine, or the fastidious. Individuals possessing minds cast in these moulds, he hath considered as inaccessible, and he hath imagined them turning from the pages of the Gleaner, with all the frigidity of apathy, with all the glooms attendant upon rigorous severity, disgust, or contempt. Nor doth he enter this remark as a complaint; he hath been *humble enough* to content himself with the esteem of the *candid* and *sincere;* in the bosom of sensibility he fondly conceives he hath obtained a place, and he is ambitious of rendering his efforts worthy that degree of consideration with which they may be regarded. Addressing then the humane, the benevolent, and the ingenuous; in one word, those who are willing to be pleased, he hardly hesitates in promising himself at least a hearing: and, he is free to own, that he possesses such a comfortable share of self complacency, as to become confident, that whenever he consecrates his efforts by the name of the daughter of his affection, he ensures a share of approbation; nor will he consent that this idea should be imputed altogether to an over-weening conceit of his own abilities; for surely it must be acknowledged that an amiable and meritorious woman, struggling with misfortunes, is an object which virtue must ever regard with commiseration and applause. For the officious length of this exordium, I supplicate the indulgence of those gentle spirits, upon whose favour I have presumed; a candidate for the patronage of benignity should hasten to gratify the feelings of susceptibility, and after narrating a few previous arrangements, without further delay, I shall pass on to a developement, which hath not only invested our daughter with high affluence, but hath, moreover, restored to her a blessing, which she entertained not the smallest conception of ever being permitted to possess.

My last communications relative to Mrs. Hamilton, crowned her with those honours which bloom most becomingly upon a female brow; the propriety of her conduct in the matrimonial career could not be questioned, and her patient merit was, in her own opinion, amply rewarded, by a discovery that neither misfortunes or caprice had robbed her of, or in the smallest degree abated the affectionate attachment of him, to whom her gentle heart was unreservedly devoted.

That tumultuous delirium of joy, of which the sketch of the scene in my reading parlour, in the month of November last, can have given but an incompetent idea, gradually subsided into an exquisitely pleasing calm. Peace, with every accompaniment, which ever clusters in the train of tranquillity, was reinstated in her bosom; rosy confidence, fruitful in the soil of conjugal complacency, again lifted its auspicious head, and the rich perfumes which it breathed around, scattered those salutary sweets that gave to every object a face of pleasure. Margaretta seemed to regard poverty as the angel of serenity: Indeed a true knowledge of her circumstances had relieved her from a mighty pressure, which, becoming quite insupportable, had well near broken the slender thread of her existence; and an assured knowledge that she still possessed those undivided regards, which she had strong reason to believe no longer reciprocated, very naturally, for a time, absorbed in her gentle bosom every other consideration.

Some days delightfully serene, thus rolled on. I knew that the bursting storm, the tremendous and uprooting hurricane must succeed; but I trembled to disturb the innocent and unreflecting felicity of the moment. Mr. Seymour, the generous young man who had extricated Hamilton from his difficulties, while hopeless love produced him a wandering fugitive in the southern States, had failed for some thousands; and although repeated letters, glowing with friendship and matchless generosity, penned by the hand of Mr. Seymour, assured us, that he would ward the blow from us, to the extremest verge of possibility; yet as he continued, for the safety of his person, a prisoner in his own house; as all his books, bonds, and papers, of every kind, were submitted to the inspection of his creditors; and, as he assured himself that a fair adjustment, producing an amicable compromise, would usher in his liberating hour, the utmost credulity could not flatter us with continued exemption. Mr. Hamilton too, had many other creditors, and they became much more suspicious, inquisitive, and troublesome, than we had expected.

The scene once opened, my knowledge of mankind induced me to fear a rapid succession of distressing events; and necessity, therefore, impelled me to obtrude upon the halcyon hours of my children considerations which threw open the avenues of uncounted cares, and great inquietude. Serafina Clifford continued unwearied in her remonstrances; she was eager to dispossess herself, in favour of her brother, of every shilling which she possessed; and against the ardour and generous impetuosity of her attack, honour, justice, and fraternal affection, although embodied for the purpose, maintained but a doubtful combat; until availing myself of the rights invested in me by my paternal authority, I was reduced to the disagreeable alternative of interposing a positive prohibition.

Miss Clifford, in a kind of frenzy, clasped the little William to her bosom, and calling upon the shade of her departed father to witness her engagements, she vowed henceforward to devote herself and fortune entirely to him; adding, "I will, my lovely child, be indefatigable in guarding the soil of thy infant mind from the admission of that fatal germ, which never fails to produce a growth of false principles, of principles that prostitute the sacred names of honour and integrity, bestowing them upon an *unsocial kind of pride,* a barbarous sentiment, which compels its adherents, although placed upon a precipice of interminable ruin, to disdain the assistance of that friendship which is warm, natural, glowing, and sincere; of that friendship, which, as it originates affinity and gratitude, as it is the result of the fondest attachment, and meliorated by deliberate esteem, can surely never be regarded as problematical. Sweet innocent! may the kindred blood that swells thy little veins, render thee one day less obdurate than thy dear inflexible parents. From this moment the interests of Serafina and thine are inseparably interwoven."

Fear not, gentle reader, by virtue of the patriarchal dignity which I have assumed, I will, *upon a proper occasion,* grant unto the said Serafina Clifford, a full and free absolution from this her inconsiderate vow, which I shall take care to impute to the irresistible impulse of an impassioned moment.

In concert with Mr. Hamilton, without delay I took measures to place the property in his possession, beyond the reach of *any single* creditor; regulating it in such a manner, as would incontestibly be most for the advantage of, and yield unto *every claimant an equal* and handsome dividend. Thus prepared for a contingency that we had but too much reason momently to expect, I requested Mary once more to call into action that admirable address which she had so repeatedly exemplified. Go, my love, said I, with all thy winning graces, and affectionate persuasion; with all thy angel softness, and reconcile our daughter to that revolution in her prospects, which must place her again a resident in this family. Margaretta was far advanced in her second pregnancy, and we judged it necessary to observe, in regard to her, the utmost delicacy; but we had not yet learned properly to appreciate the mind of our amiable child. Those particulars, which are generally so alluring to a young woman, were not considered by her, of sufficient importance to give her essential or lasting pain. An establishment, ranking as the head of a family, presiding at her table, giving laws to a train of servants, receiving visits in her own house, with a number of *et-ceteras,* which have frequently the power of fascinating a young mind, were regarded as considerations *comparatively* of little or no moment; and while conscious she possessed the affections of the man of her heart; while she retained his society; while she could clasp to her throbbing bosom her lovely infant; while indulged with the presence of Miss Clifford, now more than ever endeared to her, and bound to her soul by motives of the most delicate and indissoluble tenderness and esteem; while she enjoyed the approbating countenance of her parents, her superior understanding could scarce forbear a smile at the solicitude we discovered respecting her removal; and, relinquishing her elegant apartments, I verily believe without a single murmur, she hastened, together with her amiable friend, to those parental arms which were ever open to receive her.

Trials, however, awaited her. It was necessary that Mr. Hamilton, who was anxious to accelerate the hour that should honourably exonerate him from his embarrassments, and who was extremely desirous of making provision for the growing family which he had in prospect, should immediately apply to some business, which might afford an expectation of putting him in possession of wishes so indisputably laudable. A ship bound for Europe, in which he was offered, with the probability of great commercial advantage, a very lucrative and honorary birth, propitiously presented. Of an opening so fortunate, interest loudly called upon him to avail himself; the favourable gale of opportunity was not to be slighted. But his heart bled for his Margaretta; yet manly decision hesitated not, and every thing was in train for his departure. We conceived it adviseable to conceal our purpose from my daughter as long as possible; and it was not until two days previous to the period destined for his embarkation, that I took upon myself the painful task of disclosing to her an event, which we judged must inevitably take place. Mary, Miss Clifford, Edward and myself, seated with Margaretta, in a retired apartment, had for some time been employed in observing her; while on her part she seemed wholly absorbed in contemplating the features of the little William, who, sleeping on a pillow before her, displayed a countenance truly cherubic. Soul of sensibility! most unwillingly did I recall her from her maternal reverie! but necessity apparently impelling, I thus addressed her:

What is there that Mrs. Hamilton would not sacrifice, to advance the happiness of the little being, whom she hath introduced into existence? Margaretta started—it seemed as if her apprehensive bosom comprehended, in a single instant, the agonizing intelligence which she was about to receive. She continued, however, silent, while urged by necessity, I reluctantly proceeded—There is a duty incumbent upon parents, towards their children, and from the moment of their birth they are bound to every possible exertion, which they can rationally suppose will contribute to their *real felicity.* Upon Margaretta Hamilton claims of this sort will soon be multiplied, and the probability is, that a long train of sons and daughters will rise up and call her blessed. Margaretta will not surely be found deficient in her maternal character; the expenses attendant upon the education of young people, their advancement in life, establishment, &c. how quickly will they succeed. It is happy, that when a single means of acquiring property fails, there are others which present.

The ocean opens its hospitable arms to the unfortunate man, from whom every other resource is cut off; while the dangers, supposed peculiarly incident to a seafaring life are in reality chimeras, calculated only to appal persons unaccustomed to reflect. Those who acknowledge the superintendence of Providence, the existence of Deity, if they ascribe to him those powers and properties which are essential to the being of a God, must acknowledge, that his protecting arm is, upon all occasions, stretched forth; that he can preserve upon the mighty waters with the same facility with which he upholdeth the dweller upon the land. The truth is, we are immortal until the separating warrant passes the great seal of Heaven; and the breath arrested by a designation so inevitable, no arrangement can redeem. I flatter myself, my beloved Margaretta, that your mind, equal, energetic, and considerate, would not suffer itself to be over much depressed, should the vicissitudes of life produce contingencies, unavoidably condemning you to a few months absence from Mr. Hamilton; two or three voyages might perhaps entirely retrieve his affairs, and you would ever after have the satisfaction to reflect that you had contributed every thing in your power; every thing which fortitude and uniform exertions could achieve, in order to re-instate your Edward in that independence to which he was born. I was proceeding—but I had not been sufficiently cautious. My daughter, during my harangue, frequently changed colour; the lily and the rose seemed to chase each other upon her now mantling, and now pallid cheek; she trembled excessively; and upon my particular application to her, the agitation of her bosom, becoming insupportable, she sunk breathless into the arms of that passionately beloved, and truly afflicted husband, who hasted to prevent her fall.

"My God!" exclaimed Hamilton, "it is too much; restore, compose, and soothe this suffering angel, too often exercised by pangs of so severe a nature; and do, with a wretch who hath betrayed and undone her, whatever seemeth to thee good."

Mary and Serafina soon recalled the fleeting spirit of the lovely mourner. Hamilton once more kneeled before her, and the copious tears, with which he bedewed the hand that he alternately pressed to his bosom and to his lips, called forth a mingling stream from the eyes of the beauteous sufferer. The scene was inexpressibly tender, but the humid drops upon the face of my daughter annihilated at least one half of my fears upon her account. "And can you, Sir" in a tremulous accent she exclaimed—"can you condemn my Edward to bondage, perhaps to irretrievable slavery?" What means my love? "Ah, Sir! do you not recollect British depredations? Do you not recollect the ruthless and unrelenting rigour of that fate which awaits the captive, doomed to wear out a wretched life under the galling yoke of an Algerine[1] despot? Might I but have been spared at this time! might a step so fatal to my peace, at least have been deferred, until the face of affairs wore, to the poor, desolate, and exiled voyager, a more confirmed aspect, I think I could have acquiesced." For a moment she paused; sighs, expressive of the deepest anguish, burst from her bosom. Again she resumed—"Gracious Heaven! what an extensive and wide spreading error hath my early indiscretion proved! and perhaps its cruel consequences will follow me to the latest period of my existence! *Had I waited the parental sanction, ere I lent an ear to a wretch, practised in the arts of deception;* had I not blindly and precipitately given the reins to reprehensible inclination, I should never have listened to the pernicious voice of adulation; the faithful heart of my Edward would not have received a corroding wound; he would not have been impelled to a voluntary banishment; he would never have had recourse to an expedient, which hath too surely involved in ruin my terrestrial hopes! Forgive me, O my parents! forgive me, O thou best of men! and thou sleeping innocent, forgive, O forgive thy wretched mother! It is now indeed that Margaretta is completely undone!"

I was immeasurably affected; yet I knew that my daughter would soon become capable of reasoning. She possesses, in an uncommon degree, the power of accurately discussing points, in which she is the most deeply interested; but altogether unprepared for the present calamity, reason had been violently forced from the helm, and we unitedly endeavoured to restore her to that reflection, to which we well knew she was eminently adequate. The soothings of unquestioned friendship are the sweetest solace; they yield a balm which is endowed with the sovereign power of mitigation, and they are a consolation in almost every sorrow. It was necessary to bend the mind of Margaretta to our purpose, and a few hours accomplished our wishes; gradually we

---

1. **Algerine:** Algerian. Several acts of piracy and taking of captives had been committed by the Algerians during the late eighteenth century. See also Susanna Haswell Rowson's play, *Slaves in Algiers* (1794), and Royall Tyler 's novel, *The Algerine Captive* (1797).

opened our plan; she saw the propriety of every arrangement; the necessity for the steps we had taken, and the idea, then first held up, of the possibility that the time was not far distant, which might legally immure her Hamilton within the walls of a prison, produced the expected effect. Waving her snowy hand with peerless grace, she pressed it upon her closed lips, and bowing her afflicted head, thus tacitly gave that expressive, although melancholy assent, of which, from the beginning, considering the justness of her way of thinking, we had made ourselves sure. Two days, as I said, only remained, and they were marked by a deeper sorrow, than any which has yet pierced the bosom of my daughter! It will not be doubted, that we called into action every motive which could give energy and firmness to her feelings; yet, while pensive resignation dwelt upon her lips, her altered countenance and debilitated frame evinced the struggles of her soul. It was a trial upon which she had never reckoned; in every event, she had calculated upon the supporting presence of her husband, and that she was thus unprepared for the stroke, must apologize for the agonized emotions with which she submitted to the blow! The evening at length arrived, which we conceived destined to usher in the morning, upon which our adventurer was to depart for a neighbouring town, in order to his embarkation, and its progress was noted by the heart-felt sighs of corroding anguish.

But just at this juncture, unfortunately, as I then imagined, our Federal Government interposed the late embargo, and joy once more mantled upon the cheek of Mrs. Hamilton. Thus it is, we submit to necessity; we are convinced of the utility of certain arrangements, and we are constrained, by conviction, to yield our assent to events which, nevertheless, pierce the bosom with the barbed arrows of affliction: Yet, if an interposing hand breaks the order to which we had reluctantly submitted; if we are conscious that we have no how aided in producing the incident; if we have, in every respect, acted up to our duty, we seem to forget the good we had expected; we rejoice in a change, which emancipates us from those sorrows we had imposed upon ourselves; we seem to have attained the goal of felicity; and, for a little moment, we become unmindful of those compulsory considerations, which had urged the application of a remedy, acknowledged indispensably requisite.

Margaretta, notwithstanding the good sense of which she is mistress—
notwithstanding the remonstrances of reason—not only regarded the
embargo as a reprieve, but involuntarily breathed her wishes for its continuance; and I produce it as an irrefragable fact, that our country contains not a single partizan, whose bosom glowed with more ill-advised
zeal, for the extension or renewal of this same embargo. The 25th
instant,[1] however, arrived—it passed—the fleet and welcome footsteps
of no new commissioned express gladdened the ear of impetuosity —
and the embargo expired—Hamilton was again on the eve of his departure. Yesterday, exactly at one o'clock, we were assembled in the dining
parlour. This very morning was to have witnessed the agonized moment
of separation—and melancholy dejection brooded in the countenance
of Margaretta.

My servant, a man whom I have loved for these forty years,
entered:—"A stranger, Sir, is importunate to see you." Admit him, by all
means. Margaretta was hasting from the parlour; she was solicitous to
hide her grief from the observation of the uninterested; but the stranger
was close upon the heels of the servant, and not being able to make her
escape, she withdrew to the window.

The gentleman, the stranger, I say, entered; upon his features were
imprinted the strongest marks of perturbed and tender anxiety; and,
moreover, they were features *with which I was confident I had long been
familiar,* although, for my soul, I could not recollect at what time, or in
what place, they had met my view. He, however, fixing his inquiring
eyes, with impatient solicitude, on the face of my wife, and drawing up
a heavy sigh, thus laconically apologized:

"Excuse me, Madam, excuse me, Sir—but my feelings disdain ceremony." The scrutiny under which the countenance of Mary passed, was
soon performed; and Miss Clifford next engaged the attention of a
man, who, but for the benign ascendancy, which, amid the most tumultuous agitation I had ever witnessed, was still conspicuous in his countenance, I should have concluded, entirely deprived of reason.

"You are lovely," he exclaimed, addressing Miss Clifford, "but you are
not the angel—at least, I think you are not—of whom I am in pur-

---

1. **instant:** of this month.

suit.——Tell me, Mr. Vigillius; tell me, ye incomparable pair! ye who
have still continued the matchless guardians of my long lost and
unceasingly lamented Margaretta, what apartment in this happy dwelling contains my only surviving treasure?" Margaretta, who had sought
to hide her sorrow-marked visage from the gaze of a stranger, now, lost
in astonishment, mechanically turning from the window, presented to
his view her tearful face; she catched a glance, and, faintly shrieking,
would have sunk upon the floor, had not the stranger, whom we now
regarded with a kind of indignant horror, snatched her to his embrace!
Our resentment, however, soon gave place to all those enraptured emotions, which the accession of high and unexpected felicity originates in
the bosom, when, in a voice expressive of paternal tenderness, of paternal transport, he soothingly said—

"Compose yourself, my lovely, my admirable, my inimitable child! It
is a *father's* arms that are at length permitted to enfold his long lost Margaretta!!! Arbuthnot, thou shalt no more invade my rights; it is again
given me to possess my child, and all her beauteous mother stands confest! Sainted spirit—this hour shall render thy elysian[1] still more
blessed!"

Margaretta shrunk not from his embraces: Strange as it may appear,
her agitated spirit did not entirely suspend its functions; and while she
seemed, in the arms of the stranger, an almost lifeless corse,[2] her lips yet
moved, and every charming feature received an extatic kind of ejacula-
tory impression.

Among the trinkets belonging to her mother, which had come into
her possession on the death of Mrs. Arbuthnot, was a miniature picture
of her father: Perhaps there was not a single day, on which she did not
gaze with filial devotion upon this picture. It was a striking likeness;
and, by its general contour, her mind was strongly impressed. Hence
the effect produced, by a single glance at the original; and it was a frequent observation of this picture, that occasioned the confused
recollection, for which, upon the first appearance of the stranger, I was
at a loss to account.

---

1. **elysian:** blissfulness; referring to Elysium, or Paradise, in classical mythology.
2. **corse:** corpse.

It cannot be matter of wonder, that at an interview so astonishingly interesting, not an individual retained that self-command, so requisite to common forms: At length, however, recollection resumed, in a degree, its office. Mary conducted Mrs. Hamilton to a sofa, when, a flood of tears unlocking for her the powers of utterance, with a look of profound and dignified veneration, she quitted her seat, and suddenly kneeling before the honoured man, in this devotional attitude, with clasped hands, and in broken accents, she perturbedly questioned— "Art thou a spirit blest—dispatched from Heaven's high court to soothe thy sorrowing child?—or art thou indeed my father? Hast thou never tasted death? and, if thou hast not, by what miracle didst thou escape those tremendous waves, which we have supposed commissioned for thy destruction?" Mr. Melworth, forsooth, to say it was he, his very self, raised his kneeling child, and again clasping her to his paternal bosom, in strains of exquisite tenderness, affectionately replied—

"Be comforted, my love; be composed, my heart's best treasure; I am indeed thy father. At a proper time, thou shalt be made acquainted with every particular; and, in the interim, as I have been informed of thy embarrassed circumstances, know, that riches, more than thou canst want, are in my gift. Thou shalt introduce me to thy worthy husband. I am apprized of the whole of thy sweetly interesting story; and thy happiness shall, if possible, be equal to thy merit." Margaretta, wild with transport, now raised her eyes and hands to Heaven, and the most extravagant and incoherent expressions of joy were upon her lips. "Then he shall not go," she exclaimed—"Avaunt, ye brooding fiends, that hover round the land of murder!—ye shall not intercept the virtuous career of Hamilton—ye shall not presume to manacle those hands that have, a thousand times, been stretched forth to wipe the tear from the face of sorrow—Avaunt, ye hell-born fiends!—Algiers, united for his destruction, shall not detain him; for lo, a blessed father descends from heaven, to save his well near sinking Margaretta!"

Edward, who, from the entrance of Mr. Melworth, had remained, as it were, entranced, or petrified by astonishment, roused by his fears for the reason of Margaretta, now coming forward, prostrated himself at the feet of Mr. Melworth. No one possessed sufficient composure to introduce him—nor was this necessary; the strong sensations which pervaded his almost bursting heart, inscribing upon every manly and expressive feature, veneration, joy, gratitude, and apprehension, emphatically pointed him out, and rendered a doubt impossible.

But why continue a scene, which may, *perhaps, be conceived,* but which words can never delineate? *Our mutual congratulations; our mutual expressions of felicity; the best affections of which humanity is capable; the most rapturous sensations of delight; these were all in course—and these were all afloat;* and I will only add, that Edward will not proceed on his voyage—that Margaretta is happy—that every creditor shall be amply satisfied; and I hereby advertise—let them produce their several claims; they shall receive to the last farthing, yea, and liberal interest too. Seymour—generous Seymour!—if this Magazine shall reach thee, before thou hearest from thy friend, know, that the hour of thy emancipation is at hand, and that a full reward awaiteth thee, for all the munificent deeds which thou hast so munificently devised.

And, gentle reader, for thy consolation, I give thee my word and honour, that the very next Gleaner, by recounting to thee every particular, relative to Mr. Melworth, which shall come to my knowledge, shall, if it is within the compass of my power, amply gratify a curiosity, which thou needest not hesitate to own, and which I should have been mortified in the extreme, not to have excited.

CHAPTER 12

> The deed of worth is register'd on high,
> Own'd and approv'd in worlds beyond the sky—
> Nor only so—we feel an answering glow,
> Which but the virtuous action can bestow;
> Nor these alone—an earnest oft is given,   5
> Immediate good—the award of righteous Heaven.

The author, who leaves nothing to the imagination of his readers, is frequently accused of blameable arrogance; and it is often asserted that, puffed up by an over-weening self-conceit, he vainly supposes, that the

---

Chapter 12. Published in *The Gleaner,* 1:29.

germ of fancy can flourish no where but in the soil of his own wonderful pericranium.

Now, as the fact is, that I am anxiously solicitous to avoid every occasion of offence, I shall (taking into consideration the feelings of sensibility, and properly influenced by an idea of the ingenuity which is its accompaniment) wave the description of those delightful sensations, which, in rapturous succession, were the natural appendages of the introduction of the father of Margaretta. The extatic fondness with which he hung upon the accents of his daughter—the mingling pleasures and regrets—the big emotions which surprised his soul, as he traced each lovely feature—those well-known features, which exhibited to his view a beauteous transcript of those that he had early learned to admire in the face of her departed mother—the exquisite sensations with which he traced the kindred lineaments—comparing them separately and collectively with a miniature of his lady, which he wore in his bosom, and which might have passed for an exact copy of Mrs. Hamilton—the glowing expressions of paternal tenderness, with which he folded the little William to his bosom—the marked approbation, unequivocally demonstrated toward every movement of the husband of his Margaretta—the manly and complacent regards that he bestowed upon Miss Clifford—the sweet incense of expansive and immeasurable praise, that he addressed to me, styling me the saviour, the benefactor, the genuine father of his poor orphan girl —the elevated regards, short only of adoration, which he devoted to my dear Mary—those charming effusions, consisting in expressive looks, broken words, and unambiguous gestures; effusions which were the spontaneous growth of uncommon felicity, the reciprocity of exquisite satisfaction which we abundantly inhaled—All this, and whatever else the soul of sensibility can conceive, gladly do I refer to the glowing mind of the *feeling sentimentalist;* and I do hereby invest imagination, in the utmost latitude of its powers, with full scope; it is impossible it can paint too high; language is indeed insufficient, and the most vivid tints of fancy can alone pourtray.

Nay, gentle reader, I take upon me to assert, that however elaborately thou mayest finish thy picture, after thou has bestowed upon it thy last touches, it may, after all, fall vastly short of the original; and, right sorry am I, that my powers are so circumscribed, as to render it impossible for me to place it in its genuine lustre before thee. But, finite efforts, being doomed to submit to a necessity, the effects of which it must ever be unavailing to lament; we will, without further preamble, proceed in our narration. And here I would not have thee conceive, that I am so unreasonable as to condemn thee to the drudgery of accounting for the sudden appearance of Mr. Melworth, nor can I consent, that, setting me down as a descendant of Merlin, thou shouldst place in my hand the magic wand; invest me with the powers of incantation, the gift of working miracles, or, of summoning *"spirits from the vasty deep."*[1] No, believe me, I am no conjurer, and the better to banish every idea of a supernatural interposition, I hasten to bring forward the promised facts. Imagine then, that the tumultuous and perturbed sensations of ungovernable transport, which were consequent upon the late developement, are succeeded by that kind of satisfaction which is the result of high complacency in the present, and the most agreeable anticipations of the future; or by that state of tranquillity, which must always be considered as a desirable substitute for the hurricane of the passions, whatever may be the magnitude of the event which produced it. The extreme of joy and sorrow, originating commotions as destructive to the order of the mental system, as the uprooting storm to the apparent harmony of the natural world; the mild and equal disposition cannot but regard as a relief, the regular succession of events. Imagine that our happy circle is retired to the little apartment sacred to sentimental pleasures; to that apartment, upon which the step of inconsiderate levity, or indifference, obtrudeth not. Margaretta is seated between her enraptured father, and that husband, who experiences for her exemplary worth, with every rising hour, augmenting admiration and new esteem. Mary, Serafina and myself, complete the group, and Mr. Melworth, pressing the hand of Mrs. Hamilton, thus commences his interesting communications.

"I observed, my dear, the sweet blush that tinged thy lovely cheek, upon my mentioning in terms of reprehension, the name of Mrs.

---

1. **spirits...deep:** from William Shakespeare's *Henry IV, Part I,* 3.1.52.

Arbuthnot; yet you must allow for the feelings of a desolate father—but for her unforgiving and obdurate spirit, the probability is, that your angelic mother would, at this delightful moment, have partook, and doubled all those exquisitely charming sensations, which swell a parent's bosom, and which present such an ample compensation for every evil. From the hour which blessed me with the hand of my Margaretta, she continued sedulously intent on procuring a reconciliation with her sister; for the companion of her youth the sigh of her bosom still arose, and while the utter improbability of obtaining her wishes embittered our most pleasurable moments, her intense and unavailing solicitude visibly impaired her health!

"I flattered myself that the period which gave thee, my love, to her arms, would supply that void in her heart, which, however ardent the attachment of your sex to the man of their choice may be, such is the delicacy of the female mind, a tender and respectable *female friend* can alone fill. Your mother, my dear, was early left an orphan. Her sister had for a long period reigned supreme in her bosom. Fate presented her not a Mrs. Vigillius; goodness so unexampled is not the growth of every clime; neither was a Serafina Clifford contained in the circle of her connexions. Yet, as I had hoped, the birth of her daughter opened a source of new and exhaustless pleasure; and when she clasped her lovely infant to her bosom, she forgot, for a moment, her sister; but memory, too faithful to its office, officiously presented the mirror.—'Dear implacable Henrietta!' she exclaimed, 'why wilt thou stand aloof? why wilt thou refuse to heighten the transports of this delicious period? Thy presence, thy sanction would indeed add a completion to my felicity, which would mark me the most blessed of women!

"The novelty, however, the soft endearments, the thousand nameless perturbations, and tender interest of the maternal character, were powerful alleviations, and the tranquillity of the mother was in a measure restored. Eighteen halcyon months revolved, when fate, as if envious of our felicity, presented me with a prospect of obtaining great emolument, by engaging on board a ship bound for the East-Indies. I was flattered by the idea of obtaining for my Margaretta and her infant, an elegant independence, and that resolution which became the superstructure of a basis so proper and so deeply laid, could not be easily shaken. Margaretta, while she acknowledged the eligibility of my plan, shrunk from its execution. Her tenderly apprehensive bosom foreboded a thousand evils. Yet the heroism of her character can never be too much admired.

"'Go, my Charles'—with emotions of tender and unutterable agony, she exclaimed—'since it must be so, go!—and may the upholding hand of Heaven be, in every event, thy never-failing support!' Repeatedly she sobbed out the convulsed and agonizing adieu, while ingenious in inventions to retard my departure, she pressed me to her throbbing heart. 'Oh! my love,' in broken accents she whispered, 'if we meet again, we shall then be happy. But alas! alas!' she could not add. Yet still her clasped hands and streaming eyes continued to supplicate the protection of that God, on whom her firm reliance was invariably placed. I was inexpressibly moved. My soul was little less tempested; yet the splendour of my prospects, my previous arrangements, my pledged honour, all urged me on; and, by one violent effort, I tore myself from the most beloved of women! Our mutual sufferings may be regarded as a prediction of the fatal event. It was decreed that we never more should meet! Propitious gales attended the first part of our voyage, and I had began to anticipate the rich harvest that a few painful seasons would enable me to lay at the feet of my heart's best treasure.

"We had already doubled the southern extremity of the great continent of Africa, commonly called the Cape of Good Hope; and, shaping our course northeast to the continent of India, we were proceeding with all dispatch—when, lo! on a sudden, the scowling atmosphere gathered darkness; dreadfully portentous the winds of heaven arose. Waves beat on waves frightfully tempestuous. The tumultuous ocean seemed to lash the contending skies. Louder and louder the destructive whirlwinds bellowed round. Hoarse thunders roared terrific peals succeeding peals. The heavens poured forth a deluge of rain, and the forked lightnings were all abroad. Surrounded on every side by the tremendous world of waters, assistance was impossible—no asylum presented. The seaman's art was in vain, and death, in its most shocking form, appeared inevitable. But to describe the horrors of our situation is beyond the reach of language. In the latitude in which we then were, there is a large ridge of rocks, they are pointed out in most of our sea charts; but if our pilot was aware of them, it was not in his power to avoid them; they accelerated that fate which, imagining the ship might live many hours, I had not so speedily expected; and, bilging instantly upon one of those rocks, a second stroke severed her in twain! The shrieks of the mariners were shocking beyond expression. How long they survived, or what efforts they made, I am not able to say; for, seizing a part of a shattered raft, upon which, floating at the mercy of the winds, and waves, while I momently expected dissolution, I commended my spirit to that God whose protection and whose favour I had never ceased to invoke.

"And how many of the children of men have been constrained to ask, What circumstances are beyond the reach of Omnipotence? *He who holdeth in the hollow of his hand, the great deep,* suddenly hushed the winds; and, driven upon a small uninhabited island, my first sensations, it will not be doubted, spontaneously issued in the most grateful orisons to the God of my life, who had thus graciously interposed for my preservation. But soon the image of my Margaretta, clothed in the habiliments of immeasurable woe, harrowed up my soul; her forlorn and helpless situation —her unprotected infant!—My God! madness was in the thought. I was on the point of again plunging into that ocean from which I had so recently escaped; but the good hand of upholding Deity still prevented me, and was still my shield. Gradually the heavens resumed a serene aspect; my mind too became astonishingly calm; and, drying the only vestments which now remained to me upon a sun-beat rock, whose craggy sides received the most intense rays of that luminary, beneath the foliage of a sheltering tree I stretched my weary limbs. Sleep spread over me its downy mantle, and I obtained a temporary oblivion of those lacerating reflections, with which succeeding hours, in dreadful order, appalled my sinking spirits.

"Necessity compelled me to search out the good, if any remained, which was yet within my grasp. At the salutary stream I slaked my thirst; the nutritious berry, zested by hunger, afforded me a delicious repast, and by one soothing hope I was still buoyed up: I traced unequivocal vestiges of the human step—ships, I was positive, had recently touched there—I might yet recognize my fellow man—I might yet be borne to my native isle. Despair, however, too often gained the ascendancy, and at such intervals, inexpressible anguish overwhelmed my soul. But it is impossible to paint the unequalled calamities of his situation, who is thus circumstanced. Even the glowing imagination of a Thomson[1] could only sketch them. Yet, not a revolving hour but heard me, to the listening echo, repeat—

'Unhappy he! who from the first of joys,
Society, cut off, is left alone
Amid this world of death. Day after day,
Sad on the jutting eminence he sits,
And views the main that ever toils below;   5
Ships, dim discover'd, dropping from the clouds;
At evening to the setting sun he turns
A mournful eye, and down his *dying heart*
Sinks hopeless; while the *wonted roar* is up,
And hiss continual through the tedious night.'   10

But forever blessed be the all-gracious Disposer of events! the term of my sufferings was cut short. It was the employment of my first rational moment, after I had been thrown upon the island, to make, with a part of my clothing, a signal of distress. Upon a prominent angle ascended a small acclivity, on the summit of which stood the tall trunk of a tree, that contending storms had stripped of its branches. To this disrobed trunk I contrived to fasten the beacon of my distress, and I consecrated it, with many supplications to Him who was alone able to save.

"The morning of the fifth day (after I had so providentially escaped the waves) broke divinely serene. An amazing continuity was out-stretched before me. With folded arms, and an aching heart, I contemplated the extensive main. The frightful solitude, the awful still-ness to which I was condemned, arose dreadfully terrific to my soul. I

---

1. **Thomson:** James Thomson (1700–1748), Scottish poet; the poem cited is Thomson's *The Seasons* (1730).

threw abroad my anxiously inquiring gaze; a cloud seemed to gather at a distance—It is not a cloud—What can it be?—Swiftly it approaches—Great God! is it possible?— Saviour of sinners! it is, indeed, the white sails of a Heaven directed bark!—It is bending toward me!—Ah! it recedes, and my bounding spirit dies within me!

"Again, however, its altered course bore rapidly down upon my desolate abode. The insignia of calamity reared not in vain its petitioning head. The necessary arrangements were made. The boat was manned. My heart leaped exulting; it was too big for its prison. My tongue refused utterance, while, with that commiserating cordiality, which seamen know so well to practise, and which is a characteristic trait of their order, I was received on board the ship. To complete my joy, the captain and crew were English. The captain was a humane and venerable man, who had numbered more than threescore years: A shower of tears relieved my bursting heart. I told my tale of woe, and he regarded me with even paternal goodness. Few know how to respect the unfortunate; inestimable are the soothings of benevolence to the children of adversity.

"A tedious voyage was now to be performed; and although a proper sense of the divine interposition in my favour, forbid every murmur, yet a recurrence to those pangs which I well knew would lacerate the gentle bosom of her my soul held most dear, could not fail of pointing the keenest arrows of affliction! Ten long months (dating from the time of my departure) performed their tedious round, ere the white cliffs of Albion again met my longing gaze. With what extacy did I leap upon the strand. To the parent soil I lowly bent my head; with filial lips I kissed the kindred turf, and my bounding spirit, struggling with its mingling sensations, poured forth the rapt orisons of a shipwrecked, exiled, rescued, and restored man! On the wings of speed I hasted to my native village; to that village which I supposed contained my only treasure. But what became of me, when, posting to the apartments of Margaretta, I found them occupied by strangers!—Yet, hope still whispered she had removed to some other abode; and I hasted to the dwelling of a friend, from whom I learned the sum of my misfortunes!!

"You are, my friends, acquainted with the feelings of the heart. Every feature in your expressive countenances are vouchers of your sensibility—Why should I aim at delineation!

'When to the height of hopeless sorrow wrought,
The fainting spirit feels a pang of thought,
Which, never painted in the hues of speech,
Lives at the soul, and mocks expression's reach.'

"I drop the curtain over a train of succeeding ills; sickness, loss of reason, comfortless calamities!

"Mrs. Arbuthnot, when she accompanied her husband to Ireland, bore my child with her. My aged, widowed mother, gently remonstrated. My supposed death, and the demise of Margaretta, had centered her every remaining wish in the little prattler. Mrs. Arbuthnot plead the dying injunctions and bequest of her sister. This was decisive. The regulations suggested by the everlastingly absent should be deemed inviolably sacred, and my mother with floods of unavailing tears submitted. A few painful weeks devoted to heartfelt regret, had succeeded a separation judged unavoidable, when my unfortunate mother received a line from Mrs. Arbuthnot, acquainting her that the little Margaretta was no more. This proved a finishing stroke. So many calamities, in such swift succession, treading upon the heels of each other, brought down the grey hairs of my aged parent with sorrow to the grave. Could she have been spared to have witnessed the returning footsteps of the son of her youth, a gleam of joy would have diffused its genial and solacing influence over her parting spirit. But Heaven decreed otherwise, and she closed a life, the sorrows of which had accumulated with every added moment! What could induce Mrs. Arbuthnot to pen a misrepresentation, calculated to pierce with so keen a shaft the bosom of an aged and sorrow worn sufferer, I can only conjecture. Probably she might be influenced by her plan of passing the child for her own; or, she might imagine that my mother, being invested with the rights of a parent, would again demand the child, should the contingencies, peculiar to a soldier's life, remove Captain Arbuthnot (whom it was well known she determined to follow) to a remote or foreign destination; and it may be presumed that she made up the matter in her own mind, by a consideration that if she returned her niece to our village, the extreme age of my mother, would soon leave her destitute of every natural guide.

"For me, after a long and debilitating fever, obtaining a state of convalescence,—youth, and a constitution uncommonly good, soon completed my restoration. The same interest which had before placed me on board an East-India ship, procured me a second employment. I made several successful voyages. I accumulated riches; and at length saw myself possessed of affluence. But alas! tranquillity was not in the gift of affluence. In the variety by which I was surrounded my heart took no interest; and it refused to acknowledge a second attachment. Yet I determined to regulate my feelings by the dictates of fortitude, and to bend my wayward spirit to a state of acquiescence in the designation of that God who ruleth in the heavens. I became a citizen of the world; and, considering myself born for the universal family, and for the emolument of my fellow men, I industriously made the most of every acquisition. Under the influence of this sentiment I proceeded in the career of life; and if my path produced not those high scented perfumes, of which the exquisite succession of domestic enjoyments is susceptible, I was, notwithstanding, so far favoured, as to obtain a degree of composure. Thus rolled on succeeding years, until upon an uncommon fine night, three months since, feeling no disposition to retire to my chamber, I felt constrained to devote an hour to a contemplative walk, and after having strolled some moments upon the road-side, I bent my steps toward St. George's fields, where, experiencing an unusual kind of perturbation, with folded arms, and raised eyes, I continued my desultory aberration.

"Methought the shade of my Margaretta accompanied my steps: The ample heavens, the starry luminaries, the full orb'd moon, the blue expanse; these all combined to image the beauteous form of her, on whom fond remembrance still regretting dwelt.

"An association of ideas gave birth to a wish, to pass some moments beside a sketch of those waters, on which, bidding an eternal adieu to the injured sufferer, I had heretofore cruelly embarked; and toward Westminster bridge I rapidly took my way, which having reached, with an expedition for which I could not account, I descended the steps of the landing place; but no sooner had I put my foot upon the third stair than an unusual dash of the waters of the Thames, for which the stillness of the night rendered it impossible to assign a reason, still further accelerated my movements. I hasted forward, and was only in time to seize by his garments, an unfortunate man, who had plunged into the stream, with the unwarrantable purpose of putting a period to his existence. I remonstrated against the atrocious audacity of the deed that he had well near perpetrated, in terms expressive of the horror which it inspired. For a time he preserved an indignant kind of silence; and when he deigned to utter himself, he breathed only expressions of resentment, for what he termed my officious interposition. It was manifest that his reason was disordered, and pity grew in my soul. I addressed him in the language of commiseration, and he gradually became softened and communicative.

'Generous stranger,' he exclaimed, 'I give thee no mark of confidence in the brief recital, which as an apology for my supposed rashness, your apparent commiseration demands. To him, who is resolved on death, the disclosure of secrets which effect only himself, can be of little importance. Know then, that, born to affluence, I was bred a gentleman. Know also, that, pursuing my pleasures in a neighbouring kingdom, I saw and *loved* a beauteous woman. I *wooed* and *won* her. Her parents were no more; but her brethren, her sisters, a numerous family, her fortune, her country, her religion—all these she forsook, and fled with me to our Albion coast. Indiscretion and misfortunes have robbed me of every penny which I possessed. I have no means of obtaining the common necessaries of life; the few articles of which I have not yet disposed, will not discharge the debts already contracted. Those flatterers, who basked in the sunshine of my fortune, have now utterly forsaken me. My wife, my beloved wife, and her helpless children, are reduced to the last extremity. I have left no means unassayed, by which I could presume upon relief; but every effort hath proved ineffectual, and I have now quitted my Almira, with an expressed hope, for which, alas! there is no foundation. She will expect me with the returning sun; but she will no more behold me. I can no longer exist a witness of those ills, of which I have been the wretched cause!' Need I add, that I was eager to speak, to this son of sorrow, the words of consolation? Considering myself as the banker of the unfortunate, his draught upon me was indisputable; and the rays of night's fair empress, lent a light sufficiently strong, to evince the authenticity of its characters.

"I accompanied my new claimant, now incredulous, and now frantic with joy, to his dwelling. I had determined to keep guard the remainder of the night. We entered softly. His little family had retired to rest. I insisted that he should instantly speak peace to his beloved. I insisted that he should not revisit the parlour, until the rising sun should enable me to commence my proposed arrangements. I will repose, said I, in this easy chair; or here are books, with which I may amuse myself. Awed by that tone of authority which I had assumed, with looks of astonishment, and the most profound obeisance, he left me; and sleep being beyond my reach, I endeavoured to obtain sufficient composure to amuse myself by reading. I turned over the books—it would not do. A new and painful kind of agitation hurried my spirits; at length a parcel of Magazines seized my attention. I glanced confusedly upon the bundle. The Massachusetts Magazine caught my eye—*an American production*—curiosity was enlisted; I opened one and another; an irresistible impulse still urged me on; the first page of the Magazine for March, 1792, arrested my eye—*'Bless me, cried Margaretta,'*—you will recollect, Sir, that you thus commenced the enchanting narrative.

"The appellation *Margaretta* vibrated interestingly upon my ear; it was the sweet talisman of a thousand mingling sensations; no power on earth could have prevented my reading on. I accompanied you in your journey to South-Carolina, and I entered with you the city of Charleston. The little Margaretta's tap at the door possessed a fascinating power—the introduction of the lovely cherub penetrated my very soul; I waited impatiently for the issue; I attended at the bed of death—but, great and good God! what were my sensations when I heard from the lips of Mrs. Arbuthnot, the well known story of my Margaretta's sufferings—when I learned that the dear pledge of our sacred loves was yet alive! when I recognized her in the person of the little petitioner—when I became assured that she had been received by such protectors! I shrieked aloud, wrung my hands, wept, laughed, prostrated myself in adoration of a preserving God—traversed up and down the apartment, until, at length impelled by perturbed anxiety, I was constrained to trace my daughter's wondrous fortune through the various Magazines, which, until the close of the month of November last, presented themselves in order before me. How did my full soul bless her godlike benefactors! During the connexion with Courtland, the most tumultuous agitations tempested my bosom; but the catastrophe, I conceived, gave her honoured guardians a title to almost divine honours. Again I became a prey to all those agonizing fears which can lacerate a father's heart. Even of Miss Clifford, I must confess, that I was not a little suspicious. My feelings against thee, my son, were replete with indignation; and I bestowed upon thy supposed inconstancy a parent's malediction. But November presented the extatic eclaircissement. I saw that nothing was wanting, but what I possessed abundant ability to supply; and, in broken and almost frantic ejaculations, I sobbed out my gratitude. The dawn at length broke. Memorable, ever memorable night! Never, never can I be forgetful of the events which thou produced!

"An early hour presented the now not despairing Altamont. He led his Almira by the hand. I had cautioned him not to shock the delicacy of her feelings, by a recital of the extremity to which he had been precipitated; and he had been discreet enough to follow my advice. He had simply informed her that Heaven had sent him a friend, and this information had proved sufficient to excite the most lively emotions. Altamont began a speech expressive of his gratitude; but I cut him short, by decisively pronouncing, that fate had ordained me eternally his debtor. My disordered countenance, and the energy of my manner, alarmed him; and he in his turn became doubtful of *my* reason. I gave him, however, a simple relation of facts. I held up the divine pages. Had I not met thee; had I not consented to deliver to thee that dividend of our common Father's interest, with which he has entrusted me for thy behoof, I had not met these blessed records; I had not received intelligence, which hath communicated to my soul immeasurable felicity. *Thus amply hath our God rewarded me for designing an act of common justice.*

"Grateful tears of rapture, it will not be doubted, we mingled. Every thing was speedily adjusted to the complete satisfaction of Altamont and his Almira. With the first ship, I embarked for America. The name of Colonel Worthington, of New-Haven, was my clue; and I bore with me the heaven inspired Magazines. From Colonel Worthington I learned every necessary particular. I was told, my son, of your intended voyage, of the consequent anguish of my daughter's soul. I bless God that I am in time to prevent its prosecution. Every individual shall receive his dues; that good young man, your *forbearing friend,* the benevolent Seymour—every one shall be happy!"

Unwilling to leave the curiosity of the reader ungratified, during the tardy revolution of another month, I have felt myself necessitated to curtail the narrative of Mr. Melworth. Many useful observations are omitted. The frequent interruption, breaks, and pauses, occasioned by the susceptibility of Mrs. Hamilton, and the agitation of her father; the unbounded and venerating gratitude of Edward; and the combining admiration, and rapt felicity of our whole party; all this was in course, and to every thing of this sort, I must repeat, that the silently expressive touches of that vivid pencil, which is found in the glowing hand of fancy, can alone do justice.

Already our young people have resumed their elegant family seat. Miss Clifford is still the companion of Margaretta. Amelia Worthington is now a congratulating visitor at Hamilton-Place. Mr. Melworth is for the present a resident in that sweetly romantic mansion; and this very morning, the second day of July, one thousand seven hundred and ninety-four, witnessing the birth of a daughter to Margaretta, hath seemed to complete our family felicity.

.